Archbishop Oscar Romero

Archbishop Oscar Romero

The Making of a Martyr

By Emily Wade Will

With a foreword by
José Inocencio Alas

7/20/16
To Bill –
Mi favorita Suegro
your ever loving son
– Greg

RESOURCE *Publications* • Eugene, Oregon

ARCHBISHOP OSCAR ROMERO
The Making of a Martyr

Resource Publications
An Imprint of Wipf and Stock Publishers
199 W. 8th Ave., Suite 3
Eugene, OR 97401

www.wipfandstock.com

PAPERBACK ISBN: 978-1-4982-8355-7
HARDCOVER ISBN: 978-1-4982-8357-1
EBOOK ISBN: 978-1-4982-8356-4

Manufactured in the U.S.A.

A big thanks to Orbis Books for allowing generous quotations from both James R. Brockman's *Romero: A Life* and Maria López Vigil's *Oscar Romero: Memories in Mosaic.*

Dedicated to El Salvador's long-suffering *campesinos* and *campesinas*, whose love blessed and sustained their archbishop

Half the author's royalties from this book will go to the Foundation for Sustainability and Peacemaking in Mesoamerica.

The older one is, the more it can appear that only older people know what is true and right and the ideas of young people seem crazy and novel and so we say: *pay no attention to them!* Be very careful. Do not quench the spirit! . . . The Spirit is never old! The Spirit is always young.

—OSCAR ROMERO, HOMILY, DECEMBER 17, 1978

Contents

Foreword

History offers very few opportunities to live out the role Monseñor Oscar Romero accepted for his life. His is a story full of contradictions in which humiliation and glory are intertwined. Emily Wade Will masterfully narrates that story for us, step by step, in her book *Archbishop Oscar Romero: The Making of a Martyr*.

Having conducted thorough research, Will, a writer, takes us by the hand to visit and participate in Monseñor Oscar Romero's life from his birthplace until his beatification on May 23, 2015. The narrative rivets the reader, who bit by bit learns of the various cultural, geographic, political, and spiritual environments in which Monseñor Romero moved in his lifetime.

Through Will's pen, you'll discover how a ray of light illuminates Oscar Romero's path across the length of his life, keeping him on the same road, although he experienced dark nights and tough challenges, as well as very happy times. The light beam is his deep spirituality, evident from childhood and later flowering in a spirit of solidarity and service. He accepted his being different from others, a faith commitment for which he gave his life.

Like Oscar, I was also born in the countryside. My mother had cows, too, but no land planted in coffee. Before the proliferation of means of transportation and communications, before the expansion of educational opportunities in El Salvador—Latin America's smallest country—the life of a child born in the rural backwater was hemmed in, virtually with no future horizon beyond the child's line of vision. His fate was to grow and die in the same place. Studying provided a means of expanding one's horizons to the limit of whatever the planet offered. That was the life of the young flutist, apprentice carpenter, and priest, of Oscar.

Born in Ciudad Barrios on August 15, 1917, before the Great Depression of the '30s, he begins his studies at age thirteen at the Claretian fathers' minor seminary located in San Miguel, where he remains for five years. Oscar is in his teen years, the time of dreams. As Emily Will relates, Oscar participates in all the seminary's activities and at the same time delves into the call to the altar. The fourth and fifth years are dedicated to what are called the humanities. By then Oscar is a young man, seventeen and eighteen years old, and his worldview broadens with the study of the classics of literature, an opening to the world. This is the time of greatest human growth, the widening of the universe before studying philosophy and theology.

I have not found the story of Oscar's childhood and teen years in other books. For me at least it is new and inspiring. Through her research carried out among Oscar's family, friends, colleagues, and superiors, Emily Will gives us information of significant value.

Oscar finishes his philosophy courses in the San José de la Montaña Seminary, in San Salvador, and the question then becomes, for Bishop Dueñas of San Miguel, where to send him to continue his studies, since Oscar is an excellent student and all signs point to his becoming a model priest. He cannot send him to Spain, because it's convulsed by civil war. The Colegio Pío Latino offers three scholarships and the bishop takes advantage of them to send Oscar to Rome to study at the Gregorian University, the papal university recognized for the many bishops it has trained. Oscar finishes his theology studies, is ordained a priest, and decides to continue on for a doctorate. He must interrupt his degree work due to World War II, which involves Italy. He returns to El Salvador through Cuba, where he is imprisoned for four months because Cuba is an enemy country to Italy.

The theological training he has received is dogmatic and doctrinaire. It is applied equally to the eighth century as to the Middle Ages or the modern day. It is not committed to an historical time and place; it's abstract. It demands blind obedience to Rome's authority. Emily Will leads us admirably through the young priest's ministry in the San Miguel diocese, as secretary of the bishops' conference, auxiliary bishop of San Salvador, and, finally, bishop of Santiago de Maria. These are years of hard work, humble service, confrontations with his fellow priests because of the moral rectitude Father Oscar demands of them. They are also years of conflict with young priests, both diocesan and Jesuit, due to their interest in ministry inspired by Vatican II, the Second Latin American Episcopal Conference in Medellín, Colombia, and liberation theology. They are also years in which Oscar learns to relate to civil and economic power, although he doesn't seek personal gain.

As Emily Will relates, on February 22, 1977, Monseñor Oscar Romero takes possession of the Archdiocese of San Salvador, and Monseñor Luis Chávez y González retires after thirty-eight years as archbishop, a long period. He leaves as his legacy an archdiocese committed to Vatican II, the Second Episcopal Conference of Medellín, and, of course, to the poor.

On March 12, his friend Father Rutilio Grande is murdered and with him, an old man and a child. Monseñor immediately goes to Grande's parish, to Aguilares. At Grande's feet, he makes a *solemn commitment*, as Will shows by quoting what he told Father César Jerez, SJ, "If they killed him for what he was doing, it's my job to go down that same road." Monseñor Romero accepts the clergy's proposal to hold a single Mass with his priests in front of the cathedral on Sunday the twentieth to denounce Father Rutilio's assassination, persecution of the church, and the murders of many peasants, teachers, workers, and others. The backlash is immediate from the conservative bishops, from the Vatican's representative, Monseñor Gerada, from the government, and the oligarchy. He asks my advice and I suggest he go to the chapel to talk with Jesus. His conversation with the Teacher ends his theological understanding of blind obedience to Rome and uncritical acceptance of authority. *He understands he's responsible to and for his people*. On Sunday he's at the cathedral and with him, his clergy and more than one hundred thousand parishioners. The denunciation he makes in his sermon leads him to become the *prophet* the country needed.

Emily Will accompanies us on the journey Monseñor took for three and a half years through communities and cities, in the cathedral and on the radio, and by all other means at his disposal, defending the rights of all, particularly of the poor, denouncing oppression and injustice, and proclaiming peace. The oligarchy did not listen to him; neither did the government. On March 24, 1980, at nightfall, he is killed while celebrating the Eucharist. As Emily quotes Pope Francis, "Romero, who built peace with the power of love, bore witness to the faith in the extreme by offering his life."

—José Inocencio "Chencho" Alas

Austin, Texas
December 2015

Acknowledgements

OVER THE YEARS MANY generous souls contributed to this labor of love, sharing their devotion to Monseñor Romero by helping to mold and smooth out the rough edges of this endeavor that I began in 1998, had to set aside in 2000, and took up again in 2013.

In 1998, San Salvador-based Equipo Maíz staff members Elmer Romero and Miguel Cavada exceeded the call of duty in helping me sketch out an itinerary and coordinate interviews that would take best advantage of my time in the country. They loaded me down with valuable written resources and inveigled a family to host me in Ciudad Barrios. More recently, Marvin Hernández-López assisted with photo credits and permissions.

Many kind friends and relatives of Monseñor patiently talked with me about the young Oscar. His brothers—Mamerto and his hospitable wife, María Cristina, Arnoldo, and Gaspar—and sister Zaída warmly welcomed me into their homes. They dredged their memories to respond to the minutiae I quizzed them about, undoubtedly baffled as to why I had traveled a distance to ask them more about a long-forgotten cow than about their martyred brother's theology. They remained gracious when asked to explain words—*bahareque*, for example—and lifestyles of bygone times unfamiliar to me. Retired parish priest Bernardo Amaya blessed this work with his incredibly detailed memories of the minor seminary and his companions there, Oscar included.

I had the pleasure of spending time with a variety of individuals whose lives intersected with Monseñor's and who shared tidbits of his lighter side. Salvador Barraza, a lay friend who pulled Romero away from his duties for occasional fun and relaxation, including the circuses the archbishop loved, said the tightrope walkers were Romero's favorite act. Elvira Chacón served Romero at her small restaurant and divulged his favorite foods: *maracuyá* (passion fruit) juice, refried beans, *quesadilla* (in El Salvador, a pound cake made with two or three types of cheese), hamburgers, and hot chocolate.

Marimba player Alonso López of Ciudad Barrios, roughly the same age as Romero, treated me to a rendition of one of Monseñor's favorite songs, "Dios nunca muera" ("God never dies") on his marimba, its resonant bars fashioned of fine Guatemalan "*hormiga negra*" wood the color of dark chocolate.[1] As a girl of thirteen or fourteen, Teodora Díaz helped care for some of the Romero babies, allowing Niña Jesús to work at her sewing machine without a child on her lap. She recalled the much-appreciated aprons Niña Jesus regularly fashioned for her from leftover fabric pieces.

Pauline Martin, friend and director of the master's program in education policy and evaluation at the University of Central America, lent initial and ongoing help in making connections in El Salvador, sent helpful articles my way, and offered insightful comments on the manuscript. Without her gentle prodding, and especially her encouraging words at times when they were most needed, this work may not have come to fruition.

Over a three-year period, my online critique group uncomplainingly offered valuable suggestions for producing a readable manuscript. Throwing me lifelines while I floundered in the sea of my choppy, convoluted sentences were Kim Gore, Susan Lynn Rivera, Crystal Schubert, Chuck Robertson, Erin Fletcher, Claire Matta, and Sidney Sult-Poole.

I am immensely grateful to María López Vigil for her foresight and effort to collect remembrances after Romero's death. Gathered into a book titled *Piezas para un retrato*, they're a treasure trove of short personal accounts and anecdotes by those who knew and worked with the archbishop. Having drawn upon *Piezas* in its original Spanish for my first draft, attempting my own translations, I was delighted with Kathy Ogle's English version of this work, published in 2000 as *Monseñor Romero: Memories in Mosaic*. Her careful work made my second draft infinitely easier to write.

In addition to conducting personal interviews, James R. Brockman, SJ, Romero's first English biographer, mined mountains of paper files to extract, organize, and interpret the depth and breadth of Romero's life, providing an indispensable foundation for students and biographers. Brockman encouraged and advised me in a 1998 e-mail exchange. A big thanks to Orbis Books for allowing me to quote generously from both Brockman and López Vigil.

1. Perhaps *Platymiscium dimorphandrum* or *Dalbergia stevensonii*. In 1942, Lopez traveled three days to Guatemala to purchase the instrument. It took him another three days to get it back to Cuidad Barrios, wrapped up on a cart pulled by two oxen.

The Mennonite Central Committee played a fundamental role in forging my awareness of the world's "haves" and "have-nots" and helping me solidify and articulate my concerns for justice and human rights. While covering the organization's Latin America programs as a writer, I first met Salvadorans, who deeply impressed me with their friendliness and their ability to creatively struggle for dignity.

Several individuals read and offered corrections on the manuscript, among them Julian Filochowski, chair of the London-based Archbishop Romero Trust; José Inocencio "Chencho" Alas, a former priest who worked alongside Romero and who narrowly escaped death after the National Guard abducted him in 1970; the ever-charitable Father Carlos L. Villacorta, one of Romero's minor seminarians in San Miguel; and José Artiga, executive director of SHARE El Salvador, who encouraged me to use gender-inclusive language. I thank them for catching infelicities and errors before they had a chance to go public. I am solely responsible for any typos, misspellings, or mistakes that remain.

Carlos Colorado, who updates the world on all matters Romero on his "Super Martyrio" blog, carefully monitoring the sainthood process since 2006, recently guided me to an article about Romero's notes jotted on cards in Rome, a resource that added substance to the chapter on Romero's vital seminary years.

Last, but hardly least, my sister and her husband Annette and Bob Schiavone and my friend Tim Weber uphold me in too many ways to count; their loving concern buoys me during bouts of doubt and frustration.

Introduction

DURING THE FIRST FIVE and a half decades of Oscar Arnulfo Romero's life, little indicated he'd find a place in history books. Born in a poor hamlet with scant educational opportunities in El Salvador's remote mountains, Romero rose to leadership among his country's Roman Catholic clergy, a significant accomplishment. He was intelligent, a gifted speaker, and conscientious in fulfilling his duties.

Yet when the Vatican named the fifty-nine-year-old to fill the role of archbishop of El Salvador's most prominent diocese in 1977, few people, if any, suspected the priest, steeped in traditionalism, would become a beloved and fearless shepherd, verbalizing, defending, and broadcasting his flock's cries for justice during one of their darkest hours.

Indeed, many believed the opposite. Many thought Romero would use his new influence to back the military government in its efforts to maintain the status quo by repressing its citizens. The ballooning impoverished majority longed to shed hunger, fatigue, and misery; they desired to clothe themselves in human dignity. Many thought Romero had been named archbishop to thwart the efforts of those who were organizing to say "no more repression!"

During his years as a priest, Romero had shown little inclination to speak out against injustice. True, during his last two years as bishop he had begun to privately demand investigations into some of the more blatant abuses that occurred in his rural diocese, the poorest of El Salvador. Yet the church authorities who named him archbishop in 1977 did so expecting and wanting him to remain quiet and not make waves. Progressive priests and laity mourned his appointment, upset that the new bishop would halt or hinder their efforts for change.

Thus, it came as a jolt to onlookers when, within months of being named archbishop, Romero had morphed into a fearless and articulate spokesman of international stature who demanded his people's liberation.

That he effectively threatened the powerful was demonstrated when they hired an assassin to silence him.

What transformed Romero in his sixties, a life stage not commonly known for radical changes in ideas and attitudes? How and why did he shift from a priest of piety and prayer who shied from political confrontation to one who audaciously preached Jesus's message of justice on airwaves reaching his country's remotest corners? What caused him to leapfrog from a stalwart of the old-style Catholic Church, steeped in ritual and emphasizing personal sin, to a champion of its daring modern stance on societal sin and just human relationships?

On the surface, it appears the archbishop underwent a conversion. His transformation brings to mind the Apostle Paul, who self-righteously held the clothes of an early follower of Jesus while the believer was stoned to death as a Jewish heretic. As Paul headed off, "still breathing out murderous threats,"[1] to persecute additional followers of Jesus in Damascus, the Holy Spirit zapped him. When the scales fell from his eyes, Paul became "executive" rather than executioner of this new Jewish band.

Romero didn't just look on in the "stoning" of young priests of the Vatican II generation who preached a kingdom of God existing in the here and now rather than in some faraway heaven. He did more than observe. He hefted and hurled some rocks of his own—verbal stones. He targeted the young priests, both Jesuit and diocesan, who put Vatican II reforms into effect. They had been duped by Marxist propaganda, Romero insisted in the press, thus adding his bishop's clout to the ruling elite's justification of its brutal repression.

When questioned about his transformation, which he often was, Archbishop Romero downplayed the notion of a conversion. He acknowledged that his views and behavior had changed, but he also pointed out that he had loved God from an early age and had dedicated his entire life to the Christian church.

Perhaps a better metaphor for Romero than the "blinding light and falling away of eye scales" is that of the "surprise lily." Romero's commitment to the radical Gospel matured and strengthened underground, waiting for the right environment. Then in a burst of consolidated experience and faith, a brilliant bloom jumped two feet out of the ground overnight. Observers,

1. Acts 9:1 (NIV)

wide-eyed, asked, "Where did this come from?" They hadn't seen the burrowed amaryllis bulb as it quietly built reserves.

However it came about, the working of the Holy Spirit in Archbishop Romero's life lurks as the restless question behind this biography, as it does in most writing about Romero.

Journalist María López Vigil makes a powerful observation about Romero. He's unique, she notes, in that he broke two rules of human behavior: that old people do not change; and that the more authority an official attains, the more that official distances him- or herself from the common people.[2]

I might add that Monseñor did not conform to another common trait of aging: loss of physical energy. If Romero's schedule during his three years as archbishop were a railroad timetable, a train derailment or wreck would inevitably ensue. Yet in the midst of a packed, highly stressful agenda and dealing with one tragedy after another, Romero was never calmer and in better health and disposition in his entire life. He derived this energy and inner tranquility, I believe, from the poor who loved him and the Holy Spirit.

Most biographies of Romero concentrate on his three years as archbishop, from 1977 to 1980, when his prophetic voice rang out. A large amount of material documents these public years.

This biography fills gaps in Romero's first twenty-five years—from his birth through his ordination as priest. Because I had set out to write about Romero for young adults, I focused on Romero's family and his early years. In 1998, I was fortunate to secure interviews with the archbishop's four surviving siblings and a retired parish priest who had studied with him as a teen. Father Bernardo Amaya's prodigious memory served up details to garnish with color and personalities this formative period in Oscar's development.

Archbishop Romero's story remains as relevant today as it was several decades ago. The question he confronted in El Salvador now assumes global urgency: how can we humans best relate to one another in an unjust world of few "haves" and many "have-nots" to reduce inequalities and create sustainable communities. The answers he provided remain equally relevant. My hope is that with the passage of time Romero's witness not become solidified in dusty tomes, murals, and marble statues, as valuable as these works are to render homage and encourage memory, but rather that his journey become a dog-eared guidebook to engaging in life with faith and courage.

2. Palumbo, "María López Vigil," 8.

1. A Time to Intervene

(1977)

Monseñor Oscar Romero clung to the handgrip above the passenger seat as Father César Jerez raced, honking and weaving, through San Salvador's congested streets.

"I pray they haven't tortured him." Romero murmured, his voice as tense as his posture on this Friday morning of May 6, 1977.

"They've already tortured four and killed . . ." Jerez didn't need to complete the sentence. Romero, installed as archbishop of the San Salvador diocese two and a half months earlier, was all too aware of the violence being served upon priests in his country. He was as informed as Jerez, who served as the provincial, or superior, of Jesuits in Central America.

Since January, military officials had arrested and tortured four priests, expelling two of them. They kicked out of the country another three priests and two seminarians and refused re-entry to seven priests returning to El Salvador. Two months ago the military ambushed Father Rutilio Grande's vehicle, executing him and his two passengers.

Now Romero and Jerez rushed to see Father Jorge Sarsanedas, a Jesuit from Panama who helped with ministerial duties in the archdiocese. National Guardsmen had apprehended Sarsanedas five days ago. Today was the first time the churchmen were allowed to see him.

After parking at National Guard headquarters in the capital's hub, Jerez and Romero hurried to the monolithic gray building. Monseñor Romero shivered as he entered the center. Stories abounded of hidden torture chambers and detention cells here, and he felt certain the tales weren't rumors.

Colonel Nicolás Alvarenga, chief of the National Guard, rose partly to his feet and leaned against his enormous mahogany desk to greet the church leaders as they entered his office.

"Please be seated." The colonel, calm and cool, waved to chairs. "I'll have him brought to you." He nodded to a soldier, who saluted and left the room.

The archbishop averted his eyes from the pornographic photos under the glass sheet covering the desktop. He read a framed message on the wall next to the Salvadoran flag: "Nothing that is said, done or heard here, leaves this room!" A gleaming machete rested upon a table. Now Romero understood why others secretly called the colonel "the machete man."

A few minutes later, they heard shuffling feet.

"Here he is," the colonel said.

Romero and Jerez turned to see Father Sarsanedas enter. The young priest blinked as though adjusting to light. Bruised and gaunt, he groaned in pain as he lowered himself into a chair.

"You can see he's not hurt," the colonel said. "We haven't laid a finger on him so don't go around claiming otherwise."

Romero looked from the colonel to Sarsanedas. "How have they treated you, Father?"

"They fed me only twice in five days," Sarsanedas croaked in a parched voice. "They blindfolded me, threw me on a cement floor, and kicked me for so long I thought I'd die. At night, they cuffed both my hands and one foot to a bed frame." The dazed priest spoke in a hoarse whisper. "They pulled me out for interrogation at all times of day and night. They haven't yet even told me why I'm here and why they're treating me like this."

"Well, Monseñor, you know how subordinates can get a little carried away," the colonel harrumphed.

Sign False Document?

A soldier entered and served coffee to the colonel and two visitors. Romero stood and offered his to Sarsanedas, who downed it in a single gulp.

"Now, Monseñor, read this statement the priest has made," the colonel said. "Then sign it if you want us to turn him over to you."

Romero skimmed the paper. "This says Father Sarsanedas has been in El Salvador for sixteen years organizing subversive activities. That he was detained for inciting people to violence during the May 1 Labor Day demonstrations." Romero's voice rose in disbelief and he looked to Sarsanedas for an explanation.

"I was saying mass in a village ten miles east of the capital on Sunday morning when those demonstrations took place," the priest said. "I've not written anything. That paper contains pure lies."

Romero locked his gaze on the official. "You'll have to decide what you're going to do, Colonel, but I'm not signing this."

The colonel hesitated. "Not going to sign it?"

"I'll not put my name to a false document," Romero asserted.

The officer thought for a moment. "We're not turning him over to you, Monseñor."

Romero's heart thumped so hard he put a hand to his chest to quiet it. Do not keep this priest here, he prayed in silence.

The colonel turned to Sarsanedas. "Jesuit trouble-makers are not welcome in our country. We're sending you back to Panama."

Romero and Jerez heaved inward sighs of relief. Sarsanedas would not remain in prison. But to be sure the colonel kept his word, they followed the National Guard vehicle that drove Father Sarsanedas to the Ilopango International Airport on the city's east side. They watched as Guardsmen put the priest on a Panama-bound plane.

As they left the airport, Romero turned to Jerez. "Did you notice, Father, when earlier this morning we arrived at the Guard's headquarters, a soldier jotted down your license plate number?"

"Can't say I did. I was too worried about Padre Jorge."

"You may want to trade in this car for a new one."

Jerez considered. Romero's suggestion reminded him that priests' cars had been bombed this year.

"Good idea," he said. "A different car with different plates."[1]

Romero ruminated during the return ride from the airport. When had it become acceptable for officials to target priests? To bomb their cars and parish homes? Just yesterday government agents bombed the archdiocese's newspaper office. How and when had they come to believe they'd get off scot-free with murdering his personal friend, Father Rutilio Grande? Did they imagine they could act with impunity with him as archbishop?

Worse, now it looked as though the perpetrators might indeed go unpunished for Father Grande's murder. Seven weeks had passed since Romero urged El Salvador's president to fully investigate, and the government

1. Information of the churchmen's encounter with the military officer comes from Jorge Sarsanedas and Francisco Mena Sandoval, in López Vigil, *Mosaic*, 161–64, 177–78.

had done nothing. Romero never dreamed his country's powerful minority would carry out such a profane and dastardly act.

Falling Out

Romero now found himself at loggerheads with the government's highest officials—and the wealthy elite who controlled them. This was a problem: the Vatican had named him archbishop precisely because the privileged backed him.

Although some two hundred fifty families comprised the oligarchy, Salvadorans referred to the ruling group as "The Fourteen Families," a term rooted in the nation's history. After the wealthy class won independence from Spain in the early 1800s, prominent landowners became governors of each of the country's fourteen departments.[2] The pattern had persisted.

The elite believed Archbishop Romero would not challenge their power. He had not done so during his previous thirty-five years as priest and bishop. Some were personal friends. He had chimed in with them to oppose the "communist" progressive priests—many of them Jesuits—who preached a new doctrine. Called "liberation theology," it put the church on the side of the poor and oppressed. Liberation theology is based on the belief that Jesus did not call merely for charity to the poor but also desired a just society in which wealth and power were shared by all.

Before he became archbishop, Romero agreed with the elite who claimed liberation theology contributed to the country's ballooning unrest. Indeed, he helped rein in this new creed until governmental persecution took one of the country's best and most devoted adherents, the beloved Father Rutilio Grande. With Grande's murder, Romero began to understand why his nation's long-suffering people—now numbering almost five million—were beginning to proclaim "no more!" to those in power.

That evening, with Father Sarsanedas safe in Panama, Romero wrote to El Salvador's president. His letter reflected his growing impatience and anger:

> I remind you, Mr. President, that there exists between us an agreement that any accusation or complaint against a priest who works

2. Erdozaín named fourteen families as the rulers of El Salvador: Llach, De Sola, Hill, Dueñas, Regalado, Wright, Salaverría, García Prieto, Quiñónes, Guirola, Borja, Sol, Daglio, and Meza Ayau. While these fourteen ranked high, other families also belonged to the dominant class (*Martyr*, 3).

in our country will be communicated to and discussed with the bishop responsible before coercive measures are taken. Once again, this agreement has not been honored.

As I write this letter I hear on the radio and read in the press a statement of the Interior Ministry that basically affirms that Father Sarsanedas was expelled from the country for being found engaged in subversive activities, along with other Central American Jesuits and Salvadoran priests. . . . Mr. President, this report confirms me in the impression that facts are willfully distorted and a campaign of arbitrary persecution is being followed against priests, native and foreign. I greatly lament this . . .[3]

3. As quoted in Brockman, *A Life*, 27–28.

2. A Time to be Young

(1917–1930)

"ZAÍDA, WAKE UP," OSCAR whispered through the partition to his sister's bedroom. "Let's go!"[1]

"Too early." Zaída groaned, her voice heavy with sleep. "It's not even light yet."

"Come on! The sun's almost up," Oscar urged. "Have you forgotten what's happening today? Hurry!"

"I'm coming, I'm coming," eleven-year-old Zaída said, her voice irritable.

Oscar had pail and milking stool in hand when Zaída appeared in the doorway. They left their house on the plaza corner and strolled several blocks up the cobblestone street to the field where the family pastured its cow, mule, and horse.

Oscar basked in the dawn's beauty and nippy freshness. The rising sun transformed the clouds hovering over the valleys into a fluffy quilt of pinks and orange. The majestic mountains and nearby volcano, still night-time black, lent a stark backdrop.

"It's going to be a perfect day." Oscar, almost thirteen, considered whether God had answered his prayers for dry weather. People would be coming to their sleepy village of Ciudad Barrios from surrounding areas to

1. Chapter 2 is based on 1998 interviews the author had in El Salvador with Oscar's surviving siblings—Zaída, Mamerto, Arnoldo, and Gaspar—as well as with one of his half sisters; a first cousin on his mother's side; a woman who as a young teen had worked for Niña Jesus in the household; and a preseminary classmate who later served for two periods as parish priest of Ciudad Barrios, where he came to know the people who had known Oscar in his youth.

Many details come from Don Santos's "little black book," then in Tiberio Arnoldo Romero's possession. In the notebook, Santos jotted births and deaths, the towns and years in which he had served as telegrapher, various recipes for herbal medicines, amounts of money owed and paid, dates of major purchases, and similar details. Information was also gleaned from Jiménez and Navarrete, *Reseña;* Brockman, *A Life*; and Delgado, *Biografía*.

hear Father Nazario Monroy, twenty-five, say his first hometown mass, and the sun would keep footpaths dry to ease traveling.

Father Monroy had journeyed across the wide Atlantic Ocean, to Rome, to study to become an ordained priest. Now he was back. Oscar scarcely dared dream he might someday follow in Father Monroy's footsteps. Becoming a priest loomed as a large ambition for a boy in his circumstances.

Ciudad Barrios nestles among mountains, the cross on its central Catholic church visible from a distance. (1998 photo, Emily Will)

The visitors would include two churchmen who were even now wending their way on horseback through the twenty-five miles of steep mountain trail separating Oscar's town from the nearest city, San Miguel. It would take seven or eight hours for the vicar-general of San Miguel diocese[2] and

2. Brockman says the church official who visited Ciudad Barrios in 1930 for Father Monroy's first hometown mass was the vicar-general of the San Miguel diocese (*A Life*, 35). Jiménez and Navarrete identify him as Monseñor Daniel Ventura Cruz, who "upon learning of Oscar Arnulfo's calling, was interested in his studies and became the primary advocate of his vocation" (*Reseña*, 8). Almost two decades later, in a funeral oration for Ventura Cruz, Romero apologized for his failure to say anything at the earlier burial; he had been too torn up, mourning the loss of this prelate who had counseled and helped mold him as a young priest (*Chaparrastique*, no. 1715, April 10, 1948).

Father Benito Calvo Quinta[3] to cover the distance connecting Ciudad Barrios to the wider world in that year of 1930. Oscar prayed he'd be able to overcome his shyness long enough to talk to them about becoming a priest.

The lack of paved roads and long travel times led Oscar to believe his homeland, El Salvador, was much larger than its actual 8,260 square miles. Later he would learn why Salvadoran writer Julio Enrique Ávila dubbed the country the "Tom Thumb of America." About the size of Massachusetts, El Salvador is the smallest nation of the North and South American continents.

A Distinctive Cow

At the pasture, Zaída took the first turn to milk Vallena, a black and white cow with markings around her eyes like spectacles that gave her a distinct look.[4]

After Oscar finished the milking, he and his sister headed home, carrying the pail between them to share the weight.

"Vallena gave a full bucket today. Guess we won't have to pass by the spring." Oscar's voice contained a smile.

"Don't remind me!" Zaída replied. "It was a dumb idea."

Oscar teased Zaída about the day Vallena gave little milk. Zaida became fearful their father might think they drank or spilled some of it and would punish them with a switching or by making them kneel for hours. She therefore suggested they add some spring water. Oscar, honest to the core, would have no part of it.

The family was up, ready to simmer the milk for their breakfast *café con leche* when Oscar and Zaída returned. It was a good-sized family of six boys and one girl. Gustavo, eighteen, was the oldest. Then came Oscar and Zaída, nine-year-old Rómulo, six-year-old Mamerto, four-year-old Arnoldo, and Gaspar, an infant.[5]

3. Father Benito Calvo Quinto, a Claretian brother from Spain, had been trekking to the town every so often to offer mass following the death of Father Cecilio Morales, the parish priest who had baptized Oscar on May 11, 1919, when Oscar was going on two years old.

4. The author speculates the name may have been *Vallena*, a wordplay on *she goes full* (as in milk) or the homonym *Ballena*, meaning *whale*, or it may have had no meaning. Oscar's father named the cow; the surviving offspring did not know its meaning.

5. Names and birth dates of Oscar's siblings are: Roque Gustavo, October 19, 1911; Aminta Isabel, September 11, 1913 (died as an infant); Oscar Arnulfo, August 15, 1917;

"Papá, maybe your musician friends will be in town today." Zaída bit into a warm, thick tortilla.

"How so?" Papá asked.

Oscar's face grew warm with shame. Papá rarely set foot in church and hadn't remembered today's special service. He had had to be instructed in the basics of Roman Catholic faith before a priest would agree to marry him and Mamá in a religious marriage. True, Papá did encourage Oscar to pray daily, but it was Mamá who gathered her children at seven each evening to kneel and say the rosary.

"Don't you remember?" Mamá shook her head. She ate breakfast while she nursed the baby. "Folks will be coming into town today for Father Monroy's mass. Everyone's eager to hear him speak."

"Indeed?" Papá turned to Zaída. "Well, *m'ija*, if that's the case, perhaps we can expect one or both of my musician friends to drop by."

"Great!" Zaida said, and Oscar agreed. Mamerto clapped with excitement.

All Oscar's family enjoyed music. Papá owned a fine silver flute and Mamá possessed sheet music for some waltzes and classical pieces. Both the flute and the sheet music were prized belongings.[6] One of Papá's friends played violin and another played cello. Sometimes when one or both came to Ciudad Barrios, they got together to play. Oscar delighted in the flute's lilting tones.

As adults, Mamerto and Arnoldo would play the marimba in bands, but Oscar alone wanted to learn the flute, and Papá taught him. He'd draw notes on a dusty surface to teach Oscar how to read music. Only when

---

Zaída Emerita, October 5, 1919; Rómulo Plutarco, December 2, 1921; Mamerto Obdulio, May 15, 1924; Tiberio Arnoldo, September 13, 1926; Santos Gaspar, September 15, 1929. The children also had three *natural*, or half sisters, in town by their father and two other women. The sisters were, according to Oscar's brother Mamerto: Rubia de La O de Esperanza, Rosa Portillo Esperanza, and Candelaria Portillo. Natural, or out-of-wedlock, children were common and accepted. "We got along well and we visited one another. We didn't have any problems," Mamerto Romero said of relationships between Santos Romero's legitimate and natural children.

Father Carlos L. Villacorta, one of the seminarians Romero mentored, explained in an August 5, 1999, phone conversation with the author that churchmen didn't speak out against natural children because "75 to 80 percent of Salvadoran families have illegitimate children."

6. In addition to the concert flute, according to Tiberio Arnoldo Romero, his father owned two other fine possessions: a pocket watch and a steelyard weighing scale.

Oscar had it down pat did Papá give him some scored music paper to use. It was expensive for a family on a tight budget.

"Don't worry, Oscar," Gustavo said. "I'll deliver any telegrams that arrive today."

Oscar said a polite thanks, but inwardly he smiled. Gustavo's offer was not as magnanimous as it appeared. It was an excuse for Gustavo to stay home from church. Oscar knew he was different from Gustavo and his brothers—they preferred noisy, rambunctious games while he enjoyed quieter pursuits, such as reading. Also, unlike his brothers, Oscar had been drawn to the church and to religion since his earliest years. In this Oscar resembled his mother.

Mamá and Papá

On other days, however, Oscar willingly helped deliver telegrams and letters. Papá's work as a telegraph operator had brought him to Ciudad Barrios in the first place. Santos Romero grew up in Jocoro, a town in the adjacent department, or state, of Morazán. Beginning in 1902 and over the next eight years, the national Office of Telegraphs and Telephones posted Santos to ten towns in five of El Salvador's eastern departments. He spent from a few months to several years in any one spot.

After the telegraph office posted Santos Romero to Ciudad Barrios in August 1910, however, he wanted to stay put. He had set his eyes on Guadalupe Jesús Galdámez, a sweet young woman who received enough schooling, likely through grade three, to work as a primary school teacher. Her friends called her "Niña Jesús," using her middle name. Officials had offered her a teaching position in the village of Guatajiaqua, in neighboring Morazán department, but her parents did not want her to venture so far from home.[7]

It didn't take Don Santos and Niña Jesús long to decide to spend their lives together. They wed in a civil marriage on December 8, 1910, and again in a church marriage in January 1911. The newlyweds moved into a house provided by Niña Jesús's parents. It was one of several houses owned by members of her extended family along one side of the town's central plaza.

7. Tiberio Arnoldo Romero believed his mother had taught school locally for a period before her marriage.

Oscar's parents: Santos Romero and Guadalupe Jesús Galdámez.
(photo credit, Zolia Aurora Asturias and Eva del Carmen Asturias)

The large house—half a block in size—was modest in its construction. Its walls were *bahareque*—wood canes or laths covered with mud and whitewashed. The roof was of red clay tiles and the floors of earthen brick.

Furnishings consisted of plain but sturdy chairs and tables made mostly of *roble,* an abundant oak species. Beds were simple wood frames with rope webbings pulled between them to serve as mattresses. The Romero boys slept at least two to a bed.

Don Santos's telegraph office occupied a partitioned corner of the house, and another small area was devoted to the village post office, which Niña Jesús ran. Once the boys turned six or seven, their parents enlisted them to deliver telegrams and letters. The task was not burdensome, as the tiny town was hardly flooded with messages and mail, and they didn't have to walk far.

Oscar, about age ten. (photo credit, Elvira Chacón)

Papá taught Morse code to a few of his sons, including Gustavo, Oscar, and Mamerto, and showed them how to operate the telegraph. Oscar also learned to type after his father bought a typewriter. Oscar enjoyed both the telegraph and typewriter, and would continue an interest in communications technology throughout his life.

Still, Oscar was grateful to Gustavo that he wouldn't need to leave church today to deliver a telegram.

As if reading Oscar's mind, Mamá said, "Do you remember the outfit I sewed for you when you were a little boy and a church dignitary visited?"

Oscar shook his head. "I must have been too young. I always liked to play priest, though."

"You borrowed my aprons to wrap around your shoulders as a robe." Mamá smiled.

"Playing priest" was a common childhood activity, and it was little Oscar's favorite make-believe. Wearing his apron "cassock," Oscar created altars on chairs and "said mass" or "gave Communion." Sometimes he called his friends to march in a pretend saint's day procession. In their play-acting, Oscar reserved the role of priest for himself.

As he grew older, Oscar followed Father Cecilio Morales around. He eventually became an altar boy, and the priest gave him duties, such as ringing the church bells. Oscar stopped in the church to pray at least once a day.

In reality, however, the Romero children did not enjoy much play time. They had to help their parents with household chores and a patchwork of activities to supply their basic needs. Don Santos received a small income for running the telegraph office, as did Niña Jesus for managing the town's mail service. Niña Jesus, an adept seamstress, also sewed clothes for neighbors.

"El Pulgo"

Don Santos farmed some 104 acres of fertile land acquired from his father-in-law.[8] It was located along the skirt of the nearby volcano, some two to three miles from the family home. Since at least 1880, coffee had replaced indigo as El Salvador's "king crop," and Don Santos planted coffee bushes in the shade of the slope's oak trees, as well as some cacao, coconut palms, and *nance*, a type of fruit tree.

The boys hiked to the small farm, which Don Santos named "El Pulgo,"[9] to help their father. Coffee was a fussy crop in certain seasons. Oscar and his brothers cleared weeds and helped prune the bushes and pick the ripe red berries. Leaving the farm, Papá gave each boy a piece of firewood to carry home for the cookstove.[10]

8. At the end of the nineteenth century, Oscar's maternal grandfather, José Ángel Galdámez, purchased fertile but unused farmland ringing the base of the nearby volcano that the mayor's office of Ciudad Barrios had put up for sale. Upon Oscar's grandfather's death, he divided the land, giving his son-in-law Santos Romero some 104 acres of it (Valencia and Arias, "Plática").

9. The word *pulgo* has no meaning. Mamerto Romero described his father as quirky, a trait he said showed in his naming of his children, farm animals, and farm. At one point Don Santos had two kid goats, named Canario and Orión, whom he turned over to a local woman for two years so she could train them to pull carts. Much to his son Romulo's chagrin, who hoped to use the goats to transport firewood to sell, Don Santos sold them to buy the cow.

10. Although several biographies describe Oscar as a weak, sickly child, the author's interviews did not confirm this. Oscar suffered at least one serious early childhood

At least the Romero children were spared the burden of handcarting water from a spring to their home. In 1918, Papá had connected his house to the town's water supply. Mamá and the girl she hired to help scrub clothes were blessed with water piped into the home.

The running water and an indoor bathroom were the family's only modern conveniences, however. The town had no electricity. They lit a kerosene lamp for a couple hours each night, and Papá often read to the children then.

Later that day, Oscar held his head high as he entered the church in the central plaza for Father Monroy's mass. He had worked with others to clean the sanctuary, and townswomen decorated it with sprays of flowers.

Oscar frequently stopped in this Ciudad Barrios church to pray.
(1998 photo, Emily Will)

illness, but he was not sickly in general. The confusion may come from the word *débil*, frequently used in Spanish to describe him as a child. While *débil* often means *physical weakness*, another meaning is akin to *nerdy* or *brainiac*—a difference cleared up for me when Mamerto Romero used *débil* to describe young Oscar in our interview, but went on to explain what he meant by it. By all accounts, Oscar was shy and introverted, but he had no difficulty with the farm or other physical chores, nor in walking the distances involved to do so. "He was timid, that's the word. But for [physical] work he never had problems. He was strong," Mamerto said.

Following the service, the town mayor, Alfonso Leiva, called Oscar to speak with him and the two visitors.

"This young man has been interested in God's work since he was a *cipote*, a little lad," Mayor Leiva told the vicar-general and Father Calvo. "He's bright and would make a fine priest."

The vicar-general turned to Oscar. "Tell us about your education."

"The minor seminary requires a solid foundation," Father Calvo added. Oscar knew the priest taught at the minor seminary, or preseminary, in San Miguel city.

"I attended the public school here." Oscar cast his gaze to the ground.

"Were you a good student?" the vicar-general asked.

"Maestra Anita said I was," Oscar said quietly.

"The public school goes only through grade three," the mayor informed the vicar and priest.

"Oh?" Father Calvo said. "Oscar had only three years of school?"

"No," the mayor quickly replied. "His parents asked Anita Iglesias, the local teacher, to give Oscar private lessons for three additional years. Two hours a day."

"I went to the school for the extra classes in the afternoons after the younger children left," Oscar said.

"What's more," Mayor Leiva said, "Oscar enjoys music. He's learned how to play his father's flute."

Aspirations

"An impressive achievement." The vicar smiled at Oscar. "What do you say, Oscar? Do you want to become a priest? Learn the Gregorian chants?"

"I've always dreamt I would be a priest."

"How about your parents? What do they say about your hopes?" the vicar-general asked.

"I don't know if Papá would like it," Oscar said. "He's apprenticed me to a carpenter."

"To my brother Juan," Mayor Leiva put in.

While Oscar was dutiful in serving as Juan Leiva's apprentice, sawing boards to fashion tables, doors, and coffins wasn't what he envisioned for his future.

"Jesus worked as a carpenter before he began his ministry," the vicar said. "You'd be following his example. And how about your mother?"

"She would like me to be a priest, if that's what I want," Oscar replied.

"Let's talk with Don Santos later," the mayor said to the vicar and Father Calvo. "It's a big commitment to send a son off for many years of schooling."

The mayor turned to Oscar. "We'll see what your Papá has to say."

"Thank you." Oscar had no idea how Papá would respond to the idea. His going off to study would mean Oscar would not bring any income into the household. What's more, he'd create new expenses for his parents.

After the churchmen left to return to San Miguel, Papá spoke with Oscar. "They've offered you a half scholarship," he said. "The mayor speaks highly of your abilities and hard work."

"Can we afford the other half of the tuition?" Oscar asked.

"It'll be difficult, but we'll give it a try. Father Calvo thought I'd be able to pay in coffee beans."

"Thank you, Papá. I won't disappoint you." Oscar set his firm jaw in determination.

"Father Calvo left a list of clothing and other items you'll need to take," Papá said. "He'll be back early next year and you'll return to San Miguel with him."

In the weeks ahead, Oscar thought about the people in his life who made it possible for him to follow his dream.

Papá, for one. Oscar chafed less at Papá's iron hand at the helm of the household than did his brothers.[11] Oscar feared Papá, but he was naturally obedient and therefore avoided some of the punishments Papá imposed. He also recognized how Papá gave them advantages not available to most other village children. He read books to them, encouraged their love of music, and taught them skills such as Morse code. He had taken time to teach Oscar how to read music and play an instrument.

Then there was Mamá, patient and understanding, who involved herself with each of her children.[12] She modeled kindness. Whenever poor

11. Mamerto Obdulio Romero said about his father: "He was very strict. He didn't let us get away with anything. Therefore, we were raised in an atmosphere so immersed in fear that we didn't dare do anything disorderly in the house. And if we told him we were going out to play, he'd say, 'One hour, from seven to eight.' If we went over that time, we were punished."

12. Gaspar Romero told the author that his mother did not scold or yell at her children for misbehavior, but rather talked with and counseled them. She often did not disclose her children's misdeeds to her husband so they would avoid Papá's punishment.

people came by the house, she invited them in for coffee, never looking down on those less fortunate. Oscar hoped to show such faith and charity.

Both parents sacrificed to pay Maestra Anita for Oscar's three years of tutoring, and neither Zaída nor his brothers resented him for this extra opportunity.

Oscar owed a debt of gratitude to the mayor, who went out of his way to speak on his behalf, as did the priests who served his town.

It seemed as if God's hand brought these people together so he might take the next steps to priesthood; as a Bible verse says: "And we know that in all things God works for the good of those who love him, who have been called according to his purpose."[13] Now Oscar looked forward to God's future plans for him.

13. Rom 8:28 NIV

3. A Time to Blossom

(1931–1935)

In January 1931, after Oscar arrived at San Miguel's minor or preseminary—it also housed a small major seminary—it didn't take long for his classmates to learn he played the concert flute.[1] His father had allowed him to bring along the valuable silver instrument.

"Play it for us!" some of the boys insisted one afternoon as they chatted in the dorm room.

Just then Father Benito Calvo, the priest who had accompanied Oscar on the arduous trek to the city, passed the doorway. He served as one of their teachers.

"What's the excitement about?"

After the boys told him, he also encouraged Oscar to play a tune.

Feeling shy and awkward, Oscar opened the small leather case and assembled the instrument. He decided on one of his favorite pieces. Soon he lost himself in the lilting notes, and his nervousness lifted. When Oscar finished, the boys burst into applause.

"That's impressive, Oscar!" said classmate Mauro Yánes.

"I wish I could play the flute," said his friend Alberto Luna.

"Do you also sing?" asked schoolmate Fausto Ventura. When Oscar nodded yes, Fausto said, "I love to sing. Let's sing together sometime."

1. Most of the information in this chapter is a gift from the prodigious memory of Father Bernardo Amaya, who studied at the San Miguel minor seminary at the same time as Romero, but in an older class. Father Amaya, interviewed by the author in 1998, when Amaya was retired and living in San Salvador, recalled such details as the couplet Rafael Valladares wrote about Oscar and the opening lines of the song Oscar and Fausto Ventura sang at a Marist school performance. Amaya had also served on two occasions as parish priest in Ciudad Barrios, Oscar's hometown, and thus came to know the family. Oscar's brothers Arnoldo, Mamerto, and Gaspar Romero also provided useful information.

The specific words spoken in this chapter's conversations are the author's creative device to enliven the information; they adhere as closely as possible to what the author learned in interviews.

"Boys," Father Calvo interjected, "have you heard we sometimes entertain ourselves here by putting on musical performances and plays? A Catholic high school in the city, run by the Marist brothers, will also ask us to provide an evening's program for them. Fausto, we'll arrange for you and Oscar to sing a duet." He turned to Oscar. "Might you be willing to play your flute at the high school sometime?"

Oscar smiled. "I would like that." Already he felt welcomed and appreciated in his new home. If his brothers and sisters never quite understood him, his classmates did.

Actually, except for San Miguel's stifling heat and the pesky mosquitos that made some students and faculty so sick with malaria they had to withdraw, everything about his new home in the flat lowlands agreed with Oscar.[2] He liked his classmates, his teachers, and the seminary itself—an inviting and compact campus in the center of the bustling, growing town of about 17,500 people.

Oscar trekked over the mountains to this destination, then the San Miguel minor seminary that Oscar attended. (1998 photo, Emily Will)

2. Father Amaya said he had suffered a severe bout of malaria while a preseminarian. He also spoke of seminary director Father Benito Ibañez, who had to leave after a year due to malaria.

Some forty students, ages thirteen to eighteen, lived and studied at the preseminary, and a limited number of older students attended the major seminary. The dorms, classrooms, chapel, and dining hall formed a horseshoe around an airy tropical garden. The terra-cotta tile roofs on the long, low white buildings lent a cozy appearance. There was enough land to assign each seminarian a small plot to grow vegetables. The students also helped tend the fruit trees on the property—grapefruit, lemon, avocado, papaya, and others.

Oscar found his days full and challenging. He and his classmates rose at five thirty each morning. They washed, dressed in their long, black cassocks—Mamá had tailored Oscar's first one—and meditated and prayed until six-thirty mass in the chapel. Afterwards, they changed into yellow tunics over pants, ate breakfast, and attended classes from eight until noon, with ten-minute breaks between each fifty-minute class.

The students sat together for the noon dinner, with the teacher-priests at nearby tables. After the meal, one of the priests read from the classics. The stories engaged Oscar and his classmates and introduced them to a range of literature from various cultures. They returned to classes from two to four in the afternoon, followed by an hour of recreation. The day ended with supper, homework, and devotions.

Rebel Hair

Oscar, thirteen, and some eight to ten other boys from around El Salvador formed the youngest, or first-year, class. Oscar quickly became friends with Rafael Valladares, a witty, outgoing youth a few grades ahead of Oscar. Rafael, a bishop's nephew from Opico, a town in western El Salvador, had attended an excellent private elementary school and soon became top student. Before long, though, Oscar, with some extra math tutoring, began to rival his friend in scholarship.

Rafael churned things up with his teasing and joking. He teased Oscar about his prominent nose, proclaiming, "It looks like a *cuma*," a curved machete.

A nickname was also in the making. Oscar had been cast as an elderly manservant in a play to be given at the Marist high school. The evening of the performance, a local woman came to help the students with costumes and makeup. She brought a bottle of white talcum powder to "gray" Oscar's head. Oscar's hair was so bushy, however, that as she sprinkled it with talc, the powder settled to his scalp where it couldn't be seen.

"Ai-yai-yai! With this boy I'm going to go through the entire container!" she said in mock complaint.

Oscar's thick, unruly hair had already drawn his classmates' attention, but after this event Rafael nicknamed him *cabeza de súngano*, the equivalent of something like "shaggy head" or "mophead."[3]

Rafael had persuaded classmates to join him in producing a student newsletter. In one issue, he penned a short rhyming couplet, supposedly in Oscar's name, using the indigenous town names—Cacahuatique and Chaparrastique—by which Ciudad Barrios and San Miguel were still sometimes referred:

Como un arbusto oloroso
nací por Cacahuatique.
Y cresco súngano y hermoso
aquí por Chaparrastique.

Like a fragrant bush
in Ciudad Barrios I was born and bred.
And here in San Miguel
I grow into a handsome mophead.[4]

Oscar took Rafael's ribbing in the good-natured vein in which it was intended. Not so another classmate, who socked Rafael after Rafael turned his wit on him. But the joker knew he had it coming. "Already I'm being crucified," Rafael said with a laugh. Oscar dished out some teasing of his own but, unlike Rafael, knew when to stop.

After the priests learned Oscar could type, they sometimes asked him to put this skill to use for them.[5] Father Antonio Aguadé, in particular, who

3. The *súngano* is a brown fruit about the size of a large grapefruit with yellow or orange fibrous or "hairy" flesh. With the scientific name *Licania platypus* Fritsch, it's also known as *sunsa* in parts of El Salvador and by various other names in the region, including *zapote cabelludo, or* "shaggy *zapote*."

4. Romero recalled Valladares and his newsletters in a tribute written upon his friend's death: "In those unforgettable years in the shade of the Claretian Fathers, Valladares sowed joy, initiative, culture, piety. His fondness for journalism shone in the two newsletters he began: 'Amanecer' [Dawn] and 'El Ideal' [The Ideal]." Romero y Galdámez, "Murió como santo porque vivió como sacerdote," *Chaparrastique*, no. 2379, September 2, 1961, 1,8.

5. Oscar's father noted in his small notebook that he purchased a typewriter in 1925, the year Oscar turned eight.

handwrote the articles he contributed to the diocesan newspaper, would ask Oscar to type them. Oscar didn't mind doing so, although it meant missing the hour of outdoor activity. Later Father Aguadé repaid the favor by taking Oscar out of some classes to teach him to play the harmonium, a reed organ.

Oscar, second from right, and three minor seminary classmates.
(photo credit, Zolia Aurora Asturias and Eva del Carmen Asturias)

Oscar also developed his singing voice at the preseminary. At one of the Marist school performances, he and Fausto Ventura pleased the audience with their duet of the well-loved song *Golondrinas yucatecas*, "Yucatecan Swallows." Its sentimental lyrics compare youth with springtime when swallows arrive and nest, and old age with winter, when both dreams and swallows depart.

Family Environment

Oscar and his classmates would do just about anything for their main teachers, Father Antonio Aguadé, who also served as rector, and two young priests Fathers Benito Calvo and José Burgoa. They were from Spain, members of the Claretian order. Spanish priests in general bore a reputation for rigidity and strictness, but the youthful Calvo and Burgoa joined their students in their joking and fun. All three guided their charges through friendly support rather than rigid discipline.

After Father Aguadé's death in 1960, Romero would describe him as "the kind father, the good teacher, the sincere friend, the tireless writer" who desired first and foremost to nurture his students' gifts.[6]

Minor seminarians on an outing. Oscar, looking to his right, stands between the priests, one of whom is Monseñor Daniel Ventura Cruz. Rafael kneels in front of Oscar. Bernardo Amaya holds his hat in one hand and rolled-up towel in the other. (photo courtesy of Father Bernardo Amaya)

Fathers Calvo and Burgoa took the boys on frequent outings, often to the nearby Grande River and sometimes to Lake Olomega or beaches along the Gulf of Fonseca. Father Burgoa taught many of the boys to swim,

6. In this tribute to Father Aguadé, Romero wrote of his teacher: "He left us with this indelible memory: he strove to encourage our good qualities and talents. I'll be grateful my entire life for the time he complimented me on a little beginner's speech I gave in one of those evening events we organized in honor of our teachers. I felt his words of encouragement were so sincere they seemed to point out to me my responsibility to make good use of the gifts God gives us for God's own glory." Romero y Galdámez, "Murió el Padre Antonio Aguadé," *Chaparrastique*, no. 2304, February 20, 1960, 1,8,12.

an activity Oscar enjoyed and did well.[7] Sometimes they hiked the nearby volcano, climbing all morning to reach a chapel part way up.

Oscar and his classmates welcomed such breaks from their rigorous studies. In his five years of minor seminary studies, Oscar took classes in Spanish grammar, literature and rhetoric (composition and speech), Latin, Greek, introductory French and English, algebra and geometry, world and Salvadoran history, vocal music, including Gregorian chant, botany, zoology, human anatomy and physiology, philosophy, theology, religious practice, and law—both Roman and canon, or church, law.

The preseminarians also served as altar boys and learned how to celebrate mass. They'd practice saying "dry masses," that is, without the Communion wine and wafers.

Oscar wasn't totally cut off from his family. On extended holidays, such as Holy Week, he'd trek to Ciudad Barrios to visit his family. He also occasionally saw any two of his five brothers after they hiked through the mountains—usually at night to avoid the daytime heat—to deliver his clean, ironed clothes and to pick up his dirty ones. Sometimes, though, family friend and merchant Juan Martínez transported Oscar's laundry during his weekly buying trips to San Miguel with a cart and horse.

One day in early 1935, as Oscar, seventeen, neared the end of his minor seminary studies, he had a worrisome discussion with his brothers Gustavo, twenty-three, and Rómulo, thirteen, when they came to San Miguel on the laundry run.

"Papá had to mortgage the farm," Gustavo told Oscar.

Oscar knew of his family's growing financial troubles over the past couple of years, but news of the mortgage was unexpected. "Papá loves El Pulgo. This must break his heart. Do you think he'll be able to pay it off?" Even as he said it, Oscar had a sinking feeling Papá might lose the farm, the main source of the family income. "I didn't imagine it'd come to this."

Troubles Near and Far

Oscar was aware of tumult in the whole of El Salvador in these years of the early 1930s. Indigenous people and peasants in western El Salvador rebelled in 1932, fed up with hunger and lack of land. During the previous generation or two, owners of large coffee plantations had taken over their communal lands.

7. Oscar learned to swim as a child in streams and rivers near his home.

The ruling class responded to the revolt with a wholesale massacre. During *La matanza*, "the massacre," as it has come to be known, El Salvador's military exterminated an estimated thirty thousand people—2 percent of the country's population at the time. The atrocity would keep people silent for a long time.

In addition, the country reeled from economic upheaval after the onset of the worldwide Great Depression in 1929. Coffee prices began to plummet that year and by 1932 had dropped to one-third the average pre-Depression price.

"The government hasn't paid any of its employees, not even the teachers," Gustavo said.

"They haven't paid Papá for the telegraph or Mamá for the mail," Rómulo added. "Papá is drinking a lot." Tears clouded his eyes.

Oscar, eyebrows arched, looked to Gustavo, who nodded to confirm Rómulo's assertion.

"Not good." Oscar frowned. "How's Mamá?"

"She's worried, of course, though she doesn't say anything to Papá about his drinking," Gustavo said.

"And you know the people who rented out part of our house?" Rómulo asked. As soon as Oscar nodded, he burst out, "They're not paying their rent!"

"It's a bad time for everyone," Oscar said. Then, as he remembered Gustavo was looking for work, he turned and asked him, "What have you heard about that opening at the Potosí gold mine?"

"It involves work with the chemist," Gustavo said. "I think I have a chance of getting it. I should know soon. The pay's not bad; I'd be able to support myself. One less mouth for Papá and Mamá to worry about."

"Will Papá manage the farm work without your help?" Oscar asked.

"It's a good question because he can no longer afford to hire workers at busy times, like the coffee harvest," Gustavo said. "But our younger brothers are getting bigger and stronger. They're able to do more at the farm so my absence shouldn't hurt."

"Well, let's hope you get the job at the mine and that this year's crop is good," Oscar said. "Looks like I have lots to pray about. And promise me you'll both pray as well? You should say three Hail Marys each bedtime and three each morning when you awake."[8]

8. Oscar's counsel to pray three Ave Marias at bedtime and upon awakening come from a 1939 postcard that Oscar, twenty-two, wrote to Arnoldo on his birthday: "My

Oscar knew he'd be continuing seminary studies, but he didn't yet know where. It was up to the bishop of San Miguel diocese, Juan Antonio Dueñas y Argumedo, to decide. The bishop, who was his friend Rafael's uncle, might want him to stay on at the San Miguel seminary.

Alternately, Bishop Dueñas could have Oscar wait and begin studies at a new seminary due to open in 1936 in San Salvador, intended to serve not only future priests of El Salvador but also of Honduras, Guatemala, and Nicaragua. Or the bishop might decide to take advantage of a scholarship to send Oscar to Rome, as he had done with Father Monroy.

Whatever the future, Oscar had to think about earning money for his expenses. Fortunately, Gustavo was hired as chemist's assistant at the El Mineral Potosí, a gold mine not far south of Ciudad Barrios. Gustavo helped Oscar and his younger brother Mamerto get short-term work there.

With straps slung across their foreheads to support the leather pouches on their backs, Oscar and Mamerto spent full workdays picking up ore-containing rocks and flinging them into the ever-heavier sacks. They earned fifty cents a day and were paid every two weeks. It was grueling.

After four weeks, Oscar told his brother, "Okay, let's go. With what we've earned I have enough to buy my books and the few other things I need." Mamerto didn't argue with him.

Oscar graduated from minor seminary as a confident eighteen-year-old at the end of 1935. He had blossomed under the guidance of the Claretian brothers and with his classmates' camaraderie and acceptance. He had formed friendships that would last a lifetime. He had also acquired a broad base of knowledge and started to hone the musical and oratory gifts he'd use when he eventually became a priest.

---

dear, often-thought-of Noldo, On September 13, you will celebrate your birthday, so I'm writing you this pretty postcard to congratulate you. To always be happy, you should always do three things: Go to mass on Sundays, always take Holy Communion, love the Virgin Mary, praying to her three Hail Marys upon going to bed and rising. If you do this, God will dearly love you. If you don't, you won't be happy. I send you a hug. Your brother Oscar"

4. A Time to Prepare

(1936–1943)

"I'll be frank with you, Oscar," Bishop Dueñas said. "Now that you've graduated from minor seminary, I'm not sure where to send you for your seminary studies. You might have continued them here in San Miguel, under my guidance, but, alas . . ."

The bishop sighed as he gazed over the campus, now eerily quiet without students. "Odd, isn't it, how happenings in Spain affect us here in our little El Salvador, an ocean away?"

Oscar's heart weighed heavy with the events that recently closed the minor seminary. A few months after his graduation in late 1935, civil war erupted in Spain. The Claretian superiors recalled its order's brothers from abroad, including those who ran the San Miguel preseminary, to replace members killed in the hostilities. The San Miguel diocese lacked its own priests to staff the school.

"Any news of Father Aguadé? Of Fathers Burgoa and Calvo?" Oscar had shed tears when his beloved teachers left for their homeland, headed into violence and uncertainty. How were they faring?

"No news yet. Let's keep them in our prayers." The bishop paused and bowed his head in a moment of silence.[1] "Now back to your situation, Oscar. I have some asking around to do, but until I figure out where to send you, I suggest you go home and spend time with your family. If they don't need you, you might go help Father Monroy in his parish until I get plans lined up for you."

Oscar's posture sagged, and the bishop added, "Don't worry, Oscar, you *will* become a priest. Our country desperately needs priests, and you'll be a fine one. This period of waiting and uncertainty may be God's test of your resolve."

1. Romero would later learn that Father Aguadé had been imprisoned by one of the factions upon his return to Spain. He survived the civil war, and eventually settled in Mexico City. Romero stayed in contact with him throughout the years.

The year passed, and Oscar received no definitive news from Bishop Dueñas about his future. But in 1937, the bishop instructed Oscar to enroll in courses at the Jesuit seminary in the capital city.[2] While Oscar was there, his father died on August 14, 1937, the day after his fifty-fourth birthday and the day before Oscar's twentieth. The death resulted from Don Santos's despair over the loss of his land and livelihood when he was unable to repay a loan he had borrowed during the difficult Depression years.[3] He had also begun to drink heavily to dull his pain.[4]

Personal Loss

In his grief, Oscar wrote:

> Everything, my God, speaks of sadness, of weeping. . . .
>
> My father is dead! Dear Father, I who each evening turned my gaze to the distant east, sending you my loving distant thought, would think of you on the porch of the home I remembered, . . . would see you turning your gaze to the west where your son was. . . .
>
> Only the memories remain, memories of childhood . . . I still see you one night waiting for us to return with Mother from our trip to San Miguel, waiting with a toy for each of us made with your own hands. . . .[5]

There was yet more sad news from home. Oscar's mother suffered a malady, likely a stroke, which disabled her right arm and side. The paralysis would limit her activities for the rest of her life. Oscar, worried about his

2. The San José de la Montaña Seminary.

3. Some family members were outraged that it was a close friend and Arnoldo's godfather, Claudio Portillo, who seized the property as payment for the 2,500 colóns (US $1,000) Don Santos owed him. This left Niña Jésus and her children without a means of livelihood. Gaspar recalled that when he reached the legal age of adulthood, he confronted Portilla and demanded that he explain himself and return the land. When Portilla refused to do so, Gaspar showed him his pistol and threatened to shoot him. Portilla reconsidered and gave him back a portion of the land. After Oscar returned from Rome, and Gaspar told him what he had done, Oscar scolded him severely, telling him he had done wrong.

4. According to his son Tiberio Arnoldo Romero, in a December 2, 1998, interview with the author, in San Miguel.

5. Part of a remembrance found among Romero's papers after his death. From Brockman, *A Life*, 36.

family's future, wished he could hurry the day when he'd be working as a priest, earning a salary, however meager it might be.[6]

Bishop Dueñas eventually sent a message to Oscar. The bishop had been granted scholarships at the Colegio Pío Latino Americano in Rome and would send Oscar and his classmates Alberto Luna and Mauro Yánes to study there.

"I chose you three because you're intelligent, with common sense and the willingness to work hard," the bishop told the trio when they met to discuss plans. "*And* because you're all healthy and hardy."

"Why's that so important?" Mauro asked.

"Rome gets cold in the winter. We Salvadorans are used to our subtropical sun. When we spend extended periods in Italy, many of us return with long-term respiratory problems. I need robust priests here because, as Jesus told his disciples, 'The harvest is plentiful but the workers are few.'"[7] The bishop looked over the young men, his eyes intense. "You'll also need emotional fortitude, especially if events in Europe continue to heat up. This man Hitler in Germany seems determined to rile up people. Did I tell you he made an appearance at the three-hundred-year anniversary of the Passion Play in Oberammergau?"

They nodded. Indeed, the bishop had told them about the 1934 event, a great outdoor pageant held every ten years. Bishop Dueñas had taken his nephew, Oscar's good friend Rafael Valladares, and Abdón Arce, another San Miguel preseminarian, on his reporting trip to the Vatican that year. Rafael and Abdón stayed to study for the priesthood in Rome. They had stopped to see the famous theatrical production in Oberammergau, Bavaria, on their way.

"Adolf Hitler was named Germany's chancellor the previous year." The bishop dabbed his sweaty brow with a handkerchief. "He swooped through the town in an open black Mercedes, swastika flag on its front fender, to scattered cheers of 'Heil Hitler.' Hearing support for him chilled me. He stayed for the day-long performance and afterwards shook hands with the main actors.

6. After their father's death, two of Oscar's brothers earned money for the household by transporting firewood, coffee, and other agricultural products in an ox-drawn cart, according to Gaspar.

7. Matt 9:37 NIV

"That Hitler's a hatemonger and a rabble-rouser. Under the Versailles treaty, Germany's forbidden to rearm itself, but that's exactly what Hitler's doing. Let's pray he doesn't march Europe into another war."

To Rome

In late 1937, Oscar, Alberto, and Mauro boarded an Italian liner for Rome.[8] The ship soon anchored at a port in northern Venezuela, where another young man headed to Rome boarded.[9] Eighteen-year-old Alfonso could hardly tear himself away from the extended family members who came to see him off.[10]

Oscar, second from right, aboard the Orazio. (photo credit, Zolia Aurora Asturias and Eva del Carmen Asturias)

8. They left from Puerto Cutuco, on the Pacific. The ship was the Orazio, powered by two diesel engines. During a later trip, in January 1940, an explosion in the engine room set fire to the Orazio during a Mediterranean storm. The ship was carrying 218 crew and 431 passengers, many of them Jews escaping the Holocaust. About six hundred survivors were rescued from lifeboats, many badly burned.

9. The Venezuelan port of La Guaira.

10. His full name was Alfonso Alfonzo Vaz.

Oscar, wanting to ease the grieving newcomer's transition, introduced himself. "Would you like to see your berth?"

The distressed youth nodded.

"Come. I'll show you." Oscar led the way to their bunks.

The next morning at breakfast, Oscar sat with Alfonso and offered to help communicate with the waiter. "That's *burro* in Italian," Oscar said, pointing, and the two boys laughed. Who would have thought the Spanish word for either *donkey* or *stupid person* meant *butter* in Italian? Oscar picked up an apple. "*Mela*," he said, and Alfonso repeated it.[11]

Oscar, Alfonso, Mauro, and Alberto were four of about a dozen young Latin Americans crossing the Atlantic for seminary studies under Jesuit professors at the Gregorian University. Also aboard were some twenty priests and monks, as well as the nuncio of El Salvador.[12]

"Want to see the movie with me?" Alfonso asked Oscar one evening.

"I'm going to say the rosary on deck, if you'd like to do that instead," Oscar replied.

"Maybe some other time," Alfonso said as he headed to the theater.

Besides inviting others to pray the rosary in the evenings, Oscar assisted priests with two or three masses each morning. His devotion to spiritual matters became obvious to other passengers during the eleven-day crossing.

Once in Rome, the Latin American seminarians made their way to the Pontificial Colegio Pío Latino Americano, a fifty-year-old three-story building.[13] The neoclassical edifice, a city block in size, next to the Tiber River and close to the Vatican, served as both a home-away-from-home and a structured learning environment for the students who lived in it under the guidance of Jesuit priests.

After a three-year separation, Oscar was thrilled to meet up again with his friend Rafael Valladares, who offered to show the newcomers around. "Your new home is spacious, as you can see," Rafael told them, "but it's

11. Monseñor Alfonso Alfonzo Vaz, in a February 18, 2000, phone conversation with the author, said that even some sixty-five years after the voyage, he hadn't forgotten his first Italian words, among them *apple* and *butter*, which Oscar had taught him, nor Oscar's kind befriending of him in his homesickness.

12. From photo in Jiménez and Navarrete, *Reseña*, 10. The nuncio, the Vatican's ambassador to El Salvador, was returning home after his term of service.

13. The Colegio Pío Latino Americano was located on the road named Via Gioacchino Belli, next to the Tiber River and close to the Vatican. The *colegio* moved to a new location in 1962, and the building on Via Gioacchino Belli was eventually demolished.

drafty. So it's too hot in summer and too cold in winter. As you'll find out soon enough."

Rafael showed them the dorms and the classrooms. "We attend our course lectures at the Gregorian University, but often the real learning takes place in these classrooms."

"How so?" Oscar asked.

"Well, the university lectures aren't always easy to understand. The Jesuit scholars who give them come from many countries. Belgium, France, Germany, the Netherlands, Spain, and the United States. And of course from here in Italy."

"So, why's that a problem?" Mauro asked. "They all lecture in Latin, right?"

"Latin, yes, but accented in each professor's native tongue. Some are much easier to understand than others. We had one professor with such a thick accent we feared we'd fail his course." Rafael swiped his forehead in mock fear. "And the professors lecture old-fashioned style."[14]

"What does that mean?" one asked.

"They lecture, then leave. No time for questions."

"So what do you do when you can't understand the professor?" Oscar asked.

"That's where these classrooms come in." Rafael nodded to the blackboard at the front of the room. "The Jesuit fathers divide each year's class into four smaller groups, which they call *camerate*.[15] Then they meet with each *camerata* to review and discuss the lectures."

"In Latin or Spanish?" one asked.

Rafael rolled his eyes. "In Spanish, of course. That was one reason why the Jesuits built this *colegio*—to help us Spanish-speaking Latin Americans make it through seminary."

Oscar turned to the youth who had asked the question. "Remember. The students who attend the Gregorian University come from around the world, and Latin is our common language," he said soothingly.

The youth hit his forehead with his palm. "Of course! What a *burro* I am!"

14. Information from Father Alfonso Castro, a Mexican seminarian one year behind Oscar, in November 16, 1999, phone interview with the author.

15. The Italian word *camerata* can mean *comrade*, *companion*, or *dorm*. Its plural form is *camerate*. In this context, the Jesuits seemed to have used the word in the sense of *team*.

But can he dance?

Rafael led them to a wide double door. When he opened it, Oscar gasped to see a lovely theatre.

"Our Jesuit fathers want to make sure we learn to speak comfortably in public," Rafael told the newcomers. "They assign us weekly performances. The *camerate* compete with one another."

"What kind of performances?"

"You name it. Everything from classical plays to parodies—spoofs, that is—and musical theater, including operettas and zarzuelas."

"What's a zarzuela?" Oscar asked, baffled.

"It's like a Spanish stew, with a bit of everything thrown in. Speaking, dancing, singing. Both opera and popular music." When Oscar's brow knit, Rafael said, "Don't worry, Oscar. You'll do fine, with all your musical talent. Not as well as me, maybe, but . . ."

Rafael laughed and Oscar joined in. He was glad to be with his light-hearted friend again, even though Rafael could not allay his fear of tripping over his own feet in some dance.

"We also use this theatre to celebrate birthdays, when the *camerate* take turns performing as choruses. At Christmas, the teams compete in building *nacimientos,* nativity scenes. Some get really clever, rigging up lights for their mangers or devising ways to make some of the figures move.

"Let me show you the chapel. It's also two stories tall." Holding open its door, Rafael said, "Some of you may be ordained in this very chapel."

"Seems a long way off," Oscar commented.

"Now it does," Rafael agreed. "But once courses begin, you'll wish you had even more time to cram everything in."

"What about fun?" Alfonso asked.

"Fun? You think they sent you to Rome to have a good time?" Rafael teased. "Let me show you the area set aside for billiards, chess, and table tennis. And the soccer and basketball courts."

Rafael's tour ended in the dining room, in time for the evening meal.

The students who lodged at the Colegio Pío Latino Americano ate their meals in silence. They took turns reading aloud from classical literature while the other students ate, another exercise to help them develop ease in speaking in front of others. Even with a couple years of seminary under his belt, Oscar seemed to struggle with public speaking. On a notecard of November 23, 1940, he wrote, "[a seminary companion] tells me I'm a torrent of emotion . . . because my voice trembled nervously just reading the title of the book in my hands." Two days later, however, he wrote, "Today I read in the refectory. My nerves were calmer."[16]

The Jesuit fathers ran the combined boardinghouse and school as a large family, like the Claretian brothers at the minor seminary had done. Firm and disciplined but kind, they took every opportunity to expand the horizons of the some hundred fifty seminarians in their care. They also planned recreational outings.

On trips to the beach, Oscar, a strong swimmer, offered swim lessons to his companions. Once, he invited fellow seminarians to swim out to a rock. He arrived first. He sat on the boulder but quickly rocketed off: it was covered with spiny sea urchins. Unable to sit for several days, the stoical Oscar didn't tell his classmates what had happened. The Jesuit brother who ran the colegio's infirmary, however, leaked Oscar's "secret."[17]

In preseminary, Oscar had impressed his fellow students with his musical gifts and his academic achievement, especially remarkable considering his inadequate primary schooling in El Salvador's "boonies." He didn't stand out among the seminarians in Rome, however, where he felt most comfortable among a small group of friends.[18]

Seminary studies pushed Oscar to his limits, but he remained steadfast and determined. In November 1939, he noted, "Study is difficult, hunger humbles me, communal life torments me, my thesis worries me. It matters not! *Avanti* [onward]!!"[19]

War!

On June 10, 1940, Oscar joined some seminarians to stroll in one of Rome's lovely plazas, something they frequently did. As they chatted, enjoying the

16. These are two of Romero's two hundred fifty notecards, handwritten during his seminary days in Rome, shared in Delgado, "Joven Aspirante," 8.

17. Monseñor Alfonso Alfonzo Vaz, in February 18, 2000, phone interview with author, and in Brockman, *A Life*, 34.

18. Father Alfonso Castro, of Mexico City, a seminary contemporary of Oscar, commented in a November 16, 1999, phone interview with the author: "Oscar was very shy, introspective. He didn't speak much and had few friendships." Another co-seminarian, however, viewed Oscar as quiet but not a loner. "He was not a leader but he was cheerful and very well-integrated into the student body," said Father Rafael Montejano in a November 22, 1999, phone interview with the author. In adulthood, Montejano became a recognized historian of his native state of San Luis Potosí, Mexico.

19. Delgado, "Joven Aspirante," 8.

fresh air and bubbling fountains, a loudspeaker barked a shrill announcement. It took several repetitions for the people in the plaza to comprehend the garbled proclamation. When the import of the message hit, local women around the students broke into tears.[20]

Italy had entered the war, on the side of the Germans.[21]

World War II had begun nine months earlier when Nazi Germany occupied Poland on September 1, 1939. Oscar had been in Rome two years. Now Italy would actively participate in the bloodshed, and Rome's officials began nighttime drills to prepare citizens for possible bombing raids.

For the next six months, the seminarians awakened to one or two nightly sirens. Yawning, but with racing hearts, Oscar and his fellow students hurried to the basement. Although the alarms were meant only to ready people for possible future bombings, the earsplitting awakenings stole sleep and induced fear.

With Italy's entry into the war, the Jesuits running the *colegio* tried to find what they hoped would be safer places in other countries to send the seminarians until hostilities ended. The Latin Americans couldn't go home; war halted most transatlantic voyages to and from Europe, due to such dangers as underwater mines, German U-boats, and rapidly shifting boundaries among the major powers. Those able to relocate to other European countries did so. Sweden, which had declared itself neutral, gave haven to fifty or so Mexican seminarians.[22]

The seminarians felt more separated from their families than ever, as they were limited to twenty-five-word "letters" that were sent through the Vatican or the International Red Cross and took months to arrive in the other hemisphere.[23] Whenever one of them received a newspaper from his home country, all the others read it, too, no matter how old its news.

Oscar was among those who remained in Rome, sharing the fate of Italian civilians. Italy's farms and factories redirected their output to the war effort, leading to year-round hunger and frosty homes in the winter for the citizenry.

20. Father Alfonso Castro, November 16, 1999, phone interview with author.

21. In September 1943, Italy switched sides to back the Allied Powers against Germany.

22. Father Bernardo Amaya, December 4, 1998, interview with author.

23. The war delayed or halted usual international mail delivery for several reasons, including suspensions in service between enemy countries, rapidly changing political boundaries due to conquest and occupation, altered or no longer usable travel routes, and mail censorship by one country against another.

The two priests who served as the Pío Latino Americano rectors during the war shouldered the tough job of finding food for the young men who remained.[24] Food was rationed, and the rectors sometimes resorted to carrying in food hidden beneath their cloaks, including on occasion some meat from a farm outside of Rome.

Chestnuts from Italy's abundant chestnut trees became a staple, prepared in myriad ways. Pureed, they made pancakes or fritters, which became a frequent meal at the *colegio*.[25]

Despite the rectors' efforts, the seminarians constantly fought hunger. Every day, famished students fainted at the Gregorian University.[26] Even so, the seminarians felt fortunate; most of the civilian population endured greater hardships than they.

Out for a stroll along the Tiber River on a November day in 1940, Oscar met an impoverished man who handed him a card offering his services mending priests' vestments. "How anguished he looked!!!"[27] Oscar noted later, distressed by the man's suffering.

As he neared the *colegio* on his return that day, a pauper approached him.

"Please, food, please," the ragged man implored. "Have mercy, young man." Oscar's own empty stomach rumbled but the beggar's anguish touched him.

"Wait here," Oscar instructed the man.

Oscar went to his room and gathered scraps of bread he had been stashing—he termed it "contraband" because *colegio* rules forbade seminarians from "smuggling" food out of the dining hall. He returned to the destitute man and offered him the bread.

"God bless you," the man exclaimed.[28]

On Christmas Eve 1940, Oscar gazed out on a snowfall, a rare occurrence in Rome. His dorm was drafty but heated. "Here I am very comfortably savoring this beautiful white panorama while outside how many

24. Father Manuel Porta from 1937 to 1940, followed by Father Darío Ferioli until 1945.

25. According to Fathers Alfonso Castro and Rafael Montejano, who were seminarians at the time. (In separate 1999 phone interviews with author.)

26. A quote from Montejano, ibid.

27. Delgado, "Joven Aspirante," 8.

28. Ibid. English translations of notecards from Carlos Colorado, "Fire Brand," September 11, 2010, http://polycarpi.blogspot.com/2010/09/fire-brand-on-may-24-1941-young-oscar.html.

poor people suffer from hunger, cold, and broken spirits," he penned.[29] As difficult as his own situation might be, Oscar realized others were in even direr straits, and he felt compassion for them.

Interestingly, Oscar's note exactly one year later foreshadows his thinking of his future years as archbishop: "The poor are the incarnation of Christ. Through their tattered clothing, their darkened gazes, their festering sores, through the laughter of the mentally ill . . . the charitable soul discovers and venerates Christ."[30]

A challenge greater than hunger was to come.

In May and July 1943, Allied Powers[31] flew some 520 bombing sorties over Rome, directed at three sites—the railroad, airport, and a steel factory. Thousands of civilians were killed. Oscar and fellow residents of the Pío Latino Americano experienced fear and uncertainty. They adjusted to power outages and no lights after dark. They covered the building's windows with blackout paper to reduce the chance of being targeted by bombers.

"We got used to the fear," a classmate of Oscar's later said, "but it was very, very, difficult."[32]

By the time of Rome's bombardment, Oscar had graduated cum laude two years earlier, in 1941, with a licentiate degree in theology from the Gregorian University.[33] Unable to leave Rome, he joined Rafael in working for a doctoral degree. Oscar planned to do his dissertation, a lengthy essay, on Christian perfection, based on the teaching of Luis de la Puente.[34] A Spaniard, Puente was a sixteenth-century Jesuit and writer of ascetics who at one point in his life dedicated himself to caring for people stricken with the plague.

Oscar longed for holiness throughout his years in Rome. In March 1940, for instance, he wrote, "If I do not advance in holiness at the pace it demands, I hope to at least move toward it, albeit slowly."[35]

Three years afterward, while doing doctoral research, Oscar noted that he had been reading Puente's biography of Balthazar Alvarez, an early

29. Ibid.

30. Ibid.

31. Of the Allied Powers, primarily Great Britain and the United States flew these sorties.

32. Father Alfonso Castro, in 1999 phone interview with author.

33. Equivalent to a master's degree.

34. Brockman, *A Life*, 38.

35. Delgado, "Joven Aspirante," 7.

Jesuit mystic and the spiritual director of Saint Teresa of Avila.[36] As Oscar immersed himself in these saintly exemplars, he wrote, "The Lord has inspired me with strength . . . [and] a great desire for holiness. I've pondered how far a soul can climb if it lets itself be entirely possessed by God."[37]

Father Oscar Romero, recently ordained. (photo credit, Zolia Aurora Asturias and Eva del Carmen Asturias)

On Holy Saturday 1942, April 4, having reached the required age of twenty-four, Oscar realized his lifelong dream. He was ordained a priest in the *colegio's* chapel. Overcome with emotion, he noted:

> My Saturday of glory! On this day the Lord made, my goal is crowned as I express my hallelujahs: I am now a priest! . . . The fragrance of the holy oil spilled on priestly hands was the love of Christ lavished on the chosen. With the Lord's yoke on our shoulders, at one with the Pope, our voice, now omnipotent with the divine omnipotence of priesthood, we repeated on the altar the

36. An English version of Puente's biography of Alvarez can be found at https://ia600300.us.archive.org/9/items/lifeoffatherbalto1puen/lifeoffatherbalto1puen.pdf.

37. Delgado, "Joven Aspirante," 9. Among other things,Teresa of Avila is known for her prayers that put her in such deep communion with God that her body often levitated.

> wonder of the Cenacle [Upper Room]: *This is My Body . . .* ! And surprised by the power of our lips, the Pope kneeling with us, all of us silent, we glorify the presence of the one who came to tell us: "I no longer call you servants, but friends."[38]

Two years later, Romero would share his exalted notions of priesthood in the diocesan paper, and it became a theme he revisited occasionally. He felt inspired, and perhaps comforted, by the idea that, no matter what might happen, a priest was a priest for time without end:

> All manner of disaster may thunder over the world. They can strip [the priest] of everything he has, his flesh can succumb to illness, and even his soul can exchange Peter's fervor for Judas's betrayal . . . but always, with courage or cowardice, loyal or traitorous—the priestly character will be written at the bottom of his soul: For eternity![39]

Thirty years out, however, during a spiritual retreat, the matured Father Romero journaled about some of the doubts and mixed motives that had assailed him at the time. Like many seminarians who near ordination, he questioned whether he was suited to a life of celibacy. Yet he feared what people would think if he backed out of taking his vows at such a late date. He also worried about what he would do as a vocation after years of preparing for the priesthood.[40]

Homeward Bound

Before Romero could finish his doctorate, the new bishop of San Miguel diocese, Miguel Angel Machado, called both Romero and Valladares to return to El Salvador, either because he feared for their safety in a city under siege or, as one Salvadoran priest believed, he desperately needed clergy at home.[41]

"Well, Oscar, let's hope they don't shoot us down." Rafael tried to make light of their situation as they boarded a plane on August 16, 1943. Oscar

38. Ibid., 10.

39. Romero y Galdámez, "Juventud e ideal sacerdotal," *Chaparrastique*, no. 1521, May 27, 1944, 1.

40. Romero y Galdámez, *Ejercicios espirituales*, 60–61.

41. Father Bernardo Amaya, December 4, 1998, interview with author.

had turned twenty-six the day before and Valladares was thirty. "Hopefully God will spare two young priests," Rafael added with a laugh.

The pair had an uneventful flight to Barcelona, Spain, where they boarded a ship to Cuba. During the two weeks it took to cross the Atlantic, they relished the idea that they'd soon be back in warm, sunny weather and reunited with their families. Their final war worry, they thought, were German submarines torpedoing ships in the Caribbean.

When the ship weighed anchor in the Havana harbor, Cuban officials asked to see the papers of those disembarking.

"What's this? You're coming from Rome," a severe official asked the priests, who were dressed in their black cassocks.

"We studied for the priesthood in Rome, and we're headed home to El Salvador." Valladares spoke for both of them.

"You're arriving from Italy, an enemy country," the official said. "Here in Cuba we detain all passengers coming from Germany and Italy." Authorities arrested the young priests and took them to an internment camp.[42]

"Our plane wasn't shot down and our ship wasn't torpedoed," Valladares commented to Romero. "But it looks like we still won't get home any time soon."

"Think of the Apostle Paul," Romero said. "He was shipwrecked three times, spent a night and a day in the open sea, and imprisoned at least once."

"And don't forget how he was whipped thirty-nine lashes on five occasions, beaten with rods three times, and once pelted with stones." Valladares smiled. "Let's hope God doesn't favor us quite so generously."

The two priests weren't flogged, beaten, or stoned during their four-month internment, but, like Paul, they experienced hunger and hardship. Already undernourished, the hard labor assigned them at the camp exhausted them to the point they became ill. Valladares might have died had not Redemptorist priests in Havana heard of their plight, worked for their release, and got them admitted to a Havana hospital. With their identities and travel purposes verified, Cuban officials allowed them to leave.

42. Cuba set up four concentration camps after Japan attacked Pearl Harbor. They were Tiscornia, Torrens, and Isla de Pinos, where mostly Japanese-Cubans were interned, and Arroyo Arenas, for women. Source: http://www.cuba.com/cuba_detail_1788_world_war_ii.html. The author was unable to learn at which of these Romero and Valladares were imprisoned.

Once more they boarded a ship, in U-boat infested waters, destined for Mexico. From there, they traveled by land to El Salvador.[43] Though skinny and drained, they arrived safely in San Miguel on New Year's Eve 1943. The diocesan newspaper and its citizens heralded their arrival as "a Christmas gift."[44]

From San Miguel city, Romero headed to his hometown of Ciudad Barrios, where the townspeople turned out to give him a grand reception, proud of their native son who had studied in Rome.

He said his first mass there on January 11, 1944, undoubtedly recalling Father Monroy's first mass in the same church some thirteen years earlier, when Oscar had confided in officials his interest in the priesthood.

The eight years between Romero's 1935 graduation from minor seminary and his 1943 return to El Salvador furnished a turbulent stage on which he grew to adulthood and was ordained a priest. His reunion with his family was tinged with sadness, for the family had experienced upheaval while Oscar was faraway and correspondence nearly impossible. While Romero studied in Rome, his younger brother Rómulo died of appendicitis at age seventeen. The family lost its farmland, and the older children left town to seek their fortunes elsewhere. His mother would eventually move to San Miguel to live with her daughter and two grandsons, and Oscar helped his youngest brother, Gaspar, study in a San Miguel high school.

Valladares's uncle, Bishop Dueñas, Oscar's beloved mentor, had also died while the young men were in Rome.[45]

What Romero later said of Valladares was most certainly true for himself as well: "War's austerities strengthened his resolve to become a dedicated priest."[46]

43. Romero and Valladares traveled during the height of German U-boat activity in waters near Cuba, an island nation that held strategic importance as a portal to the Western hemisphere. Between mid-1942 and early 1944, German subs sank seven Cuban ships, killing more than eighty Cuban marines and three Americans.

Source: http://www.cuba.com/cuba_detail_1788_world_war_ii.html.

44. Romero y Galdámez, "Murió como santo porque vivió como sacerdote," *Chaparrastique*, no. 2379, September 2, 1961, 1,8.

45. The bishop died in 1941, at age seventy-three.

46. Romero y Galdámez, "Murió como santo porque vivió como sacerdote," *Chaparrastique*, no. 2379, September 2, 1961, 1,8.

5. A Time to Dig In

(1944–1967)

After Father Romero rested three months to restore his strength, the new bishop of San Miguel diocese, Miguel Angel Machado,[1] assigned him as parish priest of Anamorós. The parish lay in a poor area in the mountains of the eastern La Unión department.

Romero's youngest brother, Gaspar, then fourteen, moved with him to Anamorós to help with such tasks as toting river water to their house for bathing and shopping for food in the marketplace. Gaspar perceived his role to include that of a live-in "chaperone." He shielded the handsome young priest, who had taken a vow of lifelong celibacy, from women who might come to the house.

Gaspar also accompanied his brother on horseback to visit hamlets reachable only by trail. Although Father Romero had not yet regained his prewar heft, he possessed sufficient vigor to carry out the strenuous work of ministering to people living in all corners of the rural, rugged forty-two-square-mile parish.

1. While Bishop Machado may have acted in good faith, various sources agree the bishop's heart and energies were not in his duties. Romero's brother Gaspar said that while Machado was good-natured, he shirked responsibilities: "He didn't leave the bishop's palace except to go to and from Mass. He didn't mix with people, he didn't participate in church activities, he didn't work, he had no plans, he didn't do a thing. He was interested only in money."

One of Romero's personal acquaintances said, "Bishop Machado didn't give orders and he didn't give advice. What he gave were loans at outrageous interest rates" (Manuel Vergara, in López Vigil, *Mosaic*. 29–30). Biographer Erdozaín claims Romero suffered nervous qualms covering up the diocese's institutional sins under Machado without compromising his own integrity (*Martyr*, 6).

Father Carlos L. Villacorta, one of Romero's minor seminarians, said Migueleños knew Bishop Machado was a moneylender but the townspeople did not believe he behaved abusively in that role. In an August 5, 1999, phone interview with the author, Villacorta said Machado was basically a good and humble man but had ongoing financial worries because he supported at least four of his siblings, as well as some nieces and nephews and their families, and they all lived with him at the bishop's house.

Father Romero says an outdoor mass during his early ministry.
(photo credit, Zolia Aurora Asturias and Eva del Carmen Asturias)

The novice priest was not to stay long in Anamorós. Bishop Machado, needing a new secretary, spoke with one of his experienced priests.

"I really don't know whom to name. I can't think of anyone qualified for the position," the bishop said.

"Well, look, Monseñor, yes, you do have someone," the priest replied. "A trained person."

"Who do you have in mind?" the bishop asked.

"Have you noticed Oscar's dedication? Why don't you bring him in to serve as your secretary?"

The bishop remained pensive. "I was thinking of someone experienced, and Romero is just getting started as a parish priest."[2]

Soon afterwards, despite his doubts about the new priest's lack of experience, Bishop Machado summoned Romero to serve as his personal secretary in San Miguel, the blistering hot city in which he had attended minor seminary. Father Romero had been in Anamorós only three months.

Upon his return to San Miguel, Romero reunited with Valladares, who had been named the diocese's vicar-general, the bishop's "second-in-command." The friends collaborated in their wide-ranging activities.

2. Father Bernardo Amaya, in a December 4, 1998, interview with author, San Salvador. The experienced priest was Father Eulogio Rodríguez.

After organizing the diocesan files and records, Romero shouldered diverse secretarial and pastoral duties. The bishop assigned him as priest of the central Cathedral parish, which took in the main Cathedral–Basilica of Our Lady of Peace and the smaller San Francisco and Santo Domingo churches.[3]

The cathedral remained under construction in 1944 when Romero arrived. He would complete its building in 1962, exactly a century after its first stone was laid in 1862. Today, with its two seven-story bell towers, the cathedral ranks among the city's most prominent buildings. He also oversaw a renovation of the Santo Domingo Church.

Romero threw himself into the life and work of his parish and the larger San Miguel diocese. He organized catechism classes and first Communions and served as advisor to at least one young adult group. He began and took an active role in a long list of Catholic charitable and service groups.[4] Romero even reached out to shoeshine boys, organizing them into an association.

Perhaps because of his own father's alcohol-related death or the addiction's prevalence—his older brother, Gustavo, also became alcoholic and died before reaching middle age—Romero helped found a local Alcoholics Anonymous chapter. Father Romero was generally patient with alcoholics. If an intoxicated person impinged on church life, however, his temper could flare.

Romero and Valladares eventually got the preseminary going again, and they both lived there for a period.[5]

"With eighteen youth filled with ideals and priestly longing, the minor seminary has reopened, a beginning full of promise and special grace," Romero announced in the diocesan newspaper.[6] He urged the flock to encourage boys who felt inclined to the calling, as others had done for him. The seminarians were Romero's pride and joy. One seminarian said Romero spoiled them.

Father Romero did not overlook outreach. He visited prisoners weekly to say mass, and occasionally dropped off a movie to ease their boredom.

3. For some years, Romero resided in a room at the Santo Domingo convent.

4. These included the Legion of Mary, an organization of lay people who assist with pastoral duties in the parish, such as visiting the sick; the Knights of Christ the King, a fraternal group devoted to local service and charity; and Caritas, a relief organization that distributes food to the hungry; and many others.

5. Father Bernardo Amaya, December 4, 1998, interview.

6. Romero y Galdámez, "El espiritu sopla," *Chaparrastique*, no. 2984, February 10, 1964, 1,3.

He traveled to remote parts of the diocese to visit parishioners and participate in their baptisms, weddings, and other special church events.

Romero also became a communicator, spreading word of the Roman Catholic faith and diocese activities in several media. He helped Valladares, editor of the diocesan weekly newspaper, *Semanario Chaparrastique*, and wrote regular editorials for it. He filled in as editor when Valladares was away, and later took over the duty entirely.

Gifted in oratory, Father Romero became an admired preacher, and several radio stations eventually broadcast his Sunday morning mass. The official station of San Miguel diocese aired regular chats with Romero. In the days before television, parishioners found the programs pioneering and interesting. Even young children listened to them, as one man later recalled from his own experience:

> It wasn't just in San Miguel. All of us in the eastern part of the country knew about him because of his programs on *Radio Chaparrastique*. I was a second grader in La Unión, and I never missed an opportunity to listen to him. . . .
>
> A lot of people would write him letters asking about certain topics, asking for advice or financial help, or volunteering for his charities. And he would read that whole mess of letters on the radio. I loved that program because there was so much participation.
>
> But for me, the most impressive things were the bells. You see, when he travelled to Rome and visited places that touched his soul, he would do a summary of his trip when he returned and tell the listeners his impressions. One day he even played a recording of the bells at Saint Peter's Basilica in Rome so all of us could hear them as he had. The ringing of those bells from so far away, those chords . . . It was like I was there with him.[7]

The Queen of His Heart

Romero's frequent editorials in the diocesan paper reflect what motivated and enthused him in his early priesthood. He venerated the Virgin Mary, and was thrilled that the statue of Our Lady of Peace, the city's patroness, came under his protection.[8]

7. Miguel Vázquez, in López Vigil, *Mosaic*, 28.

8. The revered statue was temporarily housed in the San Francisco Church until the completion of a new cathedral on the site of the city's first church. The original church had been demolished to make way for a larger, more modern structure.

In an article about the statue's history, Romero said he considered himself "a humble priest allowed the immense joy of being the custodian of that invaluable treasure of the diocese."[9] According to tradition, merchants found the "invaluable treasure" in a sealed wooden box on El Salvador's Pacific coast in the 1600s, perhaps the cargo of a Spanish shipwreck.

The merchants transported it to the town of San Miguel, then undergoing bloody conflict. On a November 21, as tradition has it, the combatants, drawn to the mysterious box, opened it to behold a lovely statue of the Virgin Mary. They fell on their knees before it, forgot their grievances, and asked the Lord to forgive them. Thus, they christened the statue "Our Lady of Peace."

Ever since, Migueleños have remained devoted to Our Lady of Peace and each November hold a festival in her honor. Father Romero fostered his diocese's fervor for the Queen of Peace, as he often referred to the statue in the numerous editorials he dedicated to her.

The November celebrations united several of Romero's key interests and yearnings—his deep mystical bond with the Virgin Mary,[10] his desire that the church act as society's focal point, and his eagerness to involve all community sectors. If the 1948 festival was typical, Romero spent an extravagant amount of time to plan and coordinate it each year.

The 1948 celebration brought together the highest levels of the city's and the country's church, military, and civil leaders for an astonishing five days of pageantry and ceremony. In an exuberant and triumphal editorial, titled "The Celebrations of the Queen," Romero summarized the main events:

> November 18. The old front door of the San Francisco Church opens wide. Inside, raised on soldiers' shoulders, the Queen stands. She is adorned with impeccably white decorations, set against a backdrop of the national coat of arms and flags of the church and country.
>
> Outside, drums and bugles announce the Queen's approach. The San Miguel army, under the skillful discipline of three trim officers, orders its troops to render a queen's honor to the Queen of San Miguel, who, like a Queen, reviews her troops . . .
>
> Behind the officers stand orderly rows of soldiers. The cathedral is illuminated with the most precious treasure of San Miguel: the Virgin of the prodigals. [This year] it's the soldiers' turn to

9. Romero y Galdámez, "Nuestra Señora de la Paz," *Chaparrastique*, no. 2045, December 26, 1954, 1,4.

10. There were rumors that on one occasion, a few individuals saw Romero levitate in front of the statue while he was deep in prayer before it.

begin the harmonious pilgrimage of Peace. The Most Excellent Bishop celebrates the Mass of the soldiers, with about a hundred soldiers taking Communion. After an eloquent speech to those he called "Soldiers of Peace," he confirms twenty soldiers.

November 19. The organ arrives. A horrible worry clouded the celebrations. The program had announced the inauguration of the Wurlitzer organ. The appointed day is here, . . . the hour approaches and the organ hasn't arrived. But at one in the afternoon, there on the church doorsteps is the truck. And there's Mr. Werner Goldstaub, smiling, . . . and the church organ makes its triumphant entry while the bells peal with joy.

Four hours later the new organ envelops the crowd in a thunder of glory and harmony . . . It's the same harmony of the organ that fills the Vatican Basilica . . . the harmony of triumph.

And thanks to God and to the Peace Virgin, the church organ is now a reality. A reality that seems a dream: that day at 5 a.m. it was ship's cargo in New Orleans, and at 4 p.m. that very day, the organ was ready to burst out in classic chords in San Miguel.

[The following day.] The Supreme Head of State [the country's president] before San Miguel's Queen . . . one more high point in the celebrations of the Queen. At 10 a.m. the chief of state, General Castaneda Castro, accompanied by his wife and official entourage, entered the cathedral among thousands of spectators while the organ shook with the national anthem's vigorous strains.

The crowning glory. The 21st dawns full of emotions. It's six in the morning. November's freshness is felt in the Mass of general communion. And that morning the eastern sun provided a certain tinge of glory as it shone through the stained glass windows, and the organ became a soft morning prayer as the people of San Miguel filed before the Communion rail. . . .

The procession . . . marched blocks and blocks . . . a stunning human sea . . . and one could say that the Virgin was flooded in an ocean of candles, especially when it arrived at the cathedral, and in a pious gesture of cooperation, the electric Company shut off the lights so that only She shone . . . the candles . . . and the sparklers.

The return. The next afternoon, two long lines led the Queen to her old Franciscan sanctuary, where she remains with her kind eyes and humble smile, more than a Queen . . . Mother . . . Mother of San Miguel and of the east.[11]

11. Romero y Galdámez, "Las Fiestas de la Reina," *Chaparrastique,* no. 1747, November 26, 1948, 1,4. Romero's ellipses are retained in this excerpt translated by the author. See http://www.romeroes.com/monsenor-romero-su-pensamiento/prensa-escrita/semanario-chaparrastique.

One True Church

As a communicator, Romero aimed to uphold and spread orthodox Catholic beliefs. He filled airwaves and thousands of newsprint pages with matters of importance to the Vatican—and, thus, to himself: marital faithfulness; women's place in the home as mothers; anti–birth control; anti-euthanasia; the perils of alcoholism; the evils of communism; the need for Christian teaching in schools; the paucity of priests in El Salvador and parental duty to encourage children who exhibited interest in a religious vocation; homage to various popes, and defending Pope Pius XII against charges that he had done nothing or even supported the Nazis and fascists of the World War II era; and the obligation of Christian charity, such as that exemplified by Saint Vincent de Paul.

Father Romero with children making their first Communion in San Miguel. (photo credit, Zolia Aurora Asturias and Eva del Carmen Asturias)

Romero used editorials to lambast Freemasons and Protestants. The Freemasons, a men's organization believed to have its origins in medieval stone-builders' guilds, devotes itself to charity, moral rectitude, and mutual support. Although Masons affirm belief in a "Supreme Being," Freemasonry is not a religion. The fraternity's use of secret rituals and words often sparked criticism, as it continues to do so today.[12]

12. The Catholic Church has long opposed Freemasonry and continues to forbid

El Salvador's Catholic Church also held an historic grudge against Masons. The first Masonic lodge opened there in 1871, when the country was starting off on a long, controversial road to secularization, efforts to restrict religion's role in society. For the Catholic Church, secularization would mean a large loss of power and influence. Public schools, for example, would no longer be able to teach religion or have students pray. From the outset, Salvadoran Masons played prominent roles in business and government, including as the nation's vice-president. When the government formally adopted secularization in 1886, church officials blamed Masons and blasted them in newspapers.[13]

Romero angered some families by refusing to perform Christian burials for Masons and their relatives. Further, he prohibited local Masons from using the cathedral for a ceremony honoring the nineteenth-century military hero Gerardo Barrios.[14] (Ironically, General Barrios was not only the statesman after whom Romero's hometown was named, but he had also laid the first stone of the cathedral Romero tirelessly toiled to complete.)

But Father Romero aimed his most venomous editorials at Protestants, groups including Baptists, Lutherans, and Presbyterians that arose from a schism in Catholicism in the early 1500s. Protestants, unlike Catholics, do not recognize the pope's universal supremacy in Christian matters.

Romero considered Protestants "separated brothers" who strayed from the true church, the only church Jesus founded, with the Apostle Peter as its head. In a 1963 editorial titled, "He who is with the Pope is with Christ," he went so far as to question whether Protestants could be saved. He personally doubted the possibility.[15]

It angered Romero that Protestants were gaining converts in Latin America. Although El Salvador in the mid-1900s remained almost entirely Catholic, Baptist congregations had existed for decades. In 1926, the 156 members of Baptist churches in eastern El Salvador, including San Miguel, had united in an association. Pentecostal outreach in the country had

---

Catholics to join the fraternity.

13. Roberto Armando Valdés Valle, "Masones, liberales y ultramontos salvadoreños: debate político y constitucional en algunas publicaciones impresas, durante la etapa final del proceso de secularización del estado salvadoreño (1885–1886)" (PhD diss., UCA, 2010), http://www.uca.edu.sv/filosofia/admin/files/1260825405.pdf.

14. Brockman, *A Life*, 40. Barrios also served as El Salvador's president for several years in the mid-1800s.

15. Romero y Galdámez, "El que está con el Papa está con Cristo," *Chaparrastique*, no. 2883, January 26, 1963, 1,8.

begun in the first decade of the 1900s. Twelve Assemblies of God churches formed a national association in 1930.[16]

In his opinion piece "The Protestant Danger," Romero offered reasons for the spread of "Protestant poison": "Protestants seek out places far from parochial vigilance" and offer material advantages to lure poor people to their doors. He took special umbrage with certain Protestant statements that claimed Latin America remained superstitious and ignorant because of the gold-fevered Spanish and Portuguese colonizers who brought the Catholic Church with them.

"They show the Catholic Church as a cause of ignorance and backwardness" and "this hatred of the church is the only force that unites the different sects."[17] At different times, he asked the "separated brothers" to "purge their prejudices and grudges, sincerely review the origins of their separation and retract their errors"[18] and to "return to the fold under one pastor: *The Pope*."[19]

Despite his demanding workload, Romero did not neglect his personal spiritual life. He remained rooted in the asceticism to which he seemed naturally inclined. He observed a strict program of prayer, self-denial, and penitence, including daily meditation, Bible reading and rosary recitation; Friday fasting; and the infliction of physical discomfort by self-flagellation (lightly whipping his back with a rope cord) and by wearing, usually for an hour a day, a *cilicio*, a metal bracelet with wire barbs worn around the upper arm or thigh.

Hot Under the Clerical Collar

Although Romero worked well with people of all economic means, he was wary of the corrupting influences of wealth and materialism. When some influential society women, thinking he'd be pleased, fixed up his room at the Santo Domingo convent, furnishing it with a bed and elegant curtains, they hardly anticipated his response. A Catholic schoolgirl asked to help with the makeover recalled:

16. Information in this paragraph from Monroy, *Cien años*, 58–66.

17. Romero y Galdámez, "El peligro protestante," *Chaparrastique*, no. 2163, May 25, 1957, 1,4.

18. "Hacia la unidad del cristianismo," in ibid., no. 2299, January 16, 1960, 1,2.

19. "Hacia un solo cristianismo," in ibid., no. 1854, January 20, 1951, 1.

> When Father Romero returned he was furious. He tore down the curtains and gave them to the first person he saw passing by. He gave away his new bedspread, the sheets— everything went out! Then he returned his cot and his old chair to their old places, and put everything back in his room just the way it was before.
>
> "I may be their friend, but they're not going to start manipulating me no matter how much money they have!"[20]

His personal asceticism and self-denial sometimes led Romero to behave severely with co-workers and other priests. One morning after mass, Father Bernardo Amaya arrived at the San Francisco Church to talk with Romero. As he waited, he overheard Romero, in the vestry, lash the sacristan, the young man charged with caring for the church's sacred objects, with both his tongue and his cincture.[21]

"'You're a disgrace! Going around drunk. Man, how are you going to protect the things here that belong to the people if you go around getting drunk!' as he struck him three times, *pah! pah! pah!*" Amaya reported.[22]

One woman who knew Romero well recalled Valladares teasing Romero about his short fuse:

> "This guy stresses himself out by getting so angry! He blows his top so easily he's going to spend his entire life suffering from one sickness or another. Now, I, on the other hand, never get upset . . . "
>
> Valladares would turn everything into a joke. But Romero wouldn't. He would just burn up on the inside . . .[23]

20. Nelly Rodriguez, in López Vigil, *Mosaic*, 22.

21. Father Bernardo Amaya then served as parish priest in Chinameca, a town near San Miguel. A vestry is a small room where priests change their garments after saying Mass. A cincture is a ropelike cord tied around his waist.

22. Father Bernardo Amaya, December 4, 1998, interview.

Father Carlos L. Villacorta, who had been mentored by Romero starting at age nine or ten at the San Miguel minor seminary and through his early years of priesthood, said Romero frequently exploded in anger. He felt such outbursts were more a matter of Romero "making noise" to let others know he was angry and disappointed in them rather than of his taking out his anger in a violent fashion. "He was very easy to anger but he wasn't violent," Villacorta said in an August 5, 1999, phone interview with the author.

23. Doris Osegueda, in López Vigil, *Mosaic*, 21–22.

San Miguel parish priests, left to right, Fathers Rafael Valladares, Ruperto Ruiz Orellano, and Oscar Romero. (photo credit, Zolia Aurora Asturias and Eva del Carmen Asturias)

Rather than a faith-based frugality, Romero truly did not care much about material belongings. His youngest brother, Gaspar, recalled that a religious association bought Father Romero a modest house in San Miguel. Instead of moving into it, Romero asked his brother, "How much will they give me for this house? I need money." Gaspar sold it and gave the funds to Romero, who commented, "That will cover workers' wages for the cathedral."[24]

On another occasion, a group gave Father Romero birthday gifts: a new Jeep, a refrigerator, and a washing machine.

"He gave them all to the nursing home. I was angry with him about the Jeep." Gaspar remembered he had urged his brother to consider a vehicle's usefulness for visiting remote hamlets and taking seminarians on excursions to the volcano.

"'There are plenty of buses,' he told me," Gaspar related.[25]

Crossroads

In August 1961, Romero's mother, Niña Jesús, and his friend Rafael Valladares died within days of one another, a double-heavy personal loss.

24. Santos Gaspar Romero, in November 17, 1998, interview with author, San Salvador.

25. Ibid.

Romero must have been comforted by the huge crowd, from all walks of life, that came out for Niña Jesus's funeral, accompanying the coffin to the cemetery. Yet these deaths may also have triggered a turning point in how Romero perceived himself and his role.

Beleaguered without Valladares, likely one of few colleagues who could give him friendly counsel, Romero's relationship with many of his fellow priests grew rocky. He expected other priests to devote as much time and energy to their tasks and duties as he gave to his, and he alienated those unable or unwilling to live up to his perfectionist standards. He also disapproved of younger priests who, impatient for change in church life, became more relaxed about clerical garb—not wearing cassocks to all events—and who, he thought, interacted too familiarly or collaborated too closely with women.

Some priests began rumors that Romero, prone to melancholy, suffered mental instability. These rumors nibbled away at his self-confidence. At one point, he reached out to a priest friend to share his concern when they were in Mexico for a gathering.

> One night he came into my room, all discouraged and hanging his head.
>
> "Father Chencho, tell me. Do you think I'm crazy?"
>
> He sat down, and it was apparent that he had come for a heart-to-heart, even though that wasn't his style.
>
> "What do you think?" he asked again.
>
> I'd known him for years and knew about all the various things he was involved in.
>
> "Look, I don't believe any such thing. What I know is that you're the parish priest in San Francisco and Santo Domingo and at the cathedral . . . I know that not a day goes by that you're not giving several sermons, that there wouldn't have been a Festival for the Virgin of Peace if it weren't for you, that now you're working with Alcoholics Anonymous, and that you hardly sleep. . . . What you are is exhausted!"
>
> I also knew that some priests in San Miguel were spreading the rumor that Father Romero had mental problems in order to undermine his credibility. And since Valladares, his best priest friend had died, Romero was feeling alone. Alone and isolated.
>
> "Hey, don't let it get to you, man," I encouraged him, "Is it possible they call exhaustion madness in San Miguel?"[26]

26. José Inocencio Alas, in López Vigil, *Mosaic*, 30–31.

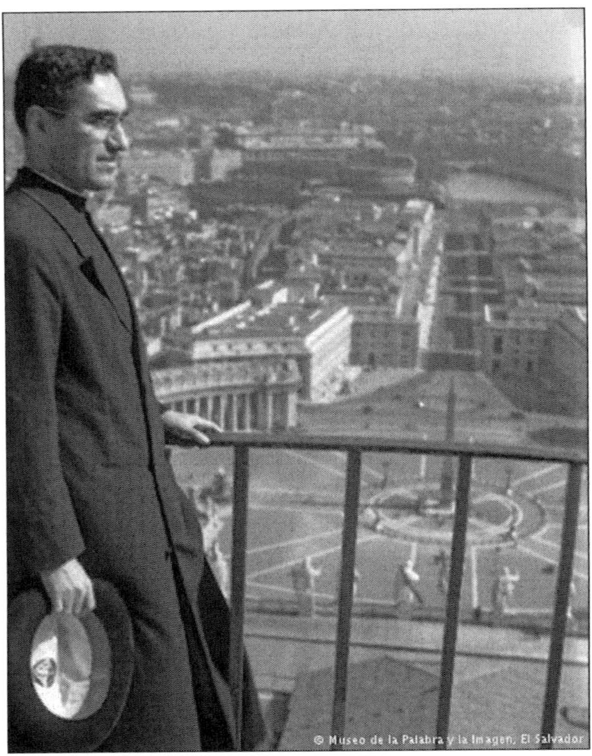

Father Romero surveys Rome from a Vatican balcony.
(Museo de la Palabra y la Imagen, El Salvador)

Interestingly, Romero demonstrated keen insight into his psychological makeup, but in trying to overcome his shortcomings, he fell into a vicious cycle. During a spiritual retreat in 1966, for example, Romero consulted a psychiatrist, who diagnosed him as an obsessive-compulsive perfectionist. Romero's solution? He proposed for himself a rigorous program of self-improvement, which, as a perfectionist, he would obsessively and compulsively follow.

Later, during a 1972 spiritual retreat, having undergone three months of psychoanalysis, Romero noted his desire to be more spontaneous and warmer in his interactions with others. He saw how his perfectionism made him rigid and angry if things were not as he wished.

"And the rigidity in turn produced insecurity, since it made him less natural and more fearful of mistakes," wrote one of his biographers. "A serious effect of all this was that he would take refuge in work, which in turn kept him from better relationships with others and intensified the problem. He resolved to try to break the cycle by regulating his work and giving time and attention to his relations with people."[27]

Personality issues aside, Romero did not seem to recognize how much power he had come to wield in San Miguel, one reason fellow priests resented him. The same biographer pointed out that by the 1960s Romero "was long established as the most powerful priest in the city, with virtually all lay movements centered in his parish, besides being the bishop's secretary, rector of the minor seminary, and editor of the diocesan newspaper."[28]

Resentment and misunderstandings inflated until, on at least one occasion, other priests asked the bishop to remove Romero from power.

Romero was indeed removed, although in a face-saving way. Bishop Machado and his newly appointed coadjutor bishop asked church officials to grant Romero the honorary title of "monseñor" in honor of his twenty-five-year anniversary as a priest in 1967.[29] The authorities agreed, and Romero became a "monseñor," which both pleased and encouraged him.[30]

A few days later, church officials named Romero secretary-general of the national bishops' conference, a promotion requiring him to move to the capital, San Salvador. A couple of biographers believe Romero was "moved up in in order to be removed."[31]

27. Brockman, *A Life*, 50–51.

28. Ibid., 42.

29. The Vatican named Lawrence M. Graziano to serve as Machado's coadjutor bishop in 1965. Coadjutor bishops are auxiliaries often appointed when a bishop nears retirement age. Graziano succeeded Machado as San Miguel's bishop in 1968.

Although Bishop Graziano told biographer Brockman in a phone interview that he had no personal conflict with Romero (*A Life*, note 41, 261), Monseñor Ricardo Urioste emphatically told this author in a December 1998 interview in San Salvador that he had personally witnessed Graziano and Romero clashing. Urioste related that on one occasion in which Graziano had invited Urioste to give a presentation to the clergy, Graziano publicly rebuked Romero, censuring Romero's attitude. (Urioste later became Archbishop Romero's "second-in-command," his vicar-general, and the two men became very close during those three years.)

Several witnesses testify that Graziano, by personality, however, would not have deliberately hurt Romero.

30. English speakers use the Italian *monsignor*, meaning *my lord*, which in Spanish is *monseñor*.

31. Delgado describes Graziano and Romero as "polar opposites" (*Biografía*, 34). Graziano, an American, represented a modern lifestyle and way of thinking at odds with Romero's traditionalism. Delgado believes Graziano was named to San Miguel in order to normalize the tensions between Romero and the younger priests. In addition to Delgado, Carranza also describes Romero's "promotion," as "*ascendido para ser removido*"

Many parishioners were unhappy with this news, and some petitioned the nuncio, the Vatican's ambassador, to allow Romero to remain in San Miguel. But the decision had been made. A huge crowd from all segments of society attended a farewell party to thank him and wish him well.

Although leaving his beloved flock could not have been easy, Romero would be the last one to question the church hierarchy. The bestowal of the honorific "monseñor" likely eased some of the sting and, publicly at least, Romero left graciously, calling on his parishioners to build unity under their pastoral leaders.

The night before Romero's departure for the capital, after his last mass at the Santo Domingo Church, he journaled: "I deeply feel the separation from so beloved a place, but I am serene and resting well without responsibilities. I ask the Lord for pardon." Then he quoted scripture: "So you also, when you have done everything you were told to do, should say, 'We are unworthy servants; we have only done our duty.' I hope so."[32]

The lengthy first chapter of Romero's priesthood closed. He had indeed done his duty, and then some. But he had also dug himself in as a stubborn traditionalist unwilling to bend during the 1960s—a decade of worldwide clamor for change.

---

or, "moved up in order to be moved out" (*Vidas*, 23).

32. Romero y Galdámez, *Ejercicios espirituales,* entry dated September 1, 1967, 12. The Bible verse Romero quotes is Luke 17:10.

Backgrounder

Two Historic Assemblies: Vatican II and Medellín and Their Impact on the Salvadoran Church

Vatican II: "Time for Fresh Air"

In 1958, newly elected Pope John XXIII perceived the Roman Catholic Church had changed little over the previous four hundred years, since the mid-1500s Council of Trent.[1]

In this post–World War II era, people everywhere faced changes on many fronts: economic, scientific and technological, environmental, medical, cultural, moral.

Pope John XXIII felt the church, too, needed to change in order to continue to serve its followers. The church's role was to guide believers in the blossoming of their faith, not to preserve the old. "We are not museum-keepers but gardeners to help things grow," the pope stated.[2] The time had come to renew the church, "to open the windows . . . and let in some fresh air" are among the phrases he used to explain his ideas.[3]

To begin the process, the pope called for a meeting of the bishops, the Second Vatican Council, in January 1959, to reach agreement on updating the church canon, or law, and in attaining Christian unity. The Council convened four times between October 1962 and December 1965. (After

1. The Council of Trent condemned Protestantism as heresy. It also defined Catholic doctrine in response to the Protestant Reformation's challenge to some of its practices and theological positions.

2. Pope John XXIII, as mentioned in the website Vatican II—Voice of the Church. http://www.vatican2voice.org/2need/advent.htm.

3. Pope John XXIII reportedly made several such informal and colorful statements during the three years after he announced plans for the Second Vatican Council, according to the New World Encyclopedia. http://www.newworldencyclopedia.org/entry/John_XXIII.

John XXIII died in 1963, his successor, Pope Paul VI, presided over the Council until its end.)

By consensus, the twenty-five hundred bishops who attended Vatican II adopted proposals for change in Catholic practice and teachings, including:

- A greater role for lay people, with a goal of creating a less hierarchical church;
- The right to say the liturgy in the local language, rather than Latin;
- Encouraging the faithful to read the Bible in their own language and to discern its meaning along with the clergy or by themselves;
- Cautioning the faithful to avoid the snare of materialism;
- Calling for religious unity among the various Christian denominations. No longer should Catholics perceive Protestants and Eastern Orthodox as "separated brethren," but should instead work together with them ecumenically, in union, as equals.

Medellín: Applying Vatican II to Latin America's "Inhuman Wretchedness"

In 1968, Latin American bishops met in Medellín,[4] Colombia, to work out how to apply Vatican II's proposed changes to their region.

The region's poverty loomed as a major concern. "The Latin American bishops cannot remain indifferent in the face of the tremendous social injustices existent in Latin America, which keep the majority of our peoples in dismal poverty, which in many cases becomes inhuman wretchedness," the bishops stated in the conference's final document.[5]

The bishops endorsed the formation of Christian base communities, some of which already existed, as a way to combat Latin America's economic poverty and social injustices. In these base communities, small groups of neighbors met to study and discuss the Bible. After Medellín, tens of thousands of the groups formed throughout the region.

4. Officially titled the "Second Conference of Latin American Bishops," the 1968 gathering is generally referred to as *Medellín*, after the Colombian city in which it took place.

5. See, for example, excerpts on justice, peace, and poverty from Medellín's final September 6, 1968, document at http://www.geraldschlabach.net/Medellín-1968-excerpts/.

Base communities placed its members, often poor and illiterate, at their core. Because clergy were scarce, priests and nuns taught lay leaders how to read, using the Bible as their primer. These lay leaders in turn taught literacy to their neighbors and guided them in interpreting the Bible on their own, deciphering its meaning for their time in history and their specific social circumstances.

The communities strove to redirect the church's flow of influence and power—from the ground, or base, up—rather than the traditional top-down course of decision-making.

Strongly influenced by liberation theology, base communities built solidarity among members as they came to understand they were poor not due to "God's will" but rather to society's injustices, in which few people control much wealth and power and many go hungry.

Thus, in humble rural shacks and in overcrowded city shanties, small groups of Christians became aware of the larger picture. Instead of asking for charity, these believers demanded more of their society and government, such as adequate wages, better health care, and education for their children. Believing Jesus did not want them hungry, ill, and uneducated, they began to speak out. Their misery could be prevented.

One result of grassroots evangelization was a raising of the average person's awareness of society's inequities and growing impatience for change. Because base communities stirred people to action, those with power viewed them as dangerous and subversive to the status quo and often labeled them "communist" in attempts to quell or squash them.

In actuality, however, the bishops' statements in Medellín decried both unchecked capitalism and Marxism (communism) as systems working against "the dignity of the human person." Capitalism sets money and profits before people, and communism concentrates power in the state, which often becomes totalitarian.

"We must denounce the fact that Latin America sees itself caught between these two options and remains dependent on one or other of the centers of power which control its economy," the Latin American bishops wrote in Medellín.

"New Breezes" Blow in El Salvador

Various parishes in El Salvador became real-life laboratories for putting into practice the theology forged in Vatican II and Medellín.

One priest of the period, José Inocencio "Chencho" Alas, credits openness to the new thinking to Archbishop Luis Chávez y González, who served in that role for thirty-eight years, from 1938 to 1977. Chávez himself promoted some of the country's first *campesino*[6] co-ops in the 1950s, a progressive action to help poor farmers work together to further their interests.

Chávez's theme during his long tenure as archbishop was, "If something will serve the good of the people, let's go ahead and do it," Alas wrote.[7]

Archbishop Chávez supported his own diocesan priests who worked on behalf of the oppressed. These diocesan priests were joined by priests belonging to religious orders, the Jesuits and Passionists in particular.

Alas lists elements of Vatican II especially vital and relevant to a radical reorientation of El Salvador's church:[8]

- Speaking the liturgy in Spanish, as suggested by the Vatican II document "Constitution on the Sacred Liturgy."[9] Masses and biblical messages became relevant to people's lives once they heard and understood them in their native language, rather than in Latin.
- Reading overlooked Bible passages. The "Constitution of the Sacred Liturgy" states, "The treasures of the Bible are to be opened up more lavishly, so that richer fare may be provided for the faithful . . . In this way a more representative portion of the holy scriptures will be read . . . "[10] Old Testament prophets who denounced oppression, sin, and injustices became new models for Salvadoran Catholics. Greater emphasis was placed on Jesus's resurrection, as opposed to his death, as had formerly been done. The gospel thus turned into a message of joy and hope, death no longer having the final word.

6. The word *campesino* derives from *campo*, Spanish for countryside or rural area. In Latin America, *campesinos* or *campesinas* (for women) refer to poor persons of the rural areas. The word lacks an adequate English translation, the closest being *peasant*. *Peasant*, however, often evokes the image of stagnant medieval farm folk, which does little justice to the dynamism, constant adaptation, and striving of Latin American *campesinos* and *campesinas*.

7. Alas, *Iglesia*, 260.

8. José Inocencio Alas, in November 24, 2015, phone conversation with author.

9. "Constitution on the Sacred Liturgy." http://www.vatican.va/archive/hist_councils/ii_vatican_council/documents/vat-ii_const_19631204_sacrosanctum-concilium_en.html.

10. Ibid., point no. 51.

- The upturning or inversion of the church hierarchy, with the laity occupying the broad top, rather than the pope at a pinnacle. This had "tremendous repercussions" in El Salvador. Many priests—and Archbishop Romero himself—were transformed when they began listening to the people instead of expecting the people to always listen to them.[11] This reversal invites the faithful to organize and to offer their prophetic visions.
- Encouraging the faithful to be concerned with the here and now rather than passively awaiting a heavenly afterlife, as suggested by the Vatican II document "Pastoral Constitution on the Church in the Modern World."[12] The church is urged to work in all realms—cultural and recreational, economic, political—in the present to create a better future for all. The faithful concerns itself with denouncing injustice and announcing what should be.

11. Point no. 12 of the Vatican II document "Dogmatic Constitution of the Church," ("*Lumen Gentium,*" in Latin) states, for example: "The holy people of God shares also in Christ's prophetic office; it spreads abroad a living witness to Him, especially by means of a life of faith and charity . . . The entire body of the faithful, anointed as they are by the Holy One, cannot err in matters of belief." http://www.vatican.va/archive/hist_councils/ii_vatican_council/documents/vat-ii_const_19641121_lumen-gentium_en.html.

12. The "Pastoral Constitution on the Church in the Modern World," is titled "*Gaudium Et Spes*" in Latin. http://www.vatican.va/archive/hist_councils/ii_vatican_council/documents/vat-ii_cons_19651207_gaudium-et-spes_en.html.

6. A Time to Dig in One's Heels

(1967–1974)

The seven years Romero lived in the capital found him unwilling or unable to embrace the changes percolating around him. It was a stressful and generally unhappy period for the priest—as well as for those he attacked with the might of his pen. He became wedged in a midlife rut that put him at odds with many colleagues and brought out a streak of hidebound stubbornness.

Arriving in San Salvador in September 1967, Romero decided to live at the San José de la Montaña Seminary, headquarters of the national bishops' conference, of which he was now secretary-general. The seminary, its students and the Jesuits who directed it, bubbled with eagerness to embrace the changes proposed by Vatican II. (*See* "Two Historic Assemblies" backgrounder.)

The old-fashioned cleric thus planted himself at the very hub of new church thinking, where he felt out of place and sensed disdain from some of those around him. This choice of residence intensified both his inner and outer conflicts.

One member of the Jesuit community also living at the seminary bluntly testified about Romero:

> I didn't like him. . . . He never ate any of his meals with us. He would go down to the dining room at different times so that he wouldn't run into us. It was clear he was avoiding us, and that he'd arrived at the seminary laden with prejudices. . . . And he didn't go to the clergy meetings. If he did go, he would hide in some corner and never open his mouth. . . . But he preferred to stay in his office buried in his papers. Or to walk down the halls dressed in his black cassock praying the breviary."[1]

1. Salvador Carranza, in López Vigil, *Mosaic*, 37–38.

A seminarian remembered once when Romero, returning from a bishops' meeting, commented, "You wouldn't believe how out of place I felt. I was the only one in the whole room wearing black."[2]

While younger priests donned jeans when not performing mass and even older clerics relaxed their dress codes, Romero continued to wear the ankle-length cassock. Giving it up would have felt like a betrayal of his lifelong loyalty to the Catholic Church.

Romero nevertheless hurled himself into his work with his trademark perfectionism. Seminarians heard his typewriter clacking into the night's wee hours, doing little to endear him to those who wanted to sleep.

Romero needed to work long hours, however. He had merely a year to assemble the voluminous documents El Salvador's bishops would need to participate in a much-anticipated meeting. In the summer of 1968, they would gather with bishops from all over Latin America in Medellín, Colombia, to discuss how to apply Vatican II's principles to their region and individual countries.

Before long, word of Romero's meticulous organizational skills reached neighboring nations, and the Central American bishops asked Romero to serve as executive secretary of their association. The position would require frequent trips to neighboring Guatemala, where the organization's president resided. Romero accepted this challenge in May 1968.

Bishop's Ordination

Two years later, perhaps to recognize Romero's contribution to these episcopal bodies, Archbishop Chávez asked his superiors at the Vatican to name Romero as his second auxiliary bishop.[3] The Holy See obliged, and Romero accepted the position. He would be ordained a bishop on June 21, 1970.

Romero asked a couple of his lay friends and Father Rutilio Grande to organize the celebration following his ordination. Grande was among the few Jesuits at the seminary able to relate to Romero. Although Grande and Romero disagreed on many issues, the two men shared a friendship. Both were of the World War II generation. Both came from families of modest

2. Miguel Ventura, in ibid., 38.

3. Bishop Arturo Rivera y Dámas had been serving as an auxiliary to Archbishop Luis Chávez y González since 1960 and would continue to do so.

means in Salvadoran villages, and each left home at a young age to attend a minor seminary.

Father Grande devoted many hours to planning Romero's ordination celebration and he served as its master of ceremonies.

"Romero shrank from publicity and ostentation. Grande assured him there would be no extraordinary costs, that the ceremony would be very ecclesial . . ." noted one biographer.[4]

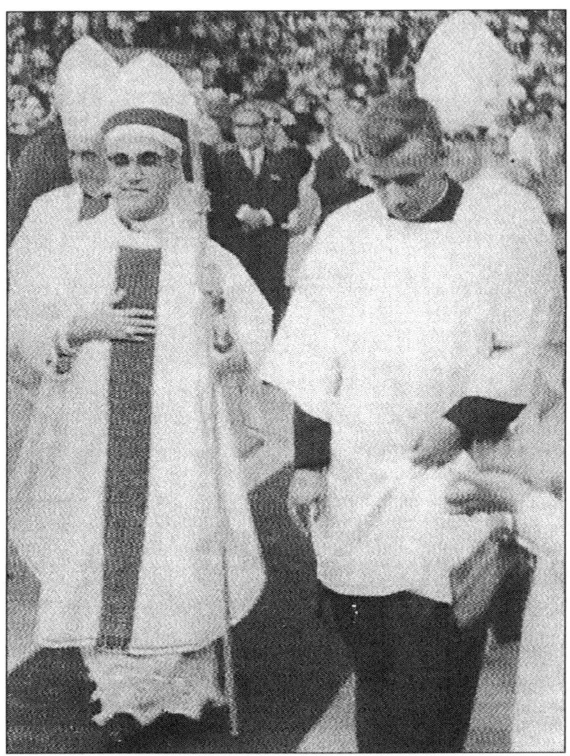

Father Rutilio Grande helped organize Romero's ordination as bishop. (photo credit, Zolia Aurora Asturias and Eva del Carmen Asturias)

A tremendous crowd turned out for the religious ceremony and for the reception afterwards on the seminary's patios.[5] Attenders included high-

4. Carranza, *Vidas*, 25.

5. The religious ceremony took place in the gymnasium of a Catholic high school, the Liceo Salvadoreño, run by Marist brothers.

level Salvadoran authorities, the nation's president and military officials, and many bishops, priests, and nuns. Busloads of friends and supporters from San Miguel also came.

Some criticized the hoopla as too extravagant at a time when many Salvadorans were suffering, but in general the event pleased Romero and its organizers. "It was a very churchly celebration, it mixed all classes of people, and there were enough tamales for everyone!" a contented Father Grande said afterwards.[6]

Castro's Shadow

Now exerting a bishop's power, Romero dove into the roiled waters of church politics, on the side of the conservative bishops. The church's turbulence mirrored larger societal unrest in El Salvador and across Latin America.

Locked in a Cold War with the Soviet Union, the United States saw in El Salvador a situation similar to that of Cuba before its revolution. A few large landowners held many landless families in their grip.[7] US officials remembered that Cuba's revolutionary leader Fidel Castro found his support among the hungry rural poor of the island's Sierra Maestra mountains. They did not want yet another communist government in the hemisphere. Cuba was already one too many.

Under President John F. Kennedy's program called Alliance for Progress, the United States poured money into its southern neighbors to promote stability. In El Salvador, the program built schools, opened clinics, and invested in industry to help provide education, health care, and jobs to the masses. At the same time, the program upgraded the five Central American nations' militaries and gathered them into a joint defense council so they could help one another put down unrest.

The two moderate army colonels who ruled in the 1960s cooperated with the United States in allowing some openness in the political process.[8]

6. Quoted in Carranza, *Vidas*, 26.

7. In the 1950s, El Salvador began small-scale industrialization, providing jobs to some of the landless people who migrated to its cities, primarily the capital. A new 1950 constitution granted factory workers the right to strike and to receive a minimum wage and social security. No such rights, however, were given *campesinos* and *campesinas* working for agricultural estate owners, who would brook no interference in their medieval "fiefdoms."

8. Colonel Julio Rivera from 1962 to 1967, followed by Colonel Fidel Sánchez Hernández until 1972.

The country's first ever political parties formed. Average Salvadorans began to believe they might at last find a voice and vote.

Democracy worked for the first time in 1967, when one colonel succeeded another as president by means of an election, rather than a coup. What's more, the elite allowed the opposition parties' candidates to take the seats they had won in the National Assembly and city governments. Optimism permeated the air.

Then an unexpected and feverish one-hundred-hour war with neighboring Honduras reversed the new parties' gains in 1970 elections. (*See* "Soccer War" backgrounder.)

The young political parties didn't give up, however. Rather, they focused on the 1972 presidential election and joined together as a single party with the acronym UNO, or "one." UNO's candidate, Napoleón Duarte, enjoyed great popularity as mayor of San Salvador, having introduced street lighting and garbage pickup and built sewers, water mains, and schools. Everything would change in 1972, Salvadorans believed.

Given El Salvador's history, however, perhaps UNO's hopeful candidates and supporters should have been reading signs indicating the rural elite would fight hard to retain its control.[9] In 1965, for example, landowners retaliated after the president hiked farmworkers' wages to ninety cents a day. Many took from workers the small plots on which they had been allowing them to plant corn and beans for family meals and they stopped serving the usual lunch.

What's more, El Salvador's armed forces created a rural paramilitary "death squad," named ORDEN, an acronym spelling the Spanish word for *order*. ORDEN became a particularly sinister weapon of repression, turning neighbor upon neighbor. In return for small favors, perhaps a job on a public works project or as a permanent farm worker, poor peasants were induced to join ORDEN to spy and inform on their neighbors' activities.[10] Observers noted that with ORDEN, "the National Guard had its own little gestapo in every village . . ."[11]

9. A few opposition members who found themselves shut out in 1970 did read the writing on the wall. They dropped out of the electoral process to form small guerrilla groups.

10. The United States played a role in ORDEN's formation. In the early 1960s, the US government sent ten Green Berets to El Salvador to help General José Alberto Medrano set up ORDEN. Sometimes *campesinos* had no choice about ORDEN membership. A local leader would merely show up and give rural men "membership cards."

11. Armstrong and Shenk, *Face of Revolution*, 77.

In 1970, those in power sent grisly warnings to Catholic priests not to help peasants organize to improve their lot. In January, soldiers detained one priest working with the poor, then drugged him and left him naked on a cliff's edge in the mountains.[12] In November, Guardsmen arrested another activist priest. Several days later, his dismembered body was found.[13]

Blinded by certainty of its party's 1972 victory, UNO supporters were stunned when, with international observers present, blatant ballot fraud prevented Duarte from taking his rightfully earned presidential seat. Instead the oligarchs handpicked a colonel as president.[14]

Full-scale repression ensued. Labor and opposition party leaders, students and professors, and progressive priests, nuns, and lay leaders all became targets.[15] "No longer restricted to the campaign or the polling date," researchers noted, "repression became a fact of everyday life, stretching from one election to the next."[16]

After the 1974 election, the government did not bother to post doctored results, as it had in 1972. It merely declared as winners all the ruling party's candidates. Armed conflict seemed inevitable. And still the agro-oligarchy would not budge, despite prodding by the US government.

El Salvador's peasants had become mired ever deeper in misery. In the 1960s, the agro-oligarchy had taken over more community land—simply by enclosing expanses of it within barbed wire fences—along the Pacific

12. Father José Inocencio Alas, parish priest of Suchitoto in Cuscatlán province, had boosted Romero's morale during his discouragement in Mexico (*see* chapter 5). Alas survived his ordeal and returned to his parish. He worked there for eight years, despite ongoing death threats, until he went into a fifteen-year exile. He later became an award-winning peacemaker based in Texas.

13. Father Nicolás Rodríguez, assassinated in Chalatenango, a department in the north of El Salvador. Archbishop Luis Chávez sent one of his auxiliary bishops—Oscar Romero—to pick up the priest's corpse.

14. Colonel Arturo Armando Molina. Romero considered Molina a personal friend.

15. Following a March 1972 protest in San Salvador, the Fourteen Families and their military partners decreed a state of siege, a curfew, and martial law for the entire country. They killed or exiled labor and opposition party leaders, including Duarte, who was tortured and banished. On July 19, 1972, the military used tanks, planes, and artillery to attack the University of El Salvador—the supposed "brains" behind popular organizations. Troops invaded, looted, and hauled off to jail hundreds of students and faculty. They banished the university's president and dean of the medical school to Nicaragua. The military closed the university, which did not reopen until the end of 1973. From Armstrong and Shenk, *Face of Revolution,* 62–64.

16. Ibid., 64.

Coast especially. With less land available and a rapidly growing population, the dispossessed swelled.

Then, in 1969, Honduras repatriated some 130,000 Salvadoran immigrants, creating yet greater need for land.[17] (*See* "Soccer War" backgrounder.)

In 1961, 12 percent of rural families possessed no land. In 1975, 41 percent were landless.[18] Over half of the rural labor force found itself unemployed more than two-thirds of the year.[19]

The Catholic Church, too, had raised hope for change in the 1960s. Although illegal to organize in the countryside, Archbishop Luis Chávez promoted agricultural cooperatives to serve the interests of small peasant farmers. Chávez and fellow clergy felt they could not sit idly by among so much hunger and poverty.

Into the Ring

Despite his archbishop's viewpoints, Bishop Romero took public stances siding with the military government. For instance, he and his fellow conservative bishops signed a paid ad in the country's newspapers defending the regime's violent occupation of the national university, agreeing with accusations that the campus represented a "hotbed of subversion."[20]

In May 1971, Archbishop Chávez made Romero editor of the diocesan weekly newspaper, *Orientación*. The former editor, Chávez felt, went too far when he editorialized in support of a Colombian priest who joined a guerrilla group after becoming convinced social equality could not be achieved nonviolently.

"If Jesus were alive today, he would be a guerrilla," the priest famously said.[21]

17. The 130,000 repatriated individuals represented about a third of the 300,000 Salvadorans living and working in Honduras at the time. Statistics from North, *Bitter Grounds*, 61.

18. Armstrong and Shenk, *Face of Revolution*, 76. Experts deemed a rural family of six needed seventeen acres of high-quality land to feed itself. In 1975, a full 96.3 percent of rural families had twelve acres or less.

19. North, *Bitter Grounds*, 50.

20. Pedro Declerc and Noemí Ortiz, in López Vigil, *Mosaic*, 47.

21. Camilo Torres Restrepo, a Colombian priest and professor, joined a guerrilla group in 1965 after several years of working for change through nonviolent actions.

Bishop Romero disagreed vehemently with such sentiments. Under his leadership, *Orientación* veered away from controversy. Instead of commenting on human rights violations and injustice, Romero lamented individual sin and problems arising from it, such as single-parent families, alcoholism, and pornography.

When Romero did address politics, he blamed everyone equally for the country's problems and provided simplistic solutions. He quoted a recent bishops' statement that identified "the true cause of our social ailments" as sinfulness on everyone's part—"in the public and private sins of our country and especially in our own sins as God's people."[22]

May all Salvadorans, Romero and his fellow bishops implored, awaken feelings of peace and harmony in their hearts as brothers and sisters of the same God and the same country:

> Above the temptations of selfishness, ambition, vengeance, and hate that kill and destroy, may fraternal feelings prevail and reign in our beloved people so that we work together to construct a country renewed by justice, peace, and mutual respect.[23]

Romero took refuge in this laudable ideal while the nation's military machine-gunned peaceful protestors and tortured and "disappeared" dissenters.

On May 27, 1973, Romero penned an *Orientación* editorial that set off a monthlong ruckus across the country. The year before, the Jesuit high school had introduced into coursework perspectives born in Medellín.[24] In sociology classes, for instance, teachers took students, most of them upper-class, on field trips into the city's slums to expose them to the harsh living conditions of most Salvadorans.

Romero had heeded grumblings about "Marxist indoctrination" from some parents and former teachers—older, more traditional Jesuits—who disliked the new teachings and wanted to oust the Jesuits from the high school. His editorial titled "Liberating Education, but Christian and without Demagoguery" lit a firestorm.

In it, Romero first acknowledged the need for profound changes in the nation's educational system. He lauded a Medellín document calling

22. "Llamamiento pastoral conjunto," *Oriente*, no. 30804. April 25, 1972, 2.

23. Ibid.

24. The high school, a private one and an arm of the Jesuit seminary, was called the Externado San José.

for a "liberating education, able to free our people from cultural, social, economic, and political servitude that impedes their development."

But such education "should not take advantage of our youth's innate generosity and concern to push them into the path of demagoguery and Marxism." Pamphlets and literature of "known red [communist] origin" had been distributed in the school, Romero asserted.

El Salvador's major newspapers reprinted Romero's editorial, some using extra-large fonts, to call attention to the "Marxist teachings." A month of heated opinion pieces ensued, on TV and radio as well as in the print media. The Jesuits responded in newspaper spreads. Romero was not to be swayed, remembered one mother who supported the Jesuits' initiative and who, with another mother, went to speak in person with Romero:

> You see, Monseñor, the Church has really been moving quickly with the Second Vatican Council and with Medellín, and we want our children to be educated in that way of thinking . . .
>
> We talked and talked. He listened to everything we had to say. He didn't contradict us or get rude with us like other bishops did. But we left with heavy hearts, and felt as if a bucket of cold water had been thrown on us because he didn't really understand anything we'd said to him. In *Orientación*, angry articles kept coming out, not only against the Jesuits now, but also against us mothers and fathers who were supposedly being manipulated by them. In the end, he didn't win that battle, but he never did anything to recognize or make up for the damage he'd caused. It seemed to me that he had his head in the clouds, away from reality, up in the trees like the avocados.[25]

It disturbed Archbishop Chávez that newspapers reprinted Romero's editorial as "the thinking of the Salvadoran church," rather than of Bishop Romero, the individual. He was angered his auxiliary did not foresee the serious consequences of the charges he leveled.

Chávez named a commission of priests to investigate the school's teachings. It found no erroneous teaching or Marxist indoctrination. What's more, 92 percent of the students' parents voted in approval of the school administration. Archbishop Chávez asked Romero to publish these findings. He did so, but on the last page and under the title, "The Archbishop Comes to the Defense of the San José School." In the same issue, he

25. Carmen Álvarez, in López Vigil, *Mosaic*, 53–54.

also attacked the commission's members, claiming their interpretations of church teaching were questionable. Hardly a heartfelt apology.

Romero had read all the documents of Vatican II and Medellín and believed he understood their true meanings. He continued to harp on the misinterpretation theme. On August 12, 1973, he published an *Orientación* editorial titled, "Medellín, Misunderstood and Mutilated." He claimed that those who were poorly acquainted with only the justice and peace portions sifted through the documents to take out whatever fit their rabble-rousing intentions, ignoring the conference's true spirit.[26]

Romero seemed curiously blind to the perils of tarring priests and church workers with the brush of "communism." It put lives at risk.

Journalist María López Vigil called Romero in the early 1970s "a little Inquisitor," referring to the infamous Medieval Inquisition. Understandably, many priests disliked him.

Romero suffered frequent illness during this period, likely related to the stresses of his many duties and his poor relationships with colleagues. In the fall of 1970 he helped lead a national Family Rosary campaign from his sick bed. He spent two months in the small home of a friend's family as he recovered from respiratory illness.[27]

"For Romero, the Barrazas became in time his family, giving him undemanding love and devotion. In their tile-floored sitting room he would tease and play with the children, take off his shoes and doze in a plastic-and-aluminum lawn chair in front of the television, and open Christmas gifts as eagerly as the children. At their dinner table he would joke and occasionally talk of his sorrows,. . ." says biographer Brockman.[28] Romero became like a second father to the couple's first daughter and the godfather of the second, born in 1972.

26. Two weeks later, Romero followed this with an editorial "The Deepest Social Revolution," a revolution arising from the "serious, mystical inner reform" of Christians, from which a reformed society would naturally flow.

27. Salvador Barraza and Romero formed an abiding friendship in 1959. In that year, Barraza had been drawn to Romero's sermons when he made regular business trips to San Miguel. Barraza helped move Romero—and his cherished books and bookshelf—to the capital in 1967. Barraza also helped organize the celebration of Romero's episcopal ordination.

28. Brockman, *A Life*, 47.

Second Up-and-Out Move

Another major life change came in October 1974, when the Holy See appointed Romero bishop of the newest and smallest of El Salvador's five dioceses, that of Santiago de María.[29] Romero would serve as its second bishop. The diocese stretched from Honduras in the north to the Pacific Ocean on the south and included Romero's hometown of Ciudad Barrios.

Was this promotion another case of Romero's being "moved up in order to be moved out," as some suspected was the case when he was named secretary to the bishops' conference and left San Miguel for the capital?

Biographer Carranza believed so.[30]

After all, while not entirely Romero's fault, under his leadership the diocesan newspaper *Orientación* fell deeply into debt. It lost many readers because, except for his controversial editorials, Romero drew heavily upon the dry, often obscure contents of the Vatican newspaper *L'Osservatore Romano*.

With Romero as rector, the San José seminary closed its doors after half a year.

Then, too, Archbishop Chávez had chafed at Romero's throwing the church into a whirlwind of controversy by labeling "communist" sincere church attempts to engage with its followers in a new, open fashion.

Because Vatican officials had promoted Romero, however, he took their action as proof of the correctness of his viewpoints. In one of his last editorials he wrote:

> The confidence the pope has placed in [*Orientacion*'s] editor must be interpreted as the Church magisterium's [authority of authentic teaching] most solemn support of the ideology that inspired the newspaper's pages under this editorship. This unspoken approval from high authority provides the best reward and satisfaction for those of us who work together for this ideal, while also reconfirming the route to follow.[31]

29. It was a promotion; a diocesan bishop holds the highest level of responsibility a bishop can assume. The Santiago de María diocese had been created twenty years earlier, when San Miguel diocese was split in two. Romero succeeded Bishop José Castro y Ramírez, who died in May 1974.

30. Carranza, *Vidas*, 38.

31. Delgado, *Biografía*, 59. Delgado takes this from an unspecified 1974 issue of *Orientación*.

6. A Time to Dig in One's Heels

During the seven years Romero lived in San Salvador, the "little Inquisitor" had remained true to his orthodoxy, reassured that he had upheld the one true faith invested in the pope, successor of the Apostle Peter, the rock upon which Jesus Christ built his church.

Never again, however, would Romero feel so certain of his beliefs.

Backgrounder

The "Soccer War"

FROM THE EARLY 1900S and especially following the 1932 *Matanza*, or massacre, many Salvadoran peasants fled across their country's long border with Honduras and settled there.

Compared to postage-stamp-size El Salvador, Honduras appeared huge. In 1930, Honduras possessed over five times more land than El Salvador—with about half as many inhabitants.[1] Initially, Honduras welcomed the extra labor on banana plantations, in mines, and to farm the nation's remote areas. Some three hundred thousand Salvadorans, most of them poor subsistence farmers, relocated to Honduras.

Since the 1880s, banana companies, mostly US-owned, received concessions on large areas of land in Honduras. By 1960, Honduran large-land owners began taking over great swaths of additional agricultural land to raise cattle and grow cotton, displacing both Honduran peasant farmers and Salvadorans living alongside them. Also in the 1960s, the United States urged land reform in Central America to avoid another "Cuba," a communist country in the region. To head off land redistribution, Honduran landowners—and the military government protecting their interests—found Salvadoran peasants a convenient scapegoat for growing land pressures.[2]

The two countries had signed immigration agreements in 1962 and 1965. When the accord ended in February 1969, they did not renew it. Honduras deported 130,000 Salvadorans to their land of origin, an action that sharpened bitterness between the neighboring nations.[3]

1. In 1930, El Salvador's population was 1.4 million, compared to Honduras's 854,000 inhabitants. By 1970, El Salvador's population had grown to roughly 5 million while Honduras's had grown to 2.6 million. El Salvador occupies about 8,000 square miles, compared to Honduras's 42,300 square miles.

2. North, *Bitter Grounds*, 62–64.

3. Trade imbalances also caused hard feelings between the two countries. El Salvador, more industrialized, fared better than did Honduras in the new Central American

The deportees returned to El Salvador at a time when 20 percent of Salvadorans were unemployed and 40 percent underemployed, working no more than one hundred twenty days per year.

In this tense atmosphere of 1969, the two countries played a series of three hotly disputed soccer matches to qualify for the 1970 World Cup. In the first match, on June 8 in Honduras' capital, the Salvadoran team contested a point scored in overtime that caused them to lose the game, 1–0.

When the Honduran team came to El Salvador for a second match on June 15, emotions ran high. Following that game, some acts of violence directed at Hondurans set off violence against Salvadorans in Honduras. Random groups of thugs threatened Salvadoran farmers in Honduras, terrorizing some and burning their homes. Some seventeen thousand refugees, up to fourteen hundred per day, fled into El Salvador.

A third soccer game, a play-off, took place, and El Salvador won 3–2. A few days later, the two countries broke off relationships amid much angry rhetoric.

On July 3, the Honduran air force sent several fighter planes over the Salvadoran border. El Salvador retaliated, and its war planes bombed the airport in the Honduran capital. Within days, the two countries engaged in both air and land warfare, killing two thousand and wounding four thousand.[4] The Honduran air force was superior to El Salvador's, while Salvadoran ground forces bested those of Honduras.

It quickly became apparent neither nation could afford protracted war, and the Organization of American States negotiated a ceasefire. The press dubbed the five-day, hundred-hour conflict the "Soccer War," a name which stuck.

Some scholars suggest the better name would be the "Landlords' War,"[5] because the tensions originated with wealthy landowners on both sides of the border who privatized land for their own use, dislodging peasant farmers.

Common Market created in 1961.

4. Armstrong and Shenk, *Face of Revolution*, 57.

5. North, *Bitter Grounds*, 64.

7. A Time to See with One's Own Eyes

(1975–1976)

On December 14, 1974, in the town of Santiago de María, a crowd of parishioners and officials turned out for Romero's installation as diocesan bishop. In addition to the church service, they celebrated the festive occasion with parades and processions.

Rural, Catholic, and impoverished described the vast majority of Santiago de María's half-million inhabitants when Romero arrived in the diocese, the poorest of the country's five. Most worked as day laborers on plantations raising export crops. Families from around the country migrated to the region to seek seasonal work on cotton and sugar plantations in the south and coffee estates in the cooler hilly north.

The diocese had just twenty-five priests, roughly one for every twenty thousand inhabitants, most of whom were assumed to be Catholic at that time. (In comparison, in 1975, there was one Roman Catholic priest for every 1,100 Catholics in the United States.[1]) Many of the priests were elderly; their average age was fifty-nine. This bode well for Romero's interpersonal relationships. Now fifty-seven himself, Romero had for years gotten along better with older, more conservative colleagues. On the downside, having few young, energetic priests curtailed pastoral activity and outreach.

What's more, Romero succeeded a bishop—a "theoretical theologian . . . of office and desk"[2]—who had let pastoral work slide, concentrating on religious celebrations that brought in income to sustain the clergy. As the new bishop, however, Romero threw himself into church outreach with the enthusiastic vigor he had shown as a new priest some thirty years earlier.

As he had done in San Miguel, Bishop Romero supported Catholic associations, visited the sick in hospitals, encouraged the area's Alcoholics

1. Sullins, *Empty Pews*. http://faculty.cua.edu/sullins/published%20articles/pshort.pdf.

2. Díez and Macho, *En Santiago*, 24. Full text of this book is at: http://servicioskoinonia.org/biblioteca/bibliodatos1.html?gralo1.

Anonymous movement and distributed alms. After a November 1975 meeting with Pope Paul VI in Rome, Romero liked to quote the pontiff regarding charity: "A father should always have his pockets full to give to his children."[3]

The new bishop began a weekly newspaper, *El Apóstol*, for the diocese. Like the periodicals he previously edited, its content drew heavily on Vatican news, much of it reprinted from a Vatican newspaper.[4]

The region lacked a powerful radio station, so Bishop Romero outfitted a Jeep with a loudspeaker and drove to rural hamlets each Sunday. He played prerecorded religious music to call people together, after which he heard confessions, said mass, baptized, and performed marriages. Sometimes he perturbed parish priests by failing to fill out the required paperwork, occasionally not even jotting down the names of those he baptized or married. On the whole, however, his priests admired the obvious zeal with which their new bishop reached out to parishioners.[5]

Romero thus found himself back in the pastoral ministry he had relished in San Miguel. But the country's political and economic tensions had intensified in the eight years since he had left San Miguel, and he faced new challenges, the first of which arrived on his doorstep six months later.

Tres Calles

In the wee hours of June 21, 1975, the phone rang in the bishop's mansion in the town of Santiago de María.

Romero, half asleep, answered. *"Sí?"*

"Sorry to wake you, but something's happened." Romero recognized the voice of Father Pedro, a Passionist priest in his diocese's Jiquilisco parish, located amid the southern cotton plantations.[6]

The tension in the priest's voice snapped Romero to attention. "*Sí*, Father Pedro. Go on."

3. As quoted in Brockman, *A Life*, 59.

4. *El Apóstol* means "The Apostle." The Vatican newspaper Romero depended on was *L'Osservatore Romano*.

5. Delgado, *Biografía*, 61–62.

6. Father Pedro Ferradas Reguero. Passionists belong to the missionary-minded Congregation of the Passion of Jesus Christ.

"We don't yet know the whole story but it seems an hour or two ago several vehicles of National Guardsmen invaded the hamlet of Tres Calles and . . ."

"*Sí?*"

". . . and killed several people. The families there are terrorized."

"They did this in the middle of the night?"

"Sometime after midnight."

"Should I come now?" the bishop asked.

"The soldiers have left and dawn's not far off, so why not wait till morning? I'll accompany you after saying the early mass. Will you concelebrate with me?"

"Of course." Once Bishop Romero hung up, he dialed the closest National Guard office and asked for the commander.

"Everyone's out on the job."

"Everyone? There's no official I can speak with?" Romero asked.

"Everyone's out on the job." The voice was curt.

The next morning after mass, Bishop Romero and Father Pedro drove to Tres Calles, a tiny hamlet of shacks among cotton plantations.

They stopped and got out when they saw people congregated at the El Zapote gully on the settlement's threshold.

As they approached, the gathering's mournful mood enveloped them. Tears ran down women's cheeks. Fearful children clung to mothers' skirts. Some of the men's eyes blazed with anger. The people parted and the churchmen saw the corpse—a young man, killed by a bullet through his temple.

"What happened here?" Bishop Romero asked.

"He's my son," a woman with graying hair said through sobs. "Juan Francisco Morales."

"And my husband," a young woman added. "Guardsmen forced him from our house last night. We found his body after daybreak." She wiped tears from her cheeks. "At least they didn't hack up his body with machetes, as they did the others."

"How many other families were attacked?" Father Pedro asked.

"One other family," someone said. "They lost four."

"Father Pedro and I would like to visit them," the bishop said, "but first let us pray for the recently departed soul of Juan Francisco Morales."

They continued to the stick-and-mud home of the Ostorga family, where they greeted José Alberto Ostorga's widow. She in turn introduced them to her daughter-in-law and, nodding to a huddle of silent, scared children, said, "My youngest and my grandchildren." The priests went to the little ones and laid their hands on their heads to greet and bless them. Like too many children in the diocese, they wore tattered clothing. The younger ones' swollen bellies spoke of malnutrition.

Doña Ostorga sent some children to fetch chairs from neighbors' homes. They soon returned with two rickety wood stools.

"Please have a seat." Doña huddled on the edge of the bed in a corner of the dirt-floor room. It served as the family's living room and dining room, as well as bedroom to some of them.

"Will you take notes?" the bishop asked Father Pedro. The priest pulled a pen and notepad from a woven bag hanging over his shoulder.

"We were sleeping," Doña Ostorga said, "when suddenly the door of our house was knocked down and soldiers began to pull us from our beds and hammocks, shining flashlights in our faces. 'Hands in the air!' they ordered. We made out many other Guardsmen in the shadows outside, surrounding our house."

"They kept demanding that we turn over our weapons, but we had none. They asked one of my sons for his identification card. They looked at it, then tied him up by his thumbs. 'Where are the weapons?' they asked, their rifles pointed at him."

"Tell us about this son," the bishop said.

"Hector David was seventeen and studying in eighth grade, a hard worker."[7]

"A youngster," Romero commented.

"Well, then," Doña Ostroga said, "another of my sons, José Alfredo, six years older than Hector, tried to hide."

"And?"

"They riddled his body with bullets. While this commotion was going on, Hector tried to leave the house. The soldiers outside machine-gunned him down in the doorway. They didn't even bother to move his body aside. Just stepped on him as they came and went." She pulled her shawl closer to her trembling body.

"They beat our Juan. Look." The thirteen-year-old showed the visitors the welts and bruises on his body.

7. That a young person of whatever age would continue to seek education despite poverty and lack of opportunities is a testament to his or her perseverance, intellect, and determination.

"Then," continued her daughter-in-law, "they tied up my husband along with my father-in-law. All the while insulting and taunting us. Dirty commies and worse names, they called us."

"And how was your husband related to Hector and José Alfredo?"

"He is—was—their older brother, twenty-eight years old. He was named after his father, my father-in law, José Alberto Ostorga Sr." After a pause, she continued. "They took them outside. 'This is just a warning,' they called to us, 'we will be back.'"

"From here, they went to the Morales home." They pointed to a house some sixty paces away. "There, they took Santos Morales and the younger Juan Francisco Morales, and lead all four away."

"We will stop by the Morales's house," Romero said.

"Not much later we heard machine guns firing."

"When we were sure the soldiers had gone, we went outside to see what we could see, using the light of a kerosene lamp. We walked to where we had heard the guns rat-a-tat-tat."

"It was horrid." She shivered.

"They had hacked up the bodies with machetes. We buried the remains along with the bodies of Hector and José Alfredo."

"It wasn't till after daylight that we found Juan Francisco's body, the one you saw in the ditch on the way in, Monseñor."

"Fathers, I don't know what we will do to survive."

"*Sí.*" Romero's voice softened. "You buried four loved ones today. Men in their prime. I'll ask the National Guard for an explanation." He turned to face some of the men clustered in the open doorway. "I know you must be very angry, but I beg you to remain levelheaded. Violence only begets violence. God will punish those who break the commandments, especially the strict law, 'Do not kill.'"

The bishop led a long responsive prayer, invoking God's healing and comforting love for the families and the community.

"To think that a bishop bothers to come to our poor little community, as insignificant and out of the way as it is," Romero overheard Doña Ostorga say as he and Father Pedro left the house.

After stopping at the Morales house and hearing a similar story, the bishop and priest drove back to Jiquilisco.[8]

8. The facts in this section are based on the two reports Bishop Romero addressed to his fellow bishops and his letter to the nation's president in the days after the massacre, included in Díez and Macho, *En Santiago*, 59–67. Romero's details vary slightly in nonessentials with Father Pedro's recounting of the event in López Vigil, *Mosaic*, 67–69.

But Why?

"Do you have any idea why the National Guard targeted these two families?" Romero asked Father Pedro. "What could they have done?"

"It may have been a member of ORDEN, one of the peasants serving as the military's local 'eyes' and 'ears' to spy on neighbors. ORDEN members have terrific power to do ill. One may have fingered these families over something they thought they heard or saw, or simply to settle a score."

"So ORDEN sets *campesinos* and *campesinas* against one another?" Bishop Romero shivered.

"I'm not saying it was ORDEN, but it could well have been. The military has upped recruitment, and there are now tens of thousands of card-carrying ORDEN members throughout the country." Father Pedro kept his eyes on the road, swerving to avoid potholes. "How will you respond to this massacre, Monseñor?"

"I'll be talking to the National Guard commander of this department. Depending on his reply, I may write to the president, who's a friend of mine."

"I can assure you the National Guard has no reason for this action other than to sow terror to keep people from getting together to defend their rights."

"How do you know the men killed were not part of a guerrilla group?" Romero asked.

"Did the soldiers find weapons at their homes?"

The bishop didn't reply.

"Even if they had found weapons, is this what passes for due process in El Salvador today? Forty Guardsmen armed with automatic guns who descend on a hamlet under the cloak of night? They ask for a teenager's identification papers and proceed to murder him, his older brothers, and father? No arrests? No trial?"

"Were they members of FECCAS?" Bishop Romero asked, referring to the Christian Peasants' Federation.[9]

The author has incorporated the facts into invented but likely dialogues between the churchmen and the Morales and Ostorga widows. The home's interior is based on those of similar communities with which the author is acquainted. Although the author ascribes the wakeup call to Father Pedro, with whom Romero visited Tres Calles, she could not learn who first phoned Romero with news of the massacre.

9. Brockman says of FECCAS and another farm workers union, UTC, which joined FECCAS in 1975: "To most of their peasant members, . . . FECCAS and UTC represented not an ideology but simply a hope for a decent piece of land to live on and to farm. To the landowning oligarchy, they were Lenin and Satan in one" (*A Life*, 3).

"And if they were?" Father Pedro replied. "I'm glad to see FECCAS expand, to see an organization give a ray of hope to families like the ones we just visited. All they ask for are little plots to raise beans and corn."

"Organizing is illegal in the countryside," Romero said.

"A law made by an illegal government. A government installed and kept in power by military officers, not elected by the people." Father Pedro glanced at the bishop. "If you write to the president, will you strongly denounce what happened here? Will you get your letter published in the nation's newspapers?"

"I'll write him as one individual to another. No point in making a public matter of something that can be handled in private. I know you and your Passionist colleagues would want a public protest, a demonstration with those new popular songs and placards . . ."

"It's the least we can do for our suffering flock." Father Pedro hit an especially bumpy section of the road and downshifted.

"The church is not a political party, however."

"But its actions certainly are political, especially its leaders' actions," Father Pedro replied. "Who do you help by your silence, the government or the people? People interpret silence in the face of injustice as support for the perpetrators."

Appealing to Authorities

The two men said their good-byes in Jiquilisco. Bishop Romero, now in his own car, headed home, stopping again in Usulután to talk with the National Guard commander and the department's governor. Neither was in, but he left messages saying he'd drop by again that evening.

Once home, he drafted a letter to the president. Then, after saying the seven o'clock evening mass, Romero met with the commander. He expressed his distress over what he had seen in Tres Calles and shared the letter he had written.

"We've already ordered an investigation," the commander assured him. "Wait to learn its outcome before sending your letter."

"The families in Tres Calles remain in fear. The Guardsmen threatened to return."

"I promise no one will bother them again," the commander said.

Romero met with the chief again the following day. Instead of a factual report on the whos and whys of the massacre, the military man contented himself with suggesting those killed were evildoers.

"They should have been arrested and given their day in court," the bishop insisted.

The commander shrugged.

A few days later, the bishop rewrote his letter to the president, using stronger language. It began:

> Mr. President:
>
> I believe I would not be fulfilling my difficult duty as Pastor of this Diocese if I were to remain silent before you, having personally witnessed, last Sunday morning, the bitter experience my dear parishioners of Tres Calles are undergoing these days.
>
> [Following two paragraphs in which he described the events, as related by the affected families, Romero continued:]
>
> Now, Mr. President, after having witnessed the despair, sown by those who should inspire trust and security in our worthy *campesinos*, I am fulfilling my duty as Diocesan Bishop by expressing to you my respectful but firm protest for the way in which a "security force" illegitimately claims the right to kill and mistreat. I am not trying to justify the behavior of those killed. Nor do I agree with those who would exploit these deplorable incidents for their political ends.
>
> My perspective is uniquely and sincerely that of the Church Pastor who laments to the President of the Republic the trampling of dignity and life, to which everyone has a right, even criminals, until they have come before a court of law that hands down, if necessary, the sentence their offenses deserve. With this same pure pastoral motive, I beg you, Mr. President, to intervene decisively to restore the peace, lost now to threats and fear, to the homes of Tres Calles, and to do justice to the victims of the abuse, somehow offering restitution to the families who have lost their breadwinners.
>
> I would not have wished, Mr. President, to use language of protest and demands in my correspondence with you, but I believe my friendship with you would not be frank or sincere if, to preserve it, I failed to obey the voice of my conscience that demands this pastoral duty of me. And because I sincerely hold in high regard your personal values, I'm confident my words, directed to you also in the name of the poor without voice, will find full harmony in your noble sentiments.

> Moreover, I want to reassure you that this letter is completely confidential, since I have no desire for the limelight, but rather wish for an effective intervention by he who has in his hands the main resources to prevent these unfortunate situations. For this reason, I would like, Mr. President, to discuss with you, more fully and without intermediaries, all I have expressed here. I am more and more convinced that direct and sincere dialogue not only wards off conflicts and misunderstandings, but above all builds, between the Supreme Government and Church Clergy, each with its own responsibilities, the country's true well-being. . . . –O.A. Romero, Bishop of Santiago de María[10]

He then sent it by special courier to the president.

There is no record of a presidential response. While Romero made no public protest over the Tres Calles massacre, his personal letter—clearly expressing his condemnation—represented a first step in addressing officials to seek justice on behalf of "the poor without voice." The missive may have been Romero's first use of this phrase he would later repeat often.

Romero's energetic pastoral response to his abused parishioners was in keeping with his essential nature as a shepherd to the humble. What's more, after hearing the widow Ostorga's parting remark, he began to realize how much his presence as a bishop, a person of stature, meant to those clinging to society's bottom rung. Perhaps most importantly, he witnessed for himself how easily the powerful abused the poor and landless. The abused lacked recourse to legal justice, and the powerful did not need to offer explanations for their behavior, not even for criminal actions.

10. The president was Colonel Arturo Armando Molina. From Romero's letter, as shared in Díez and Macho, *En Santiago*, 62–64.

8. A Time to Challenge One's Thinking

(1975–1976)

THE PASSIONIST BROTHERS WORKING in the Santiago de María diocese tested Bishop Romero's attitudes and leadership style. Father Pedro Ferradas Reguero, who had accompanied Romero to Tres Calles after the killings there, was one of three Passionists carrying out the mission of their Spain-based religious order. The Passionists had been working in the diocese since 1957.[1]

In 1971, the Passionist brothers had opened a training center for the diocese's *campesinos*, the rural poor, to prepare them as catechists, or lay leaders, in their home communities.[2] The catechists would fill some of the gaps in ministry in a country with few priests. Because many participants were illiterate or semiliterate, the center also taught literacy, Salvadoran history, and some basic life skills, such as first aid.

Romero arrived in the diocese wary of the training center, called Los Naranjos. He suspected the center used teachings like those he had confronted in the capital's Jesuit seminary and high school. He had claimed priests instructing in those educational centers used "Marxist analysis." Romero fretted because the government had already tagged Los Naranjos and two similar schools in other parts of El Salvador as "centers of subversion."

More specifically, he believed the center's teachings had "too secular and political" an emphasis, which its unschooled students couldn't properly

1. The three Passionist brothers worked in the Jiquilisco parish of Santiago de María.

2. The center's full name was "*Centro de promoción campesina Los Naranjos*," or Los Naranjos Peasant Training Center. ("*Los Naranjos*" means "Orange Grove.") Information in this section from Díez and Macho, *En Santiago*. Most, if not all, of the country's early catechists were men. In *Iglesias*, author Alas acknowledges the error he made in overlooking women as lay catechists in his parish of Suchitoto, 84.

understand. He'd prefer the Passionists teach with "a process and a language more in line with the traditional way of thinking of our rural people."[3]

In October 1975, Romero shut down the center's activities until he found time to study its plans and programs. Although the action was within his rights as bishop, he angered the Passionist brothers by taking the action without first dialoguing with them, a courtesy Romero himself had asked of the nation's president following the Tres Calles massacre.

On December 10, 1975, the center's director, Father Juan Macho, faced Romero and five other church officials to defend the Passionists' work:

> "You should already know the government doesn't at all like what you teach at the Center," said Bishop Marco René Revelo,[4] head of the bishops' education commission.
>
> "Well," Father Macho replied, addressing Revelo and Romero, "I would like the two Bishops here to tell me, as a priest, who should guide my teaching, the Government or the Bishops? If it's the Bishops, fine. But if it's the Government, for what do I need you Bishops?"
>
> "Yes, but you're running a grave risk," Bishop Revelo replied. "Any day now you could run into personal problems due to your teachings."
>
> "I knew of risks and persecution from the moment I became a priest," Father Macho replied. "It's right there in the Gospel, so they should not surprise me. . . . Further, I'd question [the validity of] my priesthood if I had no such problems."[5]

The meeting did not resolve the impasse. Two days later, the regional vicar for Passionists in Central America traveled from his home in Honduras to meet with Romero.[6]

In that encounter, which lasted over two hours, the vicar asked Romero straight out whether he could fully accept the ministry of the Passionist brothers at the training center or whether they should seek another diocese in which to labor, one that could unconditionally accept their work.[7] The

3. From Romero's letter to Padre Venancio, serving as the Passionist provincial in Zaragoza, Spain, on October 1, 1975, as cited by Díez and Macho, *En Santiago*, 90.

4. Bishop Marco René Revelo served as auxiliary bishop of Santa Ana diocese and also coordinated the work of the country's rural centers.

5. Dialogue as related by Passionist Father Juan Macho Merino, in Díez and Macho, *En Santiago*, 115–16.

6. Father Victorino Sevilla.

7. Díez and Macho supply Father Sevilla's summary document of the meeting (*En*

vicar requested that Romero reply to this question in writing before the vicar left to return home the following day.

After consulting others, Romero wrote to affirm his respect for the Passionists' work. In order to reopen the center, he requested that the Passionists invite him to their planning sessions and that Father Macho serve as pastoral, or educational, vicar for the entire diocese.

The Passionists accepted Romero's conditions, and the Los Naranjos center began its courses again. With Father Macho now his pastoral vicar, Romero worked closely with him, which allowed him to keep a close eye on teaching in the center and elsewhere in the diocese.

The two men developed a friendship and a good working relationship. Indeed, three months later, Romero used his pulpit and newspaper to encourage the faithful to gather during Lent in small groups to study God's word, using lesson plans prepared by Father Macho. After Easter, the bishop enthusiastically reported in an editorial that many groups had taken advantage of his suggestion. He acknowledged the role of Los Naranjos in preparing lay leaders. He also affirmed his belief that the Christian base communities the Passionist brothers helped create represented "the working of the Holy Spirit" in an area with so few priests.

The Passionist brothers, however, did not believe Romero had truly changed his mind about the center's teachings, still considering them to be "mutilation and misinterpretation" of Medellín documents to foment antigovernment dissent. Romero had acted out of pragmatism, they believed, not wanting to lose the energetic Passionist mission in his diocese.

In retrospect, Father Macho thought the Los Naranjos affair impelled the bishop to question his thinking on some theological issues and about his hierarchical way of interacting.[8] Never before had he been told he might be wrong, Macho said, or that his authoritarian decrees might be interpreted as unfair and condemning. The confrontation moved him toward interacting not with an "I command" or "I order" but through dialogue, discernment, and shared reflection and prayer.[9]

As the curtains closed on the Los Naranjos drama in December 1975, Pope Paul VI published his statement "Evangelization in the Modern

---

Santiago, 121–26).

8. Romero also called the Los Naranjos controversy "a tempest in a teapot," perhaps an attempt to downplay his initial overreaction to its work or what he perceived as the priests' overreaction to his wanting to study the center's work.

9. Díez and Macho, *En Santiago,* 135.

World." In it, the pope reasserted what Medellín documents had proclaimed: the church's message to the world includes liberation from sins of an unjust society, not only personal sin.[10]

Romero might not have fully accepted the statements of bishops at Medellín, but he'd not refute a pope's pronouncement. He'd have to start reevaluating his take on the Medellín documents on which the Passionist brothers based their outreach.

Campesino Wisdom

One of Romero's objections to the Los Naranjos Center had to do with his doubt that unschooled *campesinos* could adequately interpret the Bible in order to teach others. He feared they'd be manipulated by priests with "Marxist tendencies." One Sunday the bishop visited the Los Naranjos center to observe a student-led Bible study.

Father Macho took the bishop aside when he arrived. "Look, today we're reading the Gospel account of the loaves and fishes," the priest told Romero. "After it's read, the leader invites anyone who wants to comment to do so. At the end of the discussion, the presiding priest—today that's you—summarizes what's been said. You can clarify things, correct any errors, and add your own comments."

"Sounds good," the bishop replied.

After the reading, a *campesino*, a trained catechist named Juan Chicas, commented, "To me this Gospel reading shows that the boy with the loaves and fishes forced Jesus to perform the miracle."

Romero interrupted him. "Young man, no one could force Jesus to do anything. Jesus was free!"

Juan Chicas calmly stood his ground. "Give me a moment, Monseñor, and you'll see. I say he was pushed to act because five loaves and two fishes are nothing to feed a whole crowd, but, at the same time, they were all the boy had. So they were both nothing and everything at once. That's the thing! When the boy offered all he had, Jesus could do no less. He also had to do all he could. And he could do miracles!"

10. "It is impossible to accept that in evangelization one could or should ignore the importance of the problems so much discussed today, concerning justice, liberation, development, and peace in the world. This would be to forget the lesson which comes to us from the Gospel concerning love of our neighbor who is suffering and in need," the document said in its point no. 31. http://www.christlife.org/evangelization/paul6/C_evangelii.html.

"Now I understand," the bishop said.

"What I think, Monseñor, is that many times we ask God for miracles, but we hoard our bread. God will only perform miracles for us when we learn to share. Then God'll do the needed miracle, but while we're hoarding, there won't be miracles."

When the discussion ended and it was time for the bishop's wrap-up, Romero said, "I had prepared a homily for this occasion, but I see it's not needed. All I can do is repeat what Jesus said: 'I give thanks, Father, because you revealed the truth to the humble and kept it hidden from the learned.'"[11]

"So what did you think?" Father Juan later asked.

"Well, Father, as you know, I had my reservations about these *campesinos*, but I see they may be able to offer a better commentary on God's word than we can."[12]

Migrant Harvesters

During Romero's first year as bishop, he apparently did not notice the migrant coffee workers who slept sprawled over the city's sidewalks. Like Romero's hometown, Santiago de María nestles in prime coffee country in mountains higher than three thousand feet in altitude. During the November to March coffee harvest, cold temperatures produce frost at night.

"What can be done?" Romero asked his clergy in winter 1976.

"Well, there's that empty Catholic high school. You could offer it as a dorm," Father Macho suggested.

Romero opened the high school, as well as a meeting room in his own bishop's house, as shelter from the elements to exhausted coffee harvesters. He asked the Catholic charity Caritas to provide the farmworkers with a hot beverage, milk or atole, a thin corn porridge, each night.

The bishop chatted with the workers who slept in his house and thus became aware of some of the abuses they endured. By bribing Ministry of Labor inspectors to keep quiet, planters were able to pay harvesters less than the government's minimum wage. In addition, owners set their own quotas of "official pickers" to hire, and then they took on additional hands as "pickers' helpers," paying them even less.

11. Paraphrasing of Luke 10:21.

12. "Campesino Wisdom" constructed from testimonies in Díez and Macho, *En Santiago*, 152–53, and Juan Macho in López Vigil, *Mosaic*, 74–75.

The bishop visited a coffee plantation to see for himself the illegally low wages posted on a blackboard.

"How could such good, Christian people do such a thing?" Romero later asked his clergy. Ever since he was a parish priest in San Miguel, Romero's landowner friends supported his charities and church-building efforts. Now he couldn't reconcile the plantation owners he thought he knew with those who flouted the law and defrauded their workers.[13]

Bishop Romero wrote of the abuse in the diocesan newspaper:[14]

> Always lavish, God is giving us again this year that splendid rain of rubies [the red-ripe coffee beans] that brings thousands of workers from all over to gather our mountains' rich gift. [But] human sin makes the beauty of creation moan . . . For this reason the church must cry out by God's command: "God has destined the earth and all it contains for the use of the whole human race. Created wealth should reach all in just form, under the auspices of justice and accompanied by charity. Whatever the form of property-holding, we must not lose sight of this universal purpose of all wealth."[15]
>
> It saddens and troubles us to see the selfishness with which ways and means are found to cancel out the coffee pickers' just wage. We think of, for example, this new category of "helpers," being used to designate true "harvesters" in order to deprive them of their legitimate compensation.
>
> How we would wish that the joy of this rain of rubies and of all earth's harvests would not be darkened by the Bible's tragic sentence: "Look! The wages you failed to pay the workers who mowed your fields are crying out against you. The cries of the harvesters have reached the ears of the Lord Almighty."[16]

About this editorial, one biographer comments, "Romero's concern for justice for the harvesters is evident amid the flowery language, but he

13. Díez and Macho, *En Santiago,* 146–48.

14. Romero y Galdámez, "'Cortadores' y 'Ayudas,'" ["'Pickers' and 'Helpers'"] *El Apóstol*, November 28, 1976, 2. Interestingly, Romero had decried the unjust treatment of the rural poor by wealthy landowners as early as a December 13, 1952, editorial, "La Iglesia va al campesino" ["The Church Goes to the *Campesino*"] in *Chaparrastique*, no. 1946, 1.

15. Romero takes the quote from the 1975 Vatican II document *Gaudium et spes*, point no. 69. http: www.vatican.va/archive/hist_councils/ii_vatican_council/documents/vat-ii_cons_19651207_gaudium-et-spes_en.html.

16. James 5:4 NIV

offers no solution for the injustice beyond wishing that the landowners were not so selfish and fraudulent."[17]

On the other hand, the editorial testifies to Bishop Romero's learning curve. As Father Macho put it: "He gave them [the fieldworkers] blankets, beds, and a hot beverage to warm them, and they in turn gave him their shared wisdom, their worries, their sorrows, their entire lives with all their miseries."[18]

Thus, the very people to whom the bishop ministered began to open his eyes. No longer was it merely priests, but also the rural poor who instructed Bishop Romero in "Salvadoran Reality 101." Soon the student of the impoverished, Romero himself, would land in the national laboratory—as a major teacher and leader.

17. Brockman, *A Life*, 55.

18. Díez and Macho, *En Santiago*, 145.

9. A Time to be Shocked

(1977)

In 1976, when Archbishop Chávez announced he would retire, two names emerged as his possible replacement.[1] One was Chávez's auxiliary, Bishop Arturo Rivera y Damas. The other was his former auxiliary, Bishop Oscar Romero of the Santiago de María diocese.

Many of the clergy, especially the progressive and younger ones, favored Bishop Rivera. He'd continue Chávez's emphasis on a renewed church dedicated to the "opened windows" and "fresh air" proposals of Vatican II and Medellín.

The nuncio, the Vatican's ambassador to El Salvador, supported Romero. He had been impressed with Romero's handling of the Los Naranjos affair.[2] The nuncio also consulted some forty government and military leaders, businessmen, and high-society women. All favored Romero.

"For the wealthy class . . . and the government they controlled, Rivera was undesirable," said one biographer. "They did not want anyone who would continue the ways of Archbishop Chávez. . . . To some he [Rivera] was another of those communist priests who aroused the peasants and lower classes with talk of justice and liberation. They would be content with one of the known conservatives—that is, practically anyone but Rivera."[3]

The church hierarchy in Rome must have agreed with the nuncio and oligarchs. On February 10, 1977, the Vatican named Romero archbishop.

Progressive priests and laity grieved. One woman, then a student, later recalled her reaction: "My world fell apart when I found out that Romero was the new archbishop. I went to the UCA [university] crying bitterly. 'I'm

1. Luiz Chávez y González, seventy-five, had served as archbishop of San Salvador diocese for thirty-eight years, from 1938 to 1977.

2. The nuncio, Rome's ambassador to El Salvador and Guatemala, was Emanuele Gerada.

3. Brockman, *A Life*, 4.

not going to obey a church with a man like that in charge! Now we'll have to go back to the days of the catacombs!'"[4]

A priest who attended the event believed the clergy who attended Romero's installation on February 22 did so to accompany Chávez in his last act as archbishop, rather than to greet his successor. "When Monseñor Romero took the floor, the silence was sepulchral and the reaction to his words was hardly spontaneous," he wrote. "People applauded because etiquette demanded it of them."[5]

Such reactions, which may appear overblown several decades later, were justifiable in the context of the church persecution and general repression of the period. "When historians write the history of the Salvadorean revolution, the year 1977 may well be deemed the most important," claim two researchers.[6] New implausible levels of fraud in the February 1977 presidential elections sent tens of thousands into the streets in protest. The government responded with an iron fist. It imposed a state of siege, which included the prohibition of public gatherings. Soldiers obeyed orders to massacre unarmed civilians.

What's more, landowners scuttled a pilot land reform project that the nation's president, Colonel Arturo Molina, had planned the previous year. He proposed the purchase of 150,000 acres at full market price from 250 owners in order to distribute parcels to 12,000 landless families. Outraged plantation owners mounted a malicious press campaign. After being labeled a "communist in disguise" and hearing rumors of a coup to oust him, President Molina ditched the modest reform.

The people got the message: They would get no vote. They would get no land.

Further, the oligarchy would go after church leaders who had dared instill such hopes in the first place.

It lost no time in doing so. In February 1977, the government arrested and deported three priests, a former priest, and two former seminarians. It arrested and tortured another parish priest, releasing him with a fractured skull. It informed priests outside the country not to return. It hammered

4. Carmen Álvarez, in López Vigil, *Mosaic*, 82. Catacombs are underground cemeteries with multiple passageways; those below Rome served as places of refuge for early Christians fleeing their Roman persecutors.

5. Delgado, *Biografía*, 71. As a priest, Delgado was present at the installation, which took place at the San José de la Montana Church, next to the seminary of the same name.

6. Armstrong and Shenk, *Face of Revolution*, 89.

away at the church's "communist" actions in the nation's major media, owned and run by the elite.

At about eight in the evening of Saturday, March 12, 1977, the phone rang in the archdiocesan offices.[7]

"Monseñor, President Molina here. Have you heard the news?"

Romero had indeed heard the news and was in shock.[8] Two and a half hours earlier, Jesuit priest Rutilio Grande and his two passengers had been killed by gunfire as they drove through sugarcane fields on the road to say evening mass in El Paisnal, a village a few miles from their homes in Aguilares. Grande had been a good friend. The archbishop recalled his episcopal ordination seven years earlier, and Father Grande's gracious role in planning the celebration and serving as master of ceremonies.

"I want to be the first to offer condolences," Molina said.

The president's attempt at sympathy burnt Romero. He found it hollow and insincere, recalling the government's inaction after the Tres Calles massacre.

"You will investigate these latest murders, Mr. President?"

"There will be a thorough investigation."

Romero arrived in Aguilares, twenty miles from the capital, at about ten o'clock that evening. "Why?" must have rung through his mind when he saw the bodies laid out on tables in the hallway of the convent near the church.[9] The corpses were partly draped in bloodstained white sheets. A Carmelite sister used a towel to dab blood from Grande's head, which

7. Information about Grande's death from Brockman, *A Life*, 9–12, and Carranza, *Vidas*, 51–57. The phone dialogue is the author's narrative device; the actual words of the two men's conversation are not recorded. What's known is that President Molina offered condolences and Romero asked for a thorough investigation of the murders.

8. It's not known precisely when and how Romero first heard the news; the public phone in Aguilares had been sabotaged. Some individuals jumped in cars and headed to the capital to inform the YSAX radio station, the archbishop, and the Jesuit community. Whether or not it was the first Romero had learned the news, the president's phone call to him is well documented.

9. The church was El Señor de las Misericordias and the convent belonged to the Carmelite order.

still bled.[10] Alongside the Jesuit priest, pierced with eighteen bullets, lay the elderly man and teenager also killed in the assault.[11]

Stunned parishioners, distraught, many sobbing, flooded the convent doorway, blocking it so Romero had hardly been able to enter. Some priests, including the Jesuit superior for Central America[12] and recently retired archbishop Chávez—who was "confused and tremendously upset by the murder of one of his most beloved priests"[13]—had arrived in Aguilares before him.

The bodies were moved to the church and placed in front of the altar. Romero and the Jesuit superior both preached in an emotional service, which lasted till near midnight. Afterwards, Romero convened an emergency meeting with the clergy and some lay leaders present to sketch out an initial response plan. He promised to keep the public informed through the diocesan radio station, YSAX.

A doctor experienced in forensics drove from the capital to examine the corpses on behalf of the church, which he did in the early morning hours. Although the doctor lacked instruments to perform an autopsy, he said the wounds appeared to be from a type of heavy gun, .45 or .51 caliber, used by the country's security forces.

Grande and Romero had not agreed on everything, particularly on recent church reforms—Grande embraced Medellín's course while Romero mistrusted it, but the two men nevertheless connected. A seminary professor[14], Grande was one of the few Jesuits who befriended Romero and with whom Romero felt comfortable when he moved to the capital in 1967.

10. From a profile of former Carmelite nun Eva del Carmen Menjívar, present in Aguilares that night, published in Valencia, "Rutilio Grande." http://www.elfaro.net/es/201203/noticias/7949/.

11. Manuel Solórzano, seventy-two, a Delegate of the Word, and Nelson Rutilio Lemus, sixteen. Three children to whom Father Grande had offered a ride as they walked home were spared, and at least one of them was later able to offer details. A pickup had overtaken Grande's Volkswagen Safari, shooting into the vehicle as it passed. The Safari flipped on its side and crashed into a fence. Men from the pickup walked to the Safari and pumped more bullets into the priest. They allowed the three children to climb over the bleeding bodies to escape the scene. One of the children recognized a gunman, his godfather, whose "beard" had come loose as he shot; he belonged to a governmental security force (Carranza, *Vidas*, 52).

12. The Jesuit provincial was Father César Jerez.

13. Carranza, *Vidas*, 54.

14. Grande had served as prefect of the seminary as well as professor of pastoral theology and liturgy. Carranza, ibid., 28.

Kindred Souls

Both Grande and Romero had been cut from the same cloth of rural El Salvador, and they shared some key personality traits. They both struggled with low self-esteem, indecision, and natural timidity, a quality which appeared to vaporize when these two gifted orators stood behind the pulpit.[15] Despite some misunderstandings and "bumps" along the way, their friendship endured.[16] In his funeral oration for Grande, Romero said the murdered priest felt like a brother to him.

Romero knew no one could justify Grande's death by painting him with the communist brush. Grande was thoroughly Christian and utterly devoted to his flock. He and his team had built committed, informed base communities throughout the parish, modeled on what Grande had experienced in Ecuador.

Grande had spent parts of 1971 and 1972 in Quito, participating in a Catholic outreach with an indigenous group, an experience from which he returned reinvigorated and inspired.[17] Grande wanted to try to duplicate it in his homeland. Archbishop Chávez obliged and in September 1972 assigned him to the parish in which he had grown up, Aguilares.

One woman later described her reaction to Father Grande's mission: "We started going to church. The Gospel was given a different context. It

15. Carranza described Grande, in his mission in Aguilares, as "very unsure of himself and uncertain. When speaking to a crowd . . . he transformed into a warm and passionate, sometimes vehement and implacable speaker. But up to the time he stood at the pulpit . . . he obsessed over a thousand details while preparing his message" (ibid., 71). Like Romero, Grande consulted everyone, from the cook to the theologians in the capital.

16. In 1970, a new rector for the Jesuit seminary needed to be named. The Jesuit provincial superior nominated Grande, but the majority of the bishops did not support him. Feeling this lack of confidence in him and his seminary teaching—he was professor of pastoral theology and liturgy—Grande resigned from its staff and in 1972 went to Ecuador to seek a new direction for his ministerial work. It's hard to know what, if any, role Bishop Romero had in the 1970 rectorship election, as he too was nominated but rejected for the position after the bishops had vetoed Grande.

Romero did become rector, however, in 1972, when he was among the bishops who ousted the Jesuits from the seminary. Later, as archbishop, Romero would apologize to Father Amando López, rector when the bishops voted the Jesuits out.

In 1973, a dismayed Grande observed from a distance as Romero stirred up a national controversy by branding some Jesuit teachings "Marxist." The teachings were a product of the Medellín discernment, to which Grande was devoted (Ibid., 28–33).

17. As part of Monseñor Leonidas Eduardo Proaño's Instituto Pastoral Latinoamericano, a program of CELAM, the Latin American Episcopal Conference.

wasn't that contemplative Gospel of looking up at the sky and waiting for divine justice to fall, it wasn't like that."[18]

Grande and his teammates' efforts in Aguilares bore fruit in peoples' participation in organizations such as FECCAS, a peasant farmer's association. The association's strength, in turn, focused the ruling families' attention on the parish and consolidated their condemnation of it.

As he stood over his friend's murdered body, Romero concluded Grande had followed Jesus's path to the point of giving up his life for his flock. "When I saw Rutilio [Grande] dead, I thought, 'If they killed him for what he was doing, it's my job to go down that same road, . . .'" he later confided in the Jesuit superior.[19]

Romero must have questioned whether he had inadvertently strengthened the forces of death and repression by not taking strong public stands. He knew, after all, that he had been named archbishop to shore up the status quo, the powers that be, opposed to church workers like Father Grande.

Romero recalled what he had heard of Grande's sermon of a month ago, given outdoors to a packed crowd. In it, Father Grande denounced the injustice imposed on the landless peasants. He also protested the deportation of priests and one of his fellow priests in particular, a beloved Colombian. Grande's frank words had outraged the powerful, to the point some of his associates said Father Grande had signed his own death warrant:

> The enslaved masses of our people, those by the side of our road, live in a feudal system six centuries old. They own neither their land nor their own lives. . . . Mouths are full of the word "Democracy," but let us not fool ourselves. There is no democracy when the power of the people is the power of a wealthy minority, not of the people. You are Cains, and you crucify the Lord in the person of . . . the humble *campesino*.
>
> I am quite certain that very soon the Bible and the Gospel won't be allowed to cross our borders. We'll get only the bindings, because all the pages are subversive. And I think that if Jesus himself came across the border at Chalatenango, they wouldn't let him in. They would accuse him of being a rabble-rouser, a foreign Jew, one who confused the people with exotic and foreign ideas, ideas against democracy—that is, against the wealthy minority, that clan

18. Church activist Emma Landaverde in documentary film *Last Journey*, directed by Carrigan and Weber.

19. César Jerez, then Jesuit provincial, in López Vigil, *Mosaic*, 159.

> of Cains! Brothers and sisters, without any doubt, they would crucify him again.[20]

On Monday, March 14, the nuncio presided at the funeral mass for the three murder victims. More than a hundred priests concelebrated the service to a crowd that spilled out the Metropolitan Cathedral's doors into the plaza and streets.

Romero and the Jesuit provincial spoke in a two-part sermon. Romero's message stressed that Father Grande's ministry embodied Vatican II's call for church involvement to liberate people from the miseries of famine, chronic disease, illiteracy, and poverty. This liberating work, this "social gospel," carried out nonviolently, was the fruit of Christian faith and love, he said. Grande had based his mission upon Jesus's words "what you did for one of these least brothers or sisters of mine, you did for me."[21]

> True love is the gift that Father Rutilio Grande gives us in his death with the two *campesinos*. . . . It should be pointed out that it was at the time when Father Grande walked among the people, proclaiming the message of salvation and the Mass, that he was shot down. A priest with his *campesinos*, walking to meet his people, to identify himself with them, to live with them—this is an inspiration of love and not revolution. . . .
>
> Perhaps this is why God chose Father Rutilio for martyrdom because those whom he knew and those who knew him are well aware of the fact that he never called people to violence, vengeance, or hatred. He died loving and without a doubt, when he felt those first jolts that brought him death, he was able to speak those words of Jesus: Father, forgive them, they know not what they do (Luke 23:34).[22]

Raising Drawbridge to Past

That same day Romero also wrote to President Molina. Because he had not yet received the official report promised him on the phone Saturday, he "judged it most urgent" that the president order an "exhaustive investigation

20. From Father Rutilio Grande's homily at Apopa on February 13, 1977, as shared in Armstrong and Shenk, *Face of Revolution*, 82–83. The deported Colombian priest was Father Mario Bernal Londoño.

21. Matt 25:40.

22. Romero y Galdámez, *Homilies*, March 14, 1977.

of the facts."[23] The archbishop put teeth into this request, saying the church would take no part in official government acts until the government carried out the inquiry.

It was a vow upheld. The government made no serious investigation of the murders, and, while he served as archbishop, Romero attended no public government act, including the inauguration of the nation's new president.[24] This may have been the first time in El Salvador's history that one leg of the country's governing tripod—military, wealthy, church—decided to cut off its support.

The archbishop was not content to let the murders fade with the victims' burials. The next day, Tuesday, March 15, he met with his priests, many women religious, and some laity to discuss additional protest measures. Romero adopted two of the suggestions:

- Regular classes would be suspended and students at all Catholic schools in the archdiocese would devote three days to studying and reflecting upon the documents adopted at Vatican II and Medellín.
- The following Sunday, instead of individual masses in each parish, a single mass for the entire archdiocese would be held on the plaza in front the Metropolitan Cathedral and broadcast on YSAX. The action would demonstrate grief, unity, and moral indignation.

In retrospective, this Tuesday meeting with priests, women religious, and committed lay persons represents a drawbridge between Romero's past and future in a couple of ways. For one, it opened him to a method of problem-solving, of discerning God's will, within and through the body of believers, rather than through mandates handed down from on high. He sought counsel among many before making his decisions.

23. Brockman, *A Life*, 10.

24. Former journalist Julian Filochowski, chair of the London-based Archbishop Romero Trust, makes an insightful comparison of Romero's action here to a similar decision of Pope Pius XI, the pope Romero most admired: "Pius XI boycotted Hitler's visit to Rome in 1938 because of the persecution of the Catholic Church in Germany. This act, Romero has suggested [in his homily of September 3, 1978] was 'the greatest slap in the face that could have been given to Hitler.' Perhaps no surprise then that in July 1977, Romero boycotted the installation of the new Salvadoran President, General Carlos Humberto Romero, because the persecution of the Catholic Church in El Salvador was in full swing and the death squad killer of Rutilio Grande had not been brought to justice." See Julian Filochowski, "Romero: Person and His Charisma with the Pontiffs," in Pelton, *Archbishop Romero and Spiritual Leadership*, 99–110.

Equally important, the meeting's issues spotlighted Romero's open grappling to move beyond—or at least reconcile—newer currents of thought with the traditional theology in which he had been trained and immersed for the past thirty-five years. He summarized his theological problem with a single mass with this question: "If the eucharist gives glory to God, will not God have more glory in the usual number of Sunday Masses than in just one?"[25]

"I must confess that my heart sank to hear him," a prominent Jesuit theologian who attended the meeting later wrote. "Here was a theology straight out of the dark ages. But in thinking it over afterwards, and on the basis of all his actions, I finally came to interpret Archbishop Romero's words correctly. He was only showing his deep, genuine interest in the things of God. His theology was questionable. Beyond question, however, was his profound faith in God, and his surpassing concern for the glory of God in this world."[26]

After lengthy discussion, the issue was resolved when the regional Jesuit superior, Father César Jerez, affirmed Romero's concern for the glory of God. But he reminded the gathering of a teaching of the church's early patriarchs: "'*Gloria Dei, vivens homo*'—the glory of God is the living person."[27] Romero's reception to this idea "was not a mere matter of a new theological formulation. It was a matter of a new understanding of God. And Archbishop Romero had accepted that new understanding. Tirelessly he would repeat that nothing was more important to God than the life of the poor."[28]

Once decided upon, the single mass represented "so unusual and original an initiative" it "shook up church and public opinion, to say nothing of the nuncio's office," commented one participant.[29]

The initiative did not merely shake up the nuncio, it outraged him. He rightly viewed it as a confrontation with the government he served as the Vatican's ambassador. He did his best to dissuade Romero, giving him an

25. As quoted by Sobrino, *Reflections*, 15.

26. Ibid.

27. Ibid. This saying is from Saint Irenaeus, a second-century Christian thinker and leader in Lyons, France.

28. Ibid., 15–16.

29. Carranza, *Vidas*, 60.

angry "fifteen-minute scolding, calling him irresponsible, imprudent, and inconsistent in his actions as a bishop."[30]

Talking with Jesus

By Saturday, the day before the single mass, the nuncio still tried to deter Romero. He arrived at the archdiocesan offices, temporarily housed in the seminary, at about two in the afternoon with a letter marked "strictly confidential." The priest who received him, Father José Inocencio Alas, later related:

> The nuncio asked for the archbishop, and I told him he wasn't in. He looked angry and said, "He should be here. Tomorrow will be a terrible day for the church and it is his duty to be here. Available." He handed me the letter and left.
>
> At the time, Romero was out praying with some members of Opus Dei. He was a man of prayer. The conservative positions of Opus Dei, a sect within the Catholic Church, attracted him. . . .
>
> Monseñor returned at five thirty, and I immediately gave him the nuncio's letter. He went to his room for five minutes, then returned and asked me to read it. In his role as a representative of the Holy See, the nuncio warned Romero to halt the mass scheduled for the following day. He asked him to make a radio announcement that all clergy remain in their parishes.
>
> Romero was torn between his conscience and the letter's ecclesial authoritarianism. At stake was the concept of obedience to authority that Romero had learned in the Gregorian University's classrooms during World War II. . . . How could he say no to the nuncio? That was impossible.
>
> Looking worried and nervous, Romero asked me what he should do. We were leaning against the handrail in the hall of the seminary, a simple and beautiful building. Romero was suffering. I reminded him of theology. I spoke to him of his mission as a pastor, as bishop. This did not move him.
>
> I reminded him of something he himself had said when we gave *Cursillos de Cristiandad* [Christian Short Courses] together years earlier: "If we have a problem and don't know what to do, what decision to make, the best thing to do is go talk with Jesus."
>
> I suggested that he go to the seminary's chapel to speak with Jesus. I watched him walk slowly and calmly to the chapel. He

30. Brockman, *A Life*, 15.

> crossed the building from south to north, through the wide central hall festooned with bougainvillea, full of flowers and thorns, symbol of life, and he entered the chapel. The silence of the sacred invites us to make the best decisions of our lives.
>
> About an hour later, Romero returned down the same hall, approaching me. His face was serene and peaceful, and he had a smile on his lips. He said, "Tomorrow we will all be in the cathedral where we'll all celebrate the Eucharist together."[31]

A hundred thousand people attended the single mass on March 20. They arrived as parish delegations, carrying identifying banners and positioning themselves in the plaza and streets around the Metropolitan Cathedral. About one hundred fifty priests concelebrated the mass, first dispersing into the crowd as people said their confessions.

In his homily, Romero said, "I want to publicly thank all of these beloved priests. Many of them risk their lives and, like Father Grande, offer the greatest sacrifice."

The gathering erupted in applause.

"That applause ratifies the profound joy that I feel in my heart as I take possession of the Archdiocese. I also feel that my own weaknesses and my own inabilities find their complement, their power, and their courage in these united priests," Romero continued.

Then, addressing the clergy, he said, "Beloved priests, remain united in the authentic truth of the Gospel. This is another way to say to you, as Christ's humble successor and representative in the Archdiocese: the one who attacks one of my priests, attacks me."[32]

Again, the faithful clapped.

Father Alas later commented, "Thousands of people were applauding him, and something rose within him. It was then that he crossed the threshold. He went through the door. Because, you know, there is baptism by water, and there is baptism by blood. But there is also baptism by the people."[33]

Father Grande's death and the single mass defined a clear turning point for Romero, "framing a *before* and an *after* in his pastoral work."[34]

31. Alas, *Iglesia*, 261–64.
32. Romero y Galdámez, *Homilies*, March 20, 1977.
33. José Inocencio Alas, in López Vigil, *Mosaic*, 118.
34. Carranza, *Vidas*, 58.

From now on Romero would speak for the voiceless and the trampled. He would find himself at loggerheads with the nuncio, with four of his five fellow bishops, and several church officials in Rome, to say nothing of the country's governing elite.

10. A Time to Broadcast the News

(1977–1980)

Father Rutilio Grande's murder, the alarm that awoke Archbishop Romero to his country's realities, did not end the powerful elite's war on the church. Rather, the March 1977 assassination marked the onset of more dogged persecution of priests and lay people organized into base ecclesial, or Christian grassroots, communities.

Events unfolded rapidly as assaults upon the church spiraled in number and frequency. While the oligarchy dug in, new players emerged, among them groups who abandoned nonviolent change and took up arms. The archbishop found himself at the center of a nationwide maelstrom.

On May 6, 1977, Romero and the Jesuit provincial were allowed to visit Father Sarsanedas, who had endured six days of beatings and interrogations in a National Guard cell. Romero refused to sign a "confession" the priest had supposedly written saying he had been organizing subversive activities for sixteen years. The churchmen watched as soldiers put the priest on a deportation plane. Romero again wrote to President Molina, reminding him of their agreement: the government would discuss complaints against a priest with the priest's bishop before employing strong-arm tactics. (*See* chapter 1.)

In April, an armed revolutionary group kidnapped the nation's foreign minister and demanded as ransom the release of thirty-seven political prisoners.[1] The government refused to bargain. Romero appealed to both the guerillas and the military to refrain from violence.

His plea was in vain. The foreign minister's dead body was found on May 10. The elite's resolve to stamp out dissenting voices ratcheted yet higher. Copies of a leaflet appeared in the capital. Titled "The Church and

1. Foreign minister Mauricio Borgonovo Pohl, an heir to one of the country's elite families, was kidnapped by the Popular Liberation Forces (Fuerzas Populares de Liberación, or FPL), one of three guerrilla organizations then operating.

the Kidnappers," it depicted a bishop in a robe printed with slogans of various guerrilla organizations.[2]

At the foreign minister's May 11 funeral mass, Romero reiterated that the church renounced violence, just as Jesus had. "God is always shouting the commandment 'Do not kill' to the human heart,"[3] he proclaimed.

The upper-crust families who packed the church murmured in disapproval. They blamed the emergence of armed resistance on new church teachings, rather than their own unwillingness to loosen their grasp on the country's resources. Priests who told the poor that God did not want them to live in misery were advocating "communism," and therefore terrorism. More handbills littered the streets. "Be a patriot, kill a priest," they proclaimed.

Later the same day of May 11, 1977, armed men entered the rectory of the Resurrection parish house in the capital and machine-gunned Father Alfonso Navarro and a fourteen-year-old helper. As in Grande's murder, the weapons used were the type available only to government security forces. The group claiming responsibility said it had killed the priest in retaliation for the foreign minister's death.[4]

At Navarro's funeral service, Romero stated, "The [foreign minister's] life was sacred, but so was the life of the priest who is lost to us today, as was the life of Father Grande, who also was shot to death, two months ago."[5] The government had not fulfilled its promise to investigate Grande's murder; those who cover up the origins of violence are also criminal, the archbishop stated.

"In this campaign of slander, they are sinners as much as those who point the weapons to kill." The slander Romero referred to included insults and intimidations in newspapers and handbills. "How can they possibly be allowed to threaten to take more lives?"[6]

The intimidators upped the ante. On June 21, the White Warrior Union, a military-affiliated death squad that had killed Father Navarro, threatened all thirty-three Jesuits in the country:

2. Armstrong and Shenk, *Face of Revolution*, 93.

3. Romero y Galdámez, *Homilies*, May 11, 1977.

4. The White Warrior Union (Unión Guerrera Blanca) is what the group called itself. Brockman says, "The White Warrior Union seemed to have no history or identifiable members. Rightist groups were phantomlike, and to many they seemed to be simply names used by the security forces to disguise some of their actions" (*A Life*, 65).

5. As quoted in Brockman, *A Life*, 29.

6. Ibid.

> All Jesuits without exception must leave the country forever within thirty days. . . . If your order is not obeyed within the indicated time, the immediate and systematic execution of those Jesuits who remain in the country will proceed until we have finished with all of them.[7]

All institutions run by Jesuits were also declared "military targets."[8]

The Jesuit secretary general, the order's highest official, conferred with his priests in El Salvador and replied, "They may end up as martyrs, but my priests are not going to leave because they are with the people."[9]

On the July 22 deadline, Jesuits discovered that their residence in the capital, as well as Jesuit schools, were being guarded by National Police on motorcycles armed with Uzi sub-machine guns. "The White Warriors Union would not attack. Impossible. For they were sitting there in the sunlight, on motorcycles, in uniform," two observers pointed out with dark humor. "The National Police had left behind their Mr. Hyde personalities and now their alter-egos sat guarding the Jesuits."[10] In other words, those who threatened the Jesuits and those guarding them on July 22 were one and the same. The country's new president, they observed, had learned that killing priests carried a price in the international public relations arena.

The country's powerful went after the poor as well, especially those who were organized into unions and associations, both in the countryside and cities.

"But killing priests was not enough for the oligarchy," researchers said. "The peasantry was already contaminated by their ideas. They needed to be taught a lesson, and what better place than Aguilares—where the strength of the popular organizations confirmed the oligarchy's version of events: the 'communist priests' were to blame for the spirit of rebellion enveloping the land."[11]

7. Quoted in Armstrong and Shenk, *Face of Revolution*, 94.

8. Brockman, *A Life*, 65.

9. Quoted in Clarke, *Love*, 108. The Jesuit general secretary, the head of the world-wide Jesuit order, was Father Pedro Arrupe, SJ.

10. Armstrong and Shenk, *Face of Revolution*, 95.

11. Ibid., 93.

"Operation Rutilio"

Before dawn on May 17, 1977, troops were sent to forcefully remove peasant families from an estate in El Paisnal.[12] The owner, who had long rented the land to them, evicted them that year. These landless people "tried every legal way of getting work or a place to grow enough to survive; then through legal means they tried to get permission to rent some poor and unused plots of land at a price they could afford. It was useless."[13] With no alternative but to starve, the families occupied and planted the land, intending to pay what rent they could.

Their crops had begun to sprout when the army's cynically titled "Operation Rutilio" began. National Guardsmen "came in trains and trucks, and they attacked by air (parachutists) and land."[14]

The Guardsmen found the hacienda empty. The *campesinos* and *campesinas*, alerted by group members, had fled. The soldiers instead attacked nearby hamlets. They searched homes and then set many of them on fire. They threw children and women into truck beds and took them away as prisoners.

From there, tanks and armored cars carrying two thousand soldiers headed to Aguilares. National Guard officers believed the land occupation leaders had sought refuge at the parish house, but they found no one there. The three priests and a *campesino* had climbed to the church's bell tower and begun to ring the bell, hoping to alert villagers, not knowing Guardsmen were already positioned to block townspeople from leaving. Soldiers threw tear gas canisters and sprayed bullets at the bell tower. Surrounded, the priests surrendered. The *campesino* had been hit and killed.

Two days of terror ensued. Guardsmen went house to house ransacking. They arrested villagers who possessed a Bible, a parish songbook, or a photo of Father Grande. They beat many, killed some.[15]

Guardsmen arrested, thrashed, and expelled the three foreign Jesuit priests who remained in Aguilares.[16] They handcuffed a Salvadoran priest,

12. The Hacienda San Francisco Dos Cerros.

13. Erdozaín. *Martyr*, 24.

14. Ibid.

15. Father Antonio Fernández Ibáñez said leaders of Christian base communities in the Aguilares area buried their Bibles in plastic containers between meetings. "It wasn't infrequent that the army would kill someone for carrying a Bible," the priest said, in López Vigil, *Mosaic*, 271.

16. Soldiers drove the priests to the Guatemalan border, leaving them in the hands of

Father Victor Guevara, who was visiting the parish and shoved him in a truck packed with detained villagers. They were taken to National Guard headquarters, where the priest was tied to cell bars between beatings. The next day, Romero was again called to National Guard headquarters in the capital to pick up a persecuted priest.

The army occupied Aguilares for almost a month. It used the church, now battered and riddled with bullets, as a barracks. Soldiers shot open the tabernacle, scattered the Communion hosts on the floor and crushed them under their boots. "The Eucharist, the body of Christ, and the community, the people, the priests [were] all smashed and annihilated," lamented one priest.[17] This sacrilege horrified Romero, as did the deaths and disappearances of villagers and the abuse of his priests. He tried to visit the town, but the army would not let him enter.

In yet another letter to Colonel Molina, Romero wrote:

> I do not understand, Mr. President, how you can declare yourself before the nation Catholic by upbringing and by conviction and yet allow these unspeakable outrages on the part of security forces in a country that we call civilized and Christian. . . . Finally, I do not understand, Mr. President, the motives of the military authorities in not allowing me to go to the church of Aguilares to see for myself and to guarantee the church property of the Catholic people of Aguilares. Does the person of the archbishop also put in peril the security of the state?"[18]

The National Guard withdrew from Aguilares in mid-June. On June 19, Archbishop Romero visited the town and concelebrated a mass with ten priests at its violated church. He installed a new priest and three women religious to lead the parish, to continue the activities begun by Father Grande and his team five years earlier.

To the crowd of five thousand, Romero began his homily with the haunting words he would repeat often in the future: "It is my lot to gather up the trampled, the dead, and all that the persecution of the church leaves behind."[19]

---

the Guatemalan military, which was at least as brutal as El Salvador's (Erdozaín, *Martyr*, 24).

17. Ibid., 25.

18. As quoted in Brockman, *A Life*, 31–32.

19. Ibid., 62.

After the mass, Romero invited the gathering to join him in carrying through the streets the monstrance, the vessel holding the sacred Communion hosts, to cleanse the places the military had profaned.[20] A Jesuit theologian described the event:

> We left the church singing. It was a terribly hot day, and Monseñor Romero was soaked in sweat under his red rain cape. He held the monstrance high. Before him there were hundreds of people. We circled the main square singing and praying.
>
> The municipal offices across from the church were full of guardsmen watching us. When we neared, several of them went to the middle of the road and pointed their rifles at us. Then more of them came. They spread their legs defiantly and with their large boots formed a wall that we could not go through.
>
> Those at the front stopped and gradually so did those further back. The procession came to a halt. There we were, face to face with the rifles. When no one was moving anymore, we turned to look at Monseñor Romero, who was at the very back. He lifted the monstrance a little higher and said in a loud voice so that all could hear:
>
> "*Adelante*"—"Let us go forward."
>
> Then, little by little, we moved toward the soldiers, and little by little they began to back up. We moved forward. They moved backward. Eventually they backed up toward their barracks. Finally they lowered their guns and let us pass.[21]

The theologian found symbolic meaning in the event: From that day on, when any important event happened in El Salvador, people turned their eyes to the archbishop for guidance on how to act. If the church hierarchy had named Romero archbishop, now the ordinary people owned him as their leader.

Journalist of the Poor

After the events of Aguilares, people looked to Monseñor Romero for news as well as guidance. Citizens could not count on the country's private

20. The *tabernacle*, locked, holds the Communion hosts, within a container called the *pyx*, when they are not being displayed. The *monstrance*, usually placed on the altar, holds the sacrament during the mass.

21. Jon Sobrino, in López Vigil, *Mosaic*, 171.This scene was memorably reenacted in the film *Romero*, directed by Duigan and starring Raúl Juliá as Romero.

media. Its major newspapers and radio and TV stations, owned and controlled by the elite, were filled with invective, slander, and misinformation, much of it directed at the church and the archbishop. Headlines screamed false accusations: "Archbishop Romero Directs Terrorist Group" and even "Monseñor Romero Sells His Soul to Satan."[22]

The archdiocesan media, its newspaper, *Orientación,* and increasingly its radio station, YSAX, became the major means by which people received news of the country's happenings, especially of ongoing persecution. The archdiocesan offices did not need to send out reporters seeking news. Instead the offices filled with people who wanted to tell Monseñor what had happened to them and their loved ones. He also received hundreds of letters:

> From all parts of El Salvador they came, letters from the people, many laboriously traced on lined paper by hands more used to the hoe and the machete than the pen. They told of their struggles, their pains, their hopes, their faith, their confidence in him, the archbishop, the strength they drew from his words. . . .
>
> The largest number of such letters came from *campesinos,* most of whom cannot read or write. Many letters were signed with a collection of thumbprints. It is not hard to visualize a group of wiry, weather-beaten men and women gathered around the light of a candle while the one or two literate members traced the words on a tablet for all to sign and one to take over the mountain paths to a distant small-town post office.[23]

These letters moved Romero, and he jotted notes on each one to guide his small staff in answering them. He also received large quantities of hate mail, including frequent death threats. Eventually he asked the office workers to file the intimidating letters without showing them to him, saying, "out of sight, out of mind."[24]

People packed the national Metropolitan Cathedral in downtown San Salvador for Romero's Sunday morning services. "The crowd reached all

22. The full headline, which filled half the front page of an eight-page tabloid called *La Opinión* (no. 11, December 1977) was: "Archbishop Romero Directs Terrorist Group – Valiant Accusation Made by a Priest – Archbishop Great Ally of Agents of Subversion" (Brockman, *A Life,* 100). Sobrino supplies the "Satan" headline, used by a small ultra-right newspaper, "a paper which did not last very long after that" (*Reflections,* 40).

23. Brockman, *A Life,* 76–77.

24. Maria Isabel Figueroa, in López Vigil, *Mosaic,* 299.

the way to the altar; those in front were touching it. Many brought snacks with them and sat on the floor," said one biographer.[25]

Romero did not preach in a fire-and-brimstone style. He didn't yell. He didn't stride around gesticulating to punctuate his points. He stood staidly behind the pulpit and spoke in a strong but modulated tone. Yet he electrified his listeners. It might have been his cadence, the emphasis he gave certain words. It may have been the authority he carried as an old-fashioned churchman, dressed in long traditional robes. Mostly it was his courage in using the status of his prominent position to speak the prophetic "truth to power" in an open, straightforward manner, at a time when few dared do so.

Mondays, Romero frequently asked people what they thought about the previous day's homily. One acquaintance told him:

> You're always so quiet when I see you, Monseñor. And then when I hear you in the Cathedral, I feel like you turn into a different person—even in the intonation of your voice. You project such strength and certainty . . . It can't all be the microphone! . . . It's like you're two people—the everyday person, and the person who gives the homilies at the Cathedral.[26]

A professional communicator, upon hearing the buzz about the archbishop's sermons, wanted to see for himself. He related:

> That Sunday, I listened as he launched into a long theological treatise that felt too conceptual and abstract to me. . . . But the people were following him anyway, giving him their complete attention. Then the moment came that everyone was waiting for: a kind of news report in which Monseñor Romero, with all of his authority—an authority that everyone recognized— would comment on the events of the past week.
>
> To me, he seemed like an experienced broadcaster on a national news program. . . . I had never attended—and have never attended since—a Mass that was so constantly punctuated by ovations. He had achieved complete communication with the people.[27]

Romero's homilies were long, often an hour and a half. He dedicated most of them to biblical exegesis, the interpretation and explanation of

25. Erdozaín, *Martyr*, 33.

26. Coralia Godoy, in López Vigil, *Mosaic,* 207–8.

27. Mario Kaplún, in López Vigil, *Mosaic,* 209.

Scripture. The news portion, much shorter, came with details, verified dates, places, and names of particular atrocities and human rights abuses he had learned about during the week.

In his sermon of March 11, 1979, for example, at the two-year anniversary of Father Rutilio Grande's death, Romero shared the following news:

> We lament the fact that Jaime Baires, whom we spoke about last week, has died and so now we mourn.[28] His parents have stated that Jaime, before dying, spoke about being tortured by the National Guard. The Guard has issued statements about their innocence, but statements and words are not enough. The parents have asked for the case to be brought before the courts; they have the right to have their legal petition heard. Not only the parents but all of us have the right to know: what are those who wear uniforms doing?
>
> - We are also saddened by the abduction of a child in San Miguel, Carlos Villatoro Fuentes. We state: this is cruel, and we enter into solidarity with the National Association on Behalf of Children and the long list of children asking that this child be returned to his family.
> - We lament the fire in the El Fuerte sock factory.
> - We are saddened by the death of four *campesinos* and the wounding of three guardsmen that, according to official information, happened in a confrontation near San Vicente.
> - We experience as our own the uncertainty of the family members of the *campesinos* Marciano Meléndez Dueñas and Oscar Jiménez. These men were arrested in February and their whereabouts remains unknown.
> - We feel the grief of the family of Oscar Armando Interiano, the union leader, presumed to be the corpse found handcuffed and blindfolded in Güija Lake.
> - I've been very distressed by two letters I received from mothers. One mother states that her son has been a prisoner in Gotera since August, and she has no hope he will leave there alive. She is unable to visit her son because she is very poor and Gotera is far from her house. The family of Hipólito

28. Romero had visited the tortured man in the hospital the week before and believed him to be dying.

> Rolando Martínez, a teacher, asks for mercy because their son is in the same situation.[29]

These public denunciations were unique in the history of international human rights, and they helped alleviate the suffering of those still hoping for news of their "disappeared" loved ones. A journalist who provided an overview of the history of the global human rights movement explained it this way: "The word 'denunciation' did not begin to convey the psychological importance of the act. Following a disappearance, the only recourse open to a relative was to tell everything they knew. It provided an essential release from the tension."[30] El Salvador's human rights movement, centered on Romero and his legal aid office, was among the most influential on the continent, the journalist added.

As for the courageous impact of these denunciations, another reporter of the era said about Romero, "If there's any title that fits him perfectly, it's 'the journalist of the poor.'"[31]

YSAX, or "*La equis*" ("The X")

Romero remained alert to the needs of people beyond the capital, and radio transmission of his homilies felt vital to staying connected. He often opened his sermons with the greeting, "Dear brothers and sisters, esteemed radio listeners."

Broadcast on YSAX, Romero's Sunday homilies drew wider audiences than soccer matches—in a soccer-crazed country. Later, individuals would recall how they'd walk through the capital and be able to follow Romero's sermons emerging from homes, shops, and vehicles along the route. "It was a chain of radios with a broadcast as uninterrupted as if it were a single transmission" said one woman who deemed Romero's sermons the "most eagerly anticipated event of the week."[32]

Keeping YSAX on the air became one of Romero's major concerns. It was a constant challenge. The nation's powerful tried to sabotage it. Routine

29. Romero y Galdámez, *Homilies*, March 11, 1979.

30. Guest, *Disappearances*, 218.

31. Armando Contreras, in López Vigil, *Mosaic*, 298.

32. Martina Guzmán, in ibid., 205. Biographer Erdozaín says Romero's Sunday sermons drew 73 percent of the nation's radio audience in the countryside and 47 percent in cities (*Martyr*, 32).

technical issues also required expertise, and Romero wasn't above begging for help.

In April 1977, in the wake of Father Grande's assassination, fellow Jesuit Rogelio Pedraz was passing through El Salvador. For the previous six years, Father Pedraz had been involved in creating an innovative on-air school in the Dominican Republic and was exploring the possibility of setting up a similar program in El Salvador.

Pedraz, unimpressed, called YSAX, "a disaster" . . . a radio "held together by a shoestring . . . and bankrupt financially . . . beyond repair."[33] Pedraz also disliked the country in general in that tense historical period.

But Monseñor Romero had asked the Jesuit superior, or provincial, for help in saving YSAX—colloquially referred to as "*La equis*" ("The X"). The provincial, Father César Jerez, urged a reluctant Pedraz to accompany him to a meeting with Romero, as Pedraz later recalled:

> I went solely out of a sense of obligation. I didn't know Romero from Adam. César introduced me, and told him I knew a lot about radio . . .
>
> Monseñor Romero looked at me and said exactly these words: "I'm asking you to help me save the radio station. And if I have to, I'll get on my knees."
>
> No one had ever gotten on their knees to ask me for anything. Much less a bishop! . . . It really threw me for a loop. It moved me.[34]

Pedraz, a Spaniard, agreed to stay for six months. He'd later call this half year "a life-changing experience," one that ended up keeping him in El Salvador for decades.

Throughout Romero's tenure as archbishop, YSAX remained a target of intimidation. Three months after his installation as archbishop, on May 10, 1977, the nation's interior ministry called in YSAX's directors to threaten the station with a heavy fine, even closure, if it did not stop criticizing the government.[35]

In April 1978, Romero recorded in his oral diary that for more than two weeks interference disrupted broadcasts of his sermons and programs critical of the country's situation. "It is very probable that we are dealing

33. Rogelio Pedraz, in López Vigil, *Mosaic*, 131.

34. Ibid., 131–32.

35. Brockman *A Life*, 28.

with interference from the ANTEL[36] headquarters itself," he said, referring to the national telecommunications company.[37]

His suspicion of governmental sabotage was soon confirmed. It took at least one meeting of archdiocesan representatives with ANTEL officials, as well as pressure from Catholics concerned about their freedom of religious expression, to end the disruptions.

Two years later, on February 19, 1980, Romero recorded a more serious attack on the station:

> They awakened me with an urgent telephone call from Sister María . . . to tell me that a bomb had gone off in the base of the YSAX transmitter and that it has been completely destroyed. I asked if there were any injuries; I am glad that the damages were only of a material nature than can be repaired.
>
> Tonight at the same hour, around eleven o'clock, another bomb exploded in the library of the UCA [the Jesuit-run University of Central America.] Obviously, these are plots of the extreme right against the voice of the Church and against the calls for social justice.[38]

The bombings shocked the nation, as well as the international community. Letters of concern and donations for restoring the station poured in. Work to rebuild YSAX, using a broken transmitter found in storage, began almost immediately. It took more than a month, however, until March 23, to get it back on the air.

During the interim, a shortwave station in Costa Rica broadcast Romero's sermons, which heartened him:

> I heard comments that it was heard—and rather clearly—not just in this country, but also, since it was on shortwave from Central America, in the entire isthmus and also on the continent [South

36. ANTEL is an acronym for Asociación Nacional de Telecomunicaciones, or National Telecommunications Company, a governmental body. Romero's youngest brother, Gaspar, worked for ANTEL and was given an unexplained, effective-immediately demotion from an important managerial position to a petty post requiring him to work nights. About this Romero says in his diary on June 1, 1979: "Without a doubt, this [Gaspar's demotion] is revenge on the government's part because he is a relative of mine. I am sorry that my family is suffering as a result of the prophetic task I must carry out" (*Diary*, 247).

In a 2011 newspaper interview, Gaspar said he lost many friends at this time—they were afraid to associate with him—and that his house was under constant surveillance (Valencia and Arias,"Plática").

37. Romero y Galdámez, *Diary*, 186.

38. Ibid., 494.

> America]. I also learned that radios in Venezuela and Colombia had collaborated in this effort. It really impressed me to think that, for the first time, the voice of a homily given by the archbishop of San Salvador reached beyond its borders and was heard in all the continent.[39]

Following Father Grande's assassination and the military occupation of Aguilares and in the wake of increased repression, Archbishop Romero used his voice to stitch together the church and uphold the impoverished masses—on Sunday morning in the Metropolitan Cathedral and at various times throughout the week on YSAX. In today's Internet era, such communication may seem a thin and precarious thread, but it proved a surprisingly vibrant and resilient outreach and network tool in Romero's time.

39. Ibid., 505. The Costa Rican station was Radionoticias del Continente (Radio News of the Continent).

11. A Time to Harness Youthful Fervor

(1977–1980)

Romero had mentored preseminarians from his earliest days of ministry in San Miguel, taking a vibrant interest in them and their families. After Grande's death, however, he went well beyond guiding and encouraging aspirants to the priesthood. As archbishop, he embraced the same "down with the establishment" young people he had earlier feared, disparaged, and discounted as overly impressionable and misguided. He filled his archdiocesan offices with these young people, laity included, in staff and volunteer positions.

He began to see that young women, not just their male counterparts, could participate fully in the church. Romero's previous interactions with women appear to have been confined to friendships with high-society matrons who helped adorn the Peace Virgin statue and float for its annual processional—and who occasionally bothered him by trying to introduce "luxury" into his spartan quarters. Now as archbishop, he took women seriously, especially young women committed to full participation in remolding church and society.

Romero enlisted—or drafted—individuals barely in their twenties to fill major roles in the archdiocese, thereby harnessing the energy, vision, and faith commitment of those aching for change. At first, many of the young people were wary of the archbishop's intentions. They knew the old Romero. Had he really changed? Did he truly want them involved?

Guillermo Cuéllar was twenty-one in 1976 when he first met Romero, then bishop of Santiago de María. Guillermo helped lead an active and successful outreach ministry to students and youth, based in the capital's San José de la Montaña Church.[1] Guillermo's group had started meeting with

1. This group dedicated to youth outreach was hit hard by the repression of 1975 to the early 1980s, along with students, teachers, union leaders, and others voicing discontent with the status quo. Although many of the youth ministry's core group of some twenty leaders and participants took major security measures, such as moving out of

some teens in the rural, impoverished Santiago de María diocese. Now they wanted to plan a series of larger gatherings there:

> We had come to the point where we knew we had to speak with the bishop. It was church work, after all, and we didn't want to do a project on our own, as if we had something to hide.
>
> We arrived at the bishop's palace, and I had mixed impressions. The bishop's residence was large and new, a real palace. Monseñor Romero met with the four of us in an enormous—I mean enormous!—living room. I was worried about talking with a member of the church hierarchy, someone with his own way of thinking, who might have prejudices against us.
>
> At that time Monseñor Romero was a conservative, traditional churchman. He certainly was dressed as one: long black cassock, a big cross on his chest, purple sash, and purple skullcap.
>
> We explained our idea to Monseñor, and he said it sounded like a good idea. I hadn't expected that. And then he surprised me when he went even further. "Why don't you meet here? This is a very large house." We took him up on his offer and held our first youth gatherings, which were well-attended, on the expansive patio of the bishop's palace.
>
> But at some point he asked to attend a meeting. That frightened me, and I said to myself, "He's going to get upset. He's going to hear what we're saying and he's going to put an end to it."
>
> One day he dropped in at a meeting of our coordinating committee. He just sat for an hour and listened. When the coordinator asked if he'd like to say something, he began to talk about the importance of encouraging youth in devotion to the Virgin Mary. That spiritual direction was very different from our approach, and we didn't agree, but we all just said, "Okay. Of course." He didn't pursue it further.[2]

When Romero returned to San Salvador as archbishop the following year, he asked Guillermo to serve with the archdiocese's YSAX radio team. Laypeople also voted Guillermo to represent them on Romero's pastoral commission, a position that gave him, from ages twenty-two to twenty-five, an important voice in archdiocesan work. Along with a representative from

their parents' homes to go underground, nine were forced to flee to seek refuge in other countries, including Canada, Guatemala, England, Switzerland, and the United States, and four were killed by death squads. Among those killed was Guillermo's cousin Patricia Cuéllar (Guillermo Cuéllar, December 3, 1998, phone interview with author).

2. Ibid. This was the first time Romero resided in a diocesan "palace." It had been built for his predecessor, the first bishop of Santiago de María.

priests and one from women religious, "he gave us an office in the archdiocese and said, 'OK, here's where you'll work as the executive committee. I want you to provide me with a comprehensive vision for the diocese.'"[3] Romero relied on these three individuals for important decisions, such as helping to decide where to place priests—which priest would work well in which parish.

Archbishop Romero encouraged young musicians. (photo credit, Alfredo Vicente)

Guillermo, a guitarist and musician, had already written a couple of songs for the Salvadoran Popular Mass–hymns of struggle, of declaring the new church of the people, and songs commemorating recent martyrs, including Father Rutilio Grande. Romero took Guillermo's gift seriously and encouraged it. At one point Romero asked Guillermo, in front of a large gathering, to compose a hymn for the August 1980 celebrations of the country's patron saint and namesake.[4] Guillermo wasn't sure if he was up to the task but hesitated to express his uncertainty.

3. Ibid. Cuéllar's song for Romero, "*Santo, Santo, Santo,*" may be found on YouTube at https://www.youtube.com/watch?v=yWFR_uEhLq8.

4. The Transfigured Jesus, El Salvador del Mundo (the Savior of the World). The nation's co-patron is Our Lady of Peace.

Guillermo drafted a song. He was dumbfounded, but delighted, when Monseñor publicly announced it and read some of its lyrics in what would become Romero's final Sunday mass at the Metropolitan Cathedral:

> On a happier note, I want to tell you that a composer and poet has written for us a beautiful hymn in honor of Our Divine Savior. You'll soon be introduced to it: "Explosive songs ring with joy, / I will join my people in the cathedral to sing . . ."
>
> And the last stanza is very beautiful: "But the gods of power and money are opposed to transfiguration, / Therefore, Lord, you're the first to raise your arm against oppression."[5]

The crowd applauded enthusiastically, and Guillermo's spirit soared. Romero was open with Guillermo, however, when he disliked or disagreed with some of his lyrics, although he didn't ask the composer to change them. In one song, Guillermo referred to soldiers as "wild beasts in uniform," a phrase the archbishop told Guillermo he disliked.

Later, Guillermo understood why. The archbishop viewed the soldiers as pawns in the country's power structure. "They were poor peasants themselves, dressed up in army uniforms and defending interests not their own," is how one priest who worked with Guillermo's youth outreach put it.[6]

Romero wanted people to see that peasants were being set against peasants. In that same homily of March 23, 1980, the archbishop asked soldiers to disobey orders to kill their fellow Salvadorans.[7]

Managing "Martyrdom" Meetings

Another young adult, Francisco "Paco" Calles, also a layperson and part of the youth ministry based in the capital's San José de la Montaña Church, had similar experiences. "Other older members of the archdiocesan hierarchy

5. Romero y Galdámez, *Homilies*, March 23, 1980.

6. Erdozaín, *Martyr*, 24.

7. Romero also told Guillermo Cuéllar that he very much liked his song "*Vamos todos al banquete*" in honor of Father Rutilio Grande. In it, Cuéllar set to music words and images from Grande's last homily, in which the priest envisioned an entire community invited to God's feast, to creation's table, each having his or her own stool and place to sit. The word for a rustic stool, *taburete*, Cuéllar explained, is "very, very much a part of the rural world, of the *campesinos*' world. Monseñor liked Father Grande's explanation of God's kingdom in the words and images of the *campesino* mindset." (In Spanish the lyric is: "*Vamos todos al banquete, a la mesa de la creación, cada cual con su taburete, tienen un puesto y una misión.*")

didn't particularly trust me, but Romero did," Calles said. "I was surprised and astonished at how much confidence Romero put in me and how he treated me as an equal."[8]

With long hair, beard, and mustache, and wearing sandals, Calles looked like a hippie, the kind of young person adults tended to distrust.

Romero asked Calles, then in his late twenties, to work for him in the archdiocesan office. Calles scheduled Romero's meetings and generally helped out wherever he was needed, which was likely more than he had bargained for. Romero might see him in the hallway near his recording studio and buttonhole him to serve as his interviewer for a radio program. Some sobering on-the-spot tasks were not for the faint of heart. After Father Neto Barrera was killed in November 1978, Romero asked Calles to photograph the priest's mangled body at the morgue.

Monseñor Romero also asked Calles to help him survive the long, contentious bishops' meetings, which he referred to as his "martyrdom meetings," Calles said.[9]

> El Salvador had six bishops, and they were quite often in meetings that would last nearly six hours! They'd be locked inside the upper room of the archdiocesan offices in interminable discussions. Early on—practically right after the single Mass—we heard that Monseñor Romero had four bishops totally opposed to him. Only Monseñor Rivera supported him.
>
> "Paco. Do me a favor," he said to me one day at the door of the meeting room. "Come and get me out of here around midmorning, all right?" . . .
>
> I arrived around 10 a.m. to get him. . . .
>
> And we started to walk up and down those long halls, chatting about the little old lady, the little old man, the price of tea in China . . .
>
> "And another thing, Paco. Where could I find a good cassette tape of the French trumpeter Maurice André? He's extraordinary. Have you heard him?"
>
> Then we started talking about music—about trumpets and saxophones. After a while, he looked at his watch.
>
> "I'm going to go back. I really appreciate this, Paco. Thanks."
>
> He went back in. The bishop's meeting was still going on. I stood outside in the hall wondering what that had all been about.

8. Francisco Calles, in November 22, 1998, phone interview with author. (Calles had become an architect.)

9. Ibid.

> But that wasn't the only time it happened. It became the routine every time there was a meeting of the Bishops' Conference.[10]

Romero showed immense courage in confronting the country's authorities in his homilies and written statements, Calles reflected, but he outright avoided challenging his fellow bishops. "Here a mature bishop was asking a young man to help get him out of meetings by fabricating excuses. He preferred these ruses, or to remain silent, or to just put up with their reproaches and criticism rather than fight with the other bishops."[11] Romero's attitude likely related to his lifelong respect of the institutional church.

Human Rights Lawyer

Roberto Cuéllar, a lawyer, was another young professional in his midtwenties in whom Romero came to put great trust.

Roberto belonged to Servicio Jurídico (Legal Service), a lawyers' association formed in 1975 to help poor people with legal matters, including land rights. The group offered its services on the legal case concerning the assassination of Father Rutilio Grande.

In this instance, Monseñor Romero worked with young people not necessarily *because of*, but *despite*, their youth. They were the only ones bold enough to help him confront the country's judicial system, as Roberto later recalled:

> At first he really had no confidence in us. I was about twenty-six years old, and Romero seemed to have little faith in the representation of young lawyers. He didn't think our team could represent the church in a case as dangerous and difficult as the assassination of the first Jesuit priest in El Salvador. The church couldn't get other legal advice due to the intimidation and threats to any lawyer who would dare to represent the Catholic Church and the archdiocese's interests at that time.[12]

When poor people, many of them mothers and grandmothers, often weeping, began to deluge the archdiocesan offices with photos of sons and daughters who had been killed or disappeared, Romero wanted to record

10. Calles, in López Vigil, *Mosaic*, 138–39.
11. Calles, in November 22, 1998, phone interview with author.
12. Roberto Cuéllar, in documentary film *Last Journey*.

and report these events. He brought Legal Services into the church fold, offering it the protection of the archdiocese's high profile. They changed its name to Socorro Jurídico (Legal Aid).[13] Roberto Cuéllar became its director.

The first words of the first entry in Romero's tape-recorded diary relays his concern for addressing human rights abuses: "The most important meeting today was one we had with lawyers and law students we had brought together to explain to them the difficulties the Church encounters and to ask them for legal help with so many cases of abuses of human rights."[14] For that March 31, 1978, meeting, Roberto had gathered the twenty or so lawyers and law students willing to lend help and advice in a loose collaborative network.

Roberto was among the unenviable asked to go out to the mountains, beaches, and fields to witness and interview people to obtain or verify details. The work might involve looking over battered corpses buzzing with flies.

"We visited the scene of the events to check out what had been reported. Consequently no governmental or military office could contradict the information given weekly by Romero and the archdiocese," Roberto recalled.[15]

On November 1, 1979, Roberto and a seminarian[16] accompanied Romero and the country's attorney general on a harrowing rescue effort that threatened to lapse into a massacre at any moment. In the capital, they entered El Rosario Church, ringed with hostile Guardsmen, to broker the release of a soldier taken hostage by a coalition of popular organizations.[17] Roberto later related that upon their arrival, a Guard officer warned

13. Its full name was Socorro Jurídico del Arzobispado. It began in 1977 and was dismantled after Romero's assassination, at which time many of its lawyers left the country. Romero's successor, Archbishop Rivera y Damas, reopened the initiative with the name Tutela Legal in 1982. María Julia Hernández served as its director until her death in 2007. Archbishop José Luis Escobar Alas closed the office without advance notice or consulting its staff—a controversial move—on September 30, 2013. A new, independent organization, named Tutela Legal Dra. María Julia Hernández, continues to operate.

14. Romero y Galdámez, *Diary*, 19.

15. Cuéllar, in *Last Journey*.

16. Juan Bosco Palacios. In *Last Journey*, Bosco describes Romero reciting the rosary while asking the seminarian what to do if they're fired upon.

17. This took place at the El Rosario Church; the coalition Ligas Populares 28 de Febrero (February 28 Popular Leagues) had taken the hostage.

Romero's group that he was not in charge of the Guardsmen and could not guarantee what the soldiers might do.[18]

Advisor and Counselor

As archbishop, Romero became a protective figure for many young people, not only in offering sanctuary to activists but even in helping smooth over personal problems. When the woman who had worked as Romero's secretary for ten years, both in San Salvador and Santiago de María, became pregnant with an ex-seminarian, who abandoned her, she worked up her courage to tell Monseñor. She expected rejection, a scolding, loss of her job. None of these happened. Instead, the young woman recalled:

> My whole body was shaking from head to toe. And I told him everything from the beginning—from the time I'd started seeing the seminarian to the time of my swelling belly which was now beginning to show . . .
>
> "And he's going to be born in five months . . ." I was sobbing.
>
> He looked at me and smiled. . . . "It's all right, Angelita. The first time is forgiven."
>
> "What did you say, Monseñor . . .?" I was so flustered that I didn't even understand him.
>
> "Don't worry, *hija*. The first time is forgiven. Right now you have to do what you can for that baby that's going to be born."
>
> He kept smiling, and it was *me* that felt like *I* was being born again!
>
> From that day on, he helped me out with everything like a worried father. He told Silvia Arriola to help me, and so the two of us went out to talk several times. He asked his sister Zaída to take care of me until the baby was born. He even spoke with my parents to tell them what was happening, and if they ended up forgiving me, it was only because of his intercession.[19]

18. Roberto Cuéllar, in *Last Journey*.

19. Angela Morales, in López Vigil, *Mosaic*, 281. Morales named her baby Claudia Guadalupe, the Guadalupe in memory of Romero's mother. Silvia Arriola was a member of a religious order when she began to work in Christian base communities. She later joined the guerrillas as a nurse and died in combat (*Mosaic*, 123).

Losing "Sons"

As archbishop, Romero mourned the deaths of many people killed in the country's repression. Among these were several young priests he had come to know as sons, including Father Octavio Ortíz Luna.

At age thirteen, Octavio, the second of an impoverished rural couple's twelve children, left home to become one of Romero's minor seminarians in San Miguel. He became the first priest Romero, then a bishop, ordained.[20]

By 1979, Father Ortíz balanced a heavy workload. He served as priest of the San Francisco parish of the capital's Mejicanos district and temporary fill-in priest of the San Antonio Abad parish, also in the capital; vicar of the area parishes; member of the archdiocesan priests' senate; and director of spiritual life for the incoming students at the San José de la Montana Seminary.

On the evening of January 19, 1979, after an already full day of meetings and other church duties, Ortíz arrived at a retreat house in the San Antonio Abad neighborhood.[21] Under the direction of a Belgian nun and a laywoman, twenty-eight young men had gathered for a weekend "Introduction to Christianity" retreat. Father Ortíz gave his first talk late that evening.

At about six o'clock the next morning, ferocious noise and movement shook the retreat house. A small military tank and a Jeep broke through the sheet-metal fence with guns blazing. Within five minutes, the joint Treasury Police and National Guard operation had finished, leaving the dead bodies of Father Ortíz and four young men ages fifteen to twenty-two. They had been the first to emerge from the house to investigate. The police arrested the survivors, including the event's two women coordinators, the cooks, and even a cook's young children. The women, released with the children later that day, testified to what had taken place.

By the time Romero arrived at the infamous Isidro Menendez Morgue—one place where the corpses of victims of repression were

20. In López Vigil, Alejandro Ortíz said this about his sons: "Octavio . . . was the first of my sons to be killed. They killed all of them later. Angel in 1980, Santos Angel and Jesus in 1985 and Ignacio in 1990. So in the struggle for our people, I lost all my sons. The ones I have left are my daughters and grandchildren. We've named one of the little ones Octavio, thinking that maybe this little Tavito will grow up to be a priest someday" (*Mosaic*, 288).

21. The retreat center was a simple brick house owned by the archdiocese. Located in a poor neighborhood, the center was known as "El Despertar," or "The Awakening."

dumped—the entrance was already militarized. He went directly in and to the puddle of blood in which the body of the priest lay, as related by a young woman who had also arrived with her father, a friend of Father Ortíz:

> You couldn't tell it was him. His body was completely flattened, his face destroyed to the point that it looked like he didn't even have one. . . .
>
> Monseñor Romero knelt on the ground and held his shattered head.
>
> "It can't be. This isn't him. It's not him . . ."
>
> Tears streamed from Monseñor's face as he held him close . . .
>
> "They ran over him with a tank and smashed his head, Monseñor."
>
> "I can't believe they could be so savage," he said.
>
> The guardsmen looked in through the door. Monseñor's cassock was covered with blood and he was crying, cradling Father Octavio in his arms.
>
> "Octavio, my son, you have completed your mission. You were faithful . . .[22]

Meanwhile, the military concocted a cover-up. Soldiers hauled the corpses to the roof, positioned guns in their hands, and photographed them. In the army's news release, printed by major newspapers, the retreat house became a guerrilla training center. Gunfire had answered the Guardsmen's knock on the gate.

The following day, a Sunday, more than a hundred priests and a crowd of up to fifteen thousand gathered in the plaza outside the Metropolitan Cathedral.[23] The mass had to be taken outdoors; the cathedral wasn't large enough to hold all those who came. The scene was reminiscent of the single funeral mass for Father Grande almost two years earlier.

In his homily, Romero spoke bluntly of the need for telling the truth regarding the events that had taken the lives of the priest and youths lying in caskets before the outdoor altar. The official report published in the country's media was "a lie from beginning to end," he declared.

> Our Security Forces are incapable of recognizing their errors and instead make them worse by falsifying the truth with slander. Day by day they destroy our government's and our media's credibility, forcing us to resort to international organizations and media

22. Carmen Elena Hernández, in López Vigil, *Mosaic*, 283–85.

23. Film footage from Father Octavio Ortíz's funeral mass appears in the documentary *Last Journey*.

because we no longer believe in our own government's truth and justice.

[He went on to decry the social structure and values that contributed to the killings.]

Octavio found a treasure and was sharing it with these youth. This is the great message of Octavio and those killed with him: the earthly realm passes and what will be left is only the joy of having used this world to further God's reign. All earthly ostentation, triumphs, selfish capitalism, all of life's false successes will pass away. What remains is love. What remains is that which one puts into the service of others: one's money, one's assets, one's profession, the joy of having shared and the feeling that all are one's sisters and brothers. In the evening of our lives, we'll be judged by our love. God the Lord is judging Octavio and the four young men who died with him by their love.

How beautiful it is to be able to present oneself as a poor priest, one who has renounced everything with the simplicity of a *campesino* in which one glories. How beautiful to have made accessible all that can be found in the gospel concerning the poor and needy—the great message that God communicates in order to save the world. . . .

There is only one God, and that God is either the true one who asks us to renounce whatever causes us to sin, or it is the god of money that makes us turn our backs on the God of Christianity. . . . Many criticize the church and kill Octavio and try to destroy every movement attempting to overthrow the idols of false gods and to present the true God.

[He ended his sermon with these words]:

Lord, today our conversion and faith are upheld by these bodies before us here in these caskets. They are messengers of our people's reality and of the church's noble aspiration for our people's salvation. And look, Lord, upon this multitude gathered in your Cathedral. Hear the prayer of a people who cry out and weep, but does not despair, because we know Christ has not lied. The Kingdom is near, and you only ask that we convert and believe in Jesus.[24]

Romero must have been torn up emotionally that Octavio's body had to be buried in secret. He recorded in his diary that evening:

The community of San Francisco, in Mejicanos, asked permission to bury Father Octavio's body in their church. And after talking

24. Romero y Galdámez, *Homilies*, January 21, 1979.

over the situation [with Octavio's father and others], figuring out how to avoid anything that could provoke a violent situation, we decided that they should move the body secretly. His body belongs to them, since it was there that he was ordained and it was there that he worked during his five-year ministry. I was the one who ordained Father Octavio on February 3, 1974 . . .[25]

Bishop Romero found great hope, support, and strength in the many young people he mentored or simply got to know. He mourned those whose tragic fates he witnessed, bright young lives extinguished in their prime.

Romero advised his followers to remain open to young people's ideas, as in his homily of December 17, 1978:

> The older one is, the more it can appear that only older people know what is true and right, and the ideas of young people appear to be crazy and novel. And so we say, "Pay no attention to them!" Be very careful. Do not quench the spirit! Test everything and retain what is good. . . . The Bible has a very meaningful expression: "the Spirit makes all things new." We who grow old very often want everyone made to our aged pattern. The Spirit is never old! The Spirit is always young.[26]

25. Romero y Galdámez, *Diary*, 132.
26. Romero y Galdámez, *Homilies*, December 17, 1978.

12. A Time to be Disillusioned

(1977–1980)

Early on April 3, 1978, four of Romero's five fellow bishops requested his presence at "an urgent meeting," even though the sixth bishop could not attend.[1] Some two hundred priests and nuns had recently signed and delivered a letter to the apostolic nuncio, Emanuele Gerada, the Vatican's ambassador to El Salvador, in which they criticized him.[2] The four bishops seethed that church personnel, those at the bottom of the hierarchy no less, had dared to upbraid the nuncio.

The priests and nuns' letter reproached the nuncio for his support of "a repressive and unjust government" and his insensitivity "to the silent sorrow of the oppressed and persecuted peasantry."[3]

Archbishop Romero hardly desired to spend hours wrangling with fellow bishops. He and his staff were toiling to assist victims of military violence who had been arriving at church offices seeking food, shelter, and security for the past two weeks. The refugees had fled an Aguilares-type assault by security and paramilitary forces on Palm Sunday, March 19, 1978, centered in the town of San Pedro Perulapán twelve miles east of the capital.

The military blitz represented the government's deadly message to *campesinos* and *campesinas* who had organized into two rural associations—the Christian Federation of Salvadoran Peasants and the Union of

1. Romero y Galdámez, *Diary*, 23. The four bishops were: Pedro Arnoldo Aparicio, bishop of San Vicente and then president of the bishops' conference; Benjamin Barrera, elderly bishop of Santa Ana; José Eduardo Alvarez, bishop of San Miguel, also military chaplain with rank of colonel; and Marco René Revelo, auxiliary bishop of San Salvador. Missing was Arturo Rivera y Damas, who had served as auxiliary to the previous archbishop and had been the progressive priests' favorite to replace him.

2. There were then 1,125 priests and religious brothers and sisters in El Salvador, according to Huntington, "Between," 38.

3. As quoted in Brockman, *A Life*, 110.

Rural Workers.[4] Some survivors had already been given refuge at the seminary and in the parish house next to the San José de la Montaña Church.

Romero's mind and heart remained full of this latest travesty, of which he had spoken in his homily the day before: "Everyone is aware of the tragic situation that our county is now experiencing, especially the situation that has recently occurred in San Pedro Perulapán: the military operations, the high number of dead and wounded, the great number of 'disappearances,' the number of families who have abandoned their homes, and the number of people who have been taken to prison."[5]

Despite these pressures, Romero felt obligated to attend the meeting. The four bishops showed him a document they had penned to condemn the letter sent to the nuncio. "It's just a matter of our signing it," said Bishop Aparicio, president of the bishops' conference. (As archbishop, Romero presided over the country's largest diocese, which included the capital city. This gave him influence in the entire country, but he had no greater voice or vote in the bishops' conference than any of the other five bishops.[6])

"But you've read Bishop Rivera's telegram," Romero protested, referring to Rivera's request to postpone the meeting until he returned from Guatemala. The topic required all bishops to be present, wrote Rivera, who happened to be the only one who would have supported Romero. "Besides,"

4. An archdiocesan commission charged with reporting on the San Pedro Perulapán operation commented on April 7, 1978: "After hearing the testimony of numberless eyewitnesses and victims, and having analyzed the conflict attentively, we believe that the events were provoked mediately and immediately by ORDEN in close collaboration with the security forces." As quoted in ibid., 108.

ORDEN was a rural paramilitary recruited and organized by security forces, giving favors to poor peasants in exchange for their serving as "ears" and keeping people terrorized by intimidating, torturing, and even killing persons organizing for their rights in the countryside. The Christian Federation of Salvadoran Peasants (FECCAS) and the Union of Rural Workers (UTC) were technically illegal due to governmental prohibitions against political organizations in rural areas in effect since the 1920s; this prohibition did not seem to apply to ORDEN.

Brockman wrote, "By setting up its own counterorganization, ORDEN, the government created a confrontation between campesinos" (ibid., 139). He added that the division was not due to ideologies but rather to their very poverty and need to provide for their families.

5. Romero y Galdámez, *Homilies*, April 2, 1978.

6. In 1979, the archdiocese had 37 percent of El Salvador's Catholics and 60 percent of its priests (Brockman, *A Life*, 169).

the archbishop added, "we thoroughly discussed this letter in our meeting two weeks ago, right after the nuncio forwarded it to us."[7]

"The situation has turned more serious," replied Bishop Aparicio. "The letter's now been published in newspapers."

"In both Mexico City and Guatemala City," added Bishop Revelo, Romero's auxiliary.

"As bishops, we must issue a public reply," Aparicio said. "Let me review our statement's main points. We begin by expressing our grief for the attitude of the group of priests and women religious in its March 7 letter to the apostolic nuncio. Then we give specifics:

"The letter arbitrarily and ignorantly accuses the nuncio because of his diplomatic work with the government.

"It faults him for not sharing the sorrow of suffering Christians. The letter maliciously informs the nuncio he is 'outside the faith, hope and charity that our church lives and professes in communion with the universal church.'

"It 'insolently repudiates' him as a 'negative sign and a collaborator with the persecutors of the church and the Gospel.' It calls him an obstacle to the communion of the local church and the Holy See.

"It reviles him as 'contrary to the light and the truth' . . . It accuses him of submitting to politicians, to the detriment of the freedom of the children of God. It makes him 'responsible for the time of confusion and violence that the country lives in.'"

Bishop Aparicio continued to read the rebuttal's highlights: "As bishops, we condemn 'with all the energy of our mission as pastors this haughty and irreverent posture as unjust, anti-evangelical, and disrespectful to the person of the Supreme Pontiff's representative.' As bishops, we reject the charges against the nuncio and we deplore 'the effrontery of publishing the letter in the press of the country, in violation of canon law.' The zeal of many of the people who signed the letter 'does not agree with the witness of their lives as Christians, ecclesiastics, or religious.' Finally, we pledge our loyalty as bishops to the nuncio and the pope and pray for 'these children [those who wrote the letter] who have caused so much sorrow.'"

After Aparicio finished reading the proposed rebuttal, Romero said, "I personally do not agree with the style or tone of the letter sent to the

7. The author has reenacted the April 3, 1978, bishops' meeting with the help of Brockman's detailed coverage of it, including much verbatim dialogue. Brockman drew from the meeting's minutes, to which he had access (ibid., 111–13). Also consulted was Romero y Galdámez, *Diary*, 23–24.

nuncio. But a history of events lies behind its assertions. The nuncio attends functions of the military government but is not always seen at important church affairs. He did not attend Father Navarro's funeral. Further, we do not defend the pope by defending his nuncio."

"Neither do we know whether it was the letter signers who sent it to the press," Romero continued. "We should not accuse them unjustly. Doing so seems equally as unjust to me as suspending ten priests without a hearing." In saying this, Romero directly confronted Bishop Aparicio, who had suspended the ten clerics of his San Vicente diocese who had signed the missive.

"You are meddling in the affairs of my diocese!" Aparicio erupted in anger. "You support dissident priests. You allow them to come to you with their complaints."

Seeing his error in having inflamed the discussion, Romero reiterated his earlier point: "If the nuncio has indeed acted as the priests and nuns say, he does not merit our defense."

Aparicio had not finished, however. "You are harming the country and the church with your sermons, with your YSAX interviews, with editorials in *Orientación*. You're dividing the country. You've confused the nation!"

"I don't think so," Romero replied. "I am following my Christian conscience. The people come begging me for support in the great trials and tribulations they suffer."

"You're meddling in the entire country. We know your underhanded maneuvers. And then you play the victim, as if they're doing you every wrong. We're on to you!" Aparicio said.

"Please. We'll gain nothing with this type of argument among ourselves," Romero pleaded.

Bishop Revelo suggested they analyze the letter penned by various priests and nuns before rushing to condemn it.

Romero agreed and went a step further. "Before analyzing it, we should call in those responsible for it. Let them tell us their thinking."

"You insist that the author be called in. Does that mean, then, that you are the author of the letter?" Aparicio demanded.

"No."

"Then you told them to write it and send it," Aparicio said.

"That is a slander," Romero looked at his watch. He likely wondered whether Paco Calles, his office assistant, would come with an excuse to get him out of this meeting for a spell. Returning his gaze to the other bishops,

Romero said, "It seems only just that you, or preferably the nuncio himself, speak directly with the letters' authors before officially and publicly condemning its contents. Also consider that many people don't know anything of the letter's contents; this statement gives them a very good idea of it. This repudiation, naming the points of contention, may not be in the nuncio's best interest."

After more hot words, the bishops put Romero's suggestion to the vote: Should they or the nuncio speak with the priests and nuns who sent the letter before issuing a condemnation? Four voted no. Romero voted yes. The archbishop likely wished anew they had postponed the meeting until Rivera's return. He could count on Rivera's calm and constant support. The four also refrained from personally attacking Rivera, a courtesy they denied Romero.

Another round of condemning the letter writers and expressing disapproval of the archbishop's pastoral ministry ensued. Noon approached. Romero prayed they'd wrap up the business.

"Are we ready to sign the statement of condemnation?" one bishop asked. Again, Romero voted the lone no. Aparicio slowly read aloud the document's full title so their general secretary Father Fredy Delgado could record it correctly: "Condemnatory Statement of the Bishops' Conference of El Salvador in Regard to a Letter Sent to His Excellency, the Apostolic Nuncio, and the Statement of Allegiance to the Representative of the Holy Father, Paul VI."

By nightfall, still distressed by the bishops' words and action, Romero commented into his tape recorder:

> As I expected, when I arrived at the meeting, I found that everything had already been decided prior to the meeting. . . . I also protested that the document to be discussed had been prepared in advance. They told me that there was always a draft document presented, but I could see that it was not just a draft, since it was not discussed. Rather they began right away to sign it in spite of my giving my reasons against it. . . .
>
> The document was approved, and I was subjected to many false accusations by the other bishops. I was told that my preaching is subversive, violent; that my priests provoke a climate of violence among the peasants; and that we should not complain about the abuses the authorities are committing. . . .

> It has been a bitter day because of this event and I lament that the division among the bishops will be worsened by this step, which seems to me not to be very wise.[8]

Romero's rupture with these four bishops and the nuncio pained and distressed him throughout his three years as archbishop. His personal friends Salvador and Eugenia Barraza recalled that Romero had wept at least once after a bishops' meeting.

"This may have been the occasion," a biographer remarks of the April 3, 1978, row.[9]

A "Friendly Conversation" in Rome

Romero suspected the four bishops and nuncio were sending negative reports about him to Vatican officials. He received confirmation of these misgivings in a letter from Cardinal Sebastiano Baggio dated May 16, 1978. Baggio served as prefect of the Sacred Congregation for Bishops, the Vatican department responsible for naming, assigning, and overseeing bishops.[10]

In his letter, Baggio said the Congregation for Bishops was receiving letters about El Salvador, the archdiocese, and Romero "with a frequency that knows no precedents and with the most contrary reports, both good and bad." Since the situation seemed to be deteriorating, Baggio added, Romero was invited to Rome for a "friendly conversation."[11]

Romero took up the offer and traveled to Vatican City in late June with Bishop Rivera and his vicar-general.[12] After his June 20 meeting with Cardinal Baggio, Romero related, "I think I have managed to correct a great deal of information that was not accurate and that, rather, came from interests opposed to those I try to defend in the line of the pastoral work and preaching of the archdiocese."[13]

8. Romero y Galdámez, *Diary*, 23–24.
9. Brockman, *A Life*, 115.
10. The congregation's nominations needed the pope's final approval.
11. From Baggio's letter as quoted in Brockman, *A Life*, 126.
12. Monseñor Ricardo Urioste.
13. Romero y Galdámez, *Diary*, 67.

It was an attempt to put a positive spin on the "friendly conversation." In reality, said a biographer, "Baggio was severe, and Romero emerged dejected from the interview . . ."[14]

Romero made it evident that Baggio had thoroughly raked him over the coals in a thirteen-page response. Had the cardinal truly received "both good and bad reports?" the archbishop asked.

"I am left with the impression that among the reports that you had in mind the negative ones prevailed almost exclusively and that my explanations or answers did not receive official support. Naturally, I return [to El Salvador] with the worry that you will continue to receive only one-sided reports that coincide exactly with the tendentious [biased] comments of the powerful sectors of my country."[15]

In contrast, Romero felt uplifted and encouraged after a short private audience he and Bishop Rivera had with Pope Paul VI the following day, June 21, as Romero detailed in his diary:

> When our turn came, we entered the chamber where the pope was, and we greeted him with the emotion such moments produce. The pope made us sit one on each side of him and addressing himself to me in particular, he took my right hand and kept it between his two hands. I would have liked to have had a photograph of that moment, which expressed such intimate communion between a bishop and the center of Catholic unity. And holding my hands that way, he talked to me for a long time.
>
> It would be difficult for me to repeat his long message exactly because, besides being more detailed than I expected, and rather cordial, ample, generous—because of the emotion of the moment—I cannot remember it word for word. But the principal ideas of his words were these: "I understand your difficult work. It is a work that can be misunderstood; it requires a great deal of patience and a great deal of strength. I already know that not everyone thinks like you do, that it is difficult in the circumstances of your country to have this unanimity of thinking. Nevertheless, proceed with courage, with patience, with strength, with hope."
>
> I think that this moment by itself would be worth all our effort in coming to Rome: receiving comfort from our communion with the pope, being illuminated by his guidance.[16]

14. Brockman, *A Life*, 127.

15. Quoted in ibid., 130–31.

16. Romero y Galdámez, *Diary*, 69–70. Paul VI was born Giovanni Battista Enrico Antonio Maria Montini; he reigned from June 21, 1963, to his death on August 6,

The pope also knew the people of El Salvador, and Romero shared the pontiff's words in his homily of July 2, 1978:

> [. . .]He told me that since he had worked in the [Vatican's] Secretariat of State some fifty years before becoming Pontiff, he knew of the vitality, hard work and the problems of the people of El Salvador. He told me: "These people demand that their rights be respected and seek for a more just situation. You must help and love these people. . . . Tell them that the Pope loves them and cares for them and is aware of their suffering. Tell them to never seek for a solution to their problems in irrational violence. Tell them to never allow themselves to be caught up in the currents of hatred. Rather work together to build unity, peace, and justice upon a foundation of love." I was very pleased to be able to tell him: "Holy Father, this is what I have preached."[17]

Paul VI, almost eighty-two, died six weeks after he cheered up and blessed Romero. The archbishop lost a firm supporter in the Vatican.

Apostolic Visitation

In Romero's "friendly conversation" with Cardinal Baggio, the prelate mentioned Romero's possible removal, a suggestion the nuncio and four of his fellow bishops were likely advocating. A first step to this end came when the Congregation for Bishops sent an "apostolic visitor" to the archdiocese in December 1978. An apostolic visitor may have authority to carry out any number of actions to rectify a situation.

The visitor named was Bishop Antonio Quarracino of Argentina. In this case, it appears Quarracino's mission was limited to investigating and reporting his findings to Rome. He read reams of files and reports and interviewed many individuals with whom Romero interacted.

On December 19, 1978, Romero recorded in his diary: "I know that many people have come to report to him on the pastoral work of our archdiocese and the result of the visit seems to me to have been, up to now, very positive."[18]

1978. He reconvened Vatican II after his predecessor died and implemented many of its reforms.

17. Romero y Galdámez, *Homilies*, July 2, 1978.

18. Romero y Galdámez, *Diary*, 112.

Five months later, in a 1979 visit to Rome, Romero learned the outcome of the Argentinian bishop's visit.[19] After receiving a runaround from various Vatican offices, he was at last granted a short private audience with the new Holy Father, John Paul II, on May 7.[20]

The pope insisted again and again on the need for bishops' unity. The pope's position was undoubtedly based on his own experiences in Poland, where a united bishops' front had stood up to church persecution by a communist regime. Most likely due to the bishops' discord, the pope delivered the chilling news that Bishop Quarracino had recommended the appointment of an apostolic administrator *sede plena*.[21] Quarracino had proposed that Romero retain authority over the archdiocese's religious message, and an apostolic administrator be named to control relationships with the bishops and the Salvadoran government.[22] This would be an unusual action in a case in which the incumbent—Romero—remained physically and mentally capable of fulfilling the duties.

"I left, pleased by the meeting," Romero recorded, "but worried to see how much the negative reports of my pastoral work had influenced him . . ."[23]

Although Romero voiced this positive spin in his diary, he had left the meeting more devastated than pleased. In an interview in Madrid four days later, a journalist said Romero was "practically in tears" as he told her about the pope's gruffness with him.[24]

19. Romero had gone to Rome, invited by the Dominican Sisters of the Annunciation, to attend the April 29, 1979, beatification of Francisco Coll, the congregation's Catalan founder. Dominican sisters ran several schools in the San Salvador archdiocese and invited Romero as their guest.

20. The new pope was Karol Wojtyla, who took the name John Paul II; he had assumed the position on October 16, 1978. (Albino Luciani, John Paul I, succeeded Paul VI, but died suddenly after only thirty-three days, serving as pontiff from August 26 to September 28, 1978.)

21. *Sede plena* means "with the see (diocese) occupied," in contrast to *sede vacante*, "with a vacant see.") These two types of apostolic administrators fill temporary bishop assignments, and there are some restrictions on what they may do. They may not sell diocesan real estate, for example.

22. Brockman, *A Life*, 168–69.

23. Romero y Galdámez, *Diary*, 215.

Romero's colleague, the theologian Jon Sobrino, later pointed out: "I personally believe that John Paul II evolved in his estimation of Archbishop Romero. At all events, he eventually praised him, publicly, as a pastor and martyr who had given his life for the love of God and the service of his brothers and sisters" (*Reflections*, 20).

24. López Vigil *Mosaic*, 306.

The following day Romero had another conversation with Cardinal Baggio, prefect of the Congregation for Bishops, which he later described as "very cordial, even though I had expected some severity like the last time, which was last year."[25]

Baggio didn't like the idea of an apostolic administrator—not necessarily because Baggio affirmed Romero's work and appreciated his personal merits, but because he felt it was impractical. The cardinal couldn't see any of the current bishops filling the position because of their poor relationships with Romero. Bringing in "someone from outside the country also seemed an absurd idea, given the situation of our country."[26]

Baggio told the archbishop that the idea of a temporary administrator was still being studied. Somewhat surprisingly, he also said he and Romero were, in general, "ninety percent agreed already."[27]

"I told him that his words gave me great encouragement and that the depression I had been left with after my audience with the Holy Father had here, in my conversation with him, been replaced by a hope that my situation and that of my diocese have solutions if we continue to look for them in goodwill and with love of the Church," Romero recorded that evening.[28]

As Romero was leaving the cardinal's office, he bumped into a good friend, Monsignor De Nicolò. The churchman counseled Romero to be circumspect in his future interactions with officials in the Vatican's Secretariat of State. He should take care not to react too strongly to the idea of an apostolic administrator because, as Romero later put it, "The Holy Father and Cardinal Baggio could be trying to gauge my reaction . . . That if my reaction were negative, then everything might be lost."[29] Instead, he must remain humble and patient.

Nevertheless, after returning to El Salvador, Romero wrote a long letter to Baggio giving his opinion of an apostolic administrator. His main points had to do with the confusion such an appointment would sow among the archdiocesan clergy, as well as its threat to the church's unity.

25. Romero y Galdámez, *Diary*, 216.

26. Ibid.

27. Ibid., 217.

28. Ibid.

29. Ibid.

"I have suggested, as a solution that would resolve the deeper problems, the naming of some new bishops, with the criteria of Vatican II . . ." Romero said in his letter.[30]

Romero's Evaluation of Four Bishops

In correspondence with Pope John Paul II and other curia officials, Romero—likely in an attempt to round out the Vatican's opinion of his country's episcopal conflict—at various times lodged specific complaints about each of the four bishops who worked against him:

Bishop Aparicio used his position to obtain privileges from the government, such as payment for teachers' salaries in Catholic schools. "He has acted very valiantly against abuses of power and wealth when it was in his interest. But today his advantages are on the side of the government and he makes himself accomplice of its policy of persecution," Romero wrote.[31]

Bishop Benjamín Barrera, getting on in years at seventy-six, had "never chosen a pastoral policy of serious evangelical commitment to his people."[32]

Bishop José Eduardo Alvarez served as military chaplain and held the rank of colonel in the armed forces, which predisposed him in favor of the military and its actions.[33] Alvarez preferred to "maintain privileges with authorities, high-ranking military, and powerful persons," Romero said.[34] He was also deficient in his pastoral duties in the army and his diocese, according to complaints from those he was supposed to serve, the archbishop charged.

Bishop René Revelo, Romero's auxiliary, had committed an act of insubordination—an infraction of church and also civil law—in November 1978. Taking advantage of Romero's absence and acting under his title of vicar-general, Revelo had contrived to sign away Romero's right to head the Catholic relief organization Caritas and confer the authority instead on

30. Ibid., 241.

31. From a six-page letter Romero wrote to the new pope, John Paul II, on November 7, 1978, in which he describes the conditions of his country and ministry. As shared by Brockman, *A Life*, 146.

32. Ibid.

33. In 1981, Bishop Alvarez would garner international commentary when he blessed new war planes that arrived in El Salvador.

34. From Romero's six-page letter to the new pope. From Brockman, *A Life*, 146.

the president of the bishops' conference, then Aparicio. Revelo may have attempted this action to get around Romero's desire to tighten distribution of Caritas food aid; he wanted to prevent the government from using it to pay members of ORDEN, its rural paramilitary organization.

At the formal request of the priests' senate, Romero removed Revelo as vicar-general on November 23, although Revelo remained his auxiliary—as well as a sharp thorn in his side.

In May 1979, the four bishops wrote ten tightly spaced pages condemning Romero. Although they gave it the neutral-sounding title "Political-Religious Situation of El Salvador," biographer Brockman says:

> Despite the history of conflict and accusations on the part of the four bishops, the document is shocking. It ignores most of what Romero had been saying and doing publicly, in order to present a warped view of his teaching and practice. It distorts beyond recognition his attitude and actions in relation to the popular organizations. It accepts wild theories about the priests and lay workers killed in order to explain away the persecution of the part of the church that was trying to follow Medellín and Puebla.[35] That some bishops should have a different vision of what the church should be is understandable. That they should search so hard to find fault and should rely on such a hollow argument seems small-minded and mean.[36]

By May 1979, Romero appeared to be coming to terms with the possibility of meeting a violent end. Death threats from shadowy right-wing death squads continued unabated as the country's overall situation grew ever more explosive and bloody. After a May 3 visit to Saint Peter's Basilica while in Rome, Romero related in his diary, "I asked for great faithfulness to my Christian faith and the courage, should it be necessary, to die as those martyrs [early apostles, including Peter] died . . ."[37]

The next day, frustrated with the runaround various officials were giving him in his quest for an appointment to see the pope, Romero commented in his diary that, while he would always love and be faithful to

35. A January 25 to February 13, 1979, bishops' meeting in Puebla, Mexico, reconfirmed the direction set a decade earlier in Medellín, Colombia. Romero attended this gathering, titled the Third General Conference of the Latin American Bishops, as did Bishop Aparicio. Pope John Paul II visited Mexico at the outset of the conference.

36. Brockman, *A Life*, 180.

37. Romero y Galdámez, *Diary*, 210.

the Vatican, "I understand the human, limited, defective part of his Holy church . . ."[38]

His new understanding and acknowledgement of the church's flaws allowed the archbishop to accept the four bishops with greater equanimity. He commented on their ten-page denunciation: "In spite of how serious this [series of accusations] is, I feel great peace. I acknowledge my deficiencies before God, but I believe that I have worked with goodwill and that I am not guilty of the serious things of which they accuse me."[39]

He had evidently found serenity in the thought that, when all was said and done, his accountability would be to God, not to the "human, limited" institutional church.

On December 31, 1979, Romero received another envoy sent by the Vatican to look into the archdiocese's affairs.[40] This time the visitor was Cardinal Aloísio Lorscheider of Brazil. The cardinal, like Romero, was appalled by the misery of Latin America's masses and the power of the few. Lorscheider took bold stances condemning the abuses of the Brazilian military and he too struggled against Brazil's traditional church. The cardinal was one of the few people to stay at Romero's little two-room bungalow on the grounds of a cancer hospital. "This way I show that I am with you," Lorscheider told Romero about his choice of host.[41]

38. Ibid., 211.

39. Ibid., 229.

40. "Two of these official [apostolic] visitors in just three years had to be a world's record," commented Father Plácido Erdozaín, "to say nothing of the 'unofficial' visit of the papal nuncio from Costa Rica [in early 1980]" (*Martyr*, 43).

41. Brockman, *A Life*, 217. For his sixtieth birthday on August 15, 1977, the sisters in charge of the Divine Providence Hospital, a small care-center for indigent cancer patients, had a modest two-room residence built for the archbishop on the hospital grounds. Romero had hammock hooks installed in the outer room; this allowed him to use the hammock while a guest slept in the little bedroom. The sisters were members of the order Carmelite Missionaries of Saint Teresa.

During his first five months as archbishop, Romero had slept in a room across from the sacristy (room behind the altar) of the chapel on the cancer hospital's grounds. Romero had also used the room when he visited the capital while bishop of Santiago de María. He had close relationships with the sisters who ran the hospital and had designated to the hospital the offering taken up in his ordination as bishop in 1970, as well as the $10,000 that accompanied a Swedish peace price he was awarded in early March 1980. During his time as archbishop, he ate with the sisters in their dining room and served as their chaplain, celebrating a daily 6:30 a.m. mass and prayers.

The cardinal spent a couple of days talking with a variety of people and told Romero he planned to tell Vatican officials that his work in the archdiocese deserved support.

Romero spent the last three days of January 1980 in Rome en route to Belgium, where he was to receive an honorary doctorate from the University of Louvain. Upon his arrival in Rome, evidently expecting more chastisement, and reflecting his new awareness of the church's imperfections, he recorded in his diary: "I have asked the Lord to preserve my faith and my loyalty to Rome, which Christ chose to be the seat of the universal pastor, the pope."[42]

This simple statement reflects a huge change of stance in a person who for sixty years had held the Vatican on a reverent pedestal. He now worried that Vatican officials might erode, rather than enhance, his Christian faith.[43]

42. Romero y Galdámez, *Diary*, 464.

43. Filochowski believes Lorscheider's positive report to Rome led Pope John Paul II to receive Romero more cordially in their January 1980 meeting. At the end of the meeting, John Paul embraced Romero and told him he prayed daily for El Salvador, which Romero took as confirmation of his ministry. See Julian Filochowski, "Romero: Person and His Charisma with the Pontiffs," in Pelton, *Archbishop Romero and Spiritual Leadership*, 99–110.

13. A Time to Tread a Tightrope

(1977–1980)

El Salvador's powerful right wing aggressively persecuted Archbishop Romero and others who shared his conviction that the church must stand with the poor. This is the story most frequently told about Romero.

Less well-known are the frustrations, run-ins, and criticism—at times hostile—Romero dealt with from the left.

Disagreements with the left often had more to do with methods than with desired outcomes. Romero shared the desire of most leftist groups to create a country in which justice and human rights prevailed. A Jesuit close to the archbishop wrote that Romero did not even call the popular organizations "forces of the left" but rather "forces of the people."[1]

Despite his basic sympathy with the "forces of the people," Romero recoiled at the idea of violence. He believed revolutionary organizations using kidnapping and other forms of violence put their own agendas first, making idols of their views and goals. Such groups were leading people away from their Christian values, fomenting hatred rather than love of enemies.

Romero faced three conundrums with the left during his time as archbishop. Church occupations frustrated and angered him, although he learned to cope with them. The case of Father Neto mired him in confusion. How to relate to the civilian-military junta that governed after an October 1979 coup brought him criticism, some of it intense, from the left, including from some of his own priests, which wounded him.

Church Occupations

When soldiers opened fire on peaceful demonstrations, participants often fled into nearby churches to take refuge, both in the capital city and in

1. Sobrino, *Reflections*, 35.

towns. Romero and leftist leaders did not debate how to act in such church sanctuary cases. They spoke with security force commanders to obtain permission to take food and supplies into the occupiers and to evacuate the injured. Longer term, they mediated with military officials to allow demonstrators to leave the church to return to their homes without being arrested or fired upon.

Other times, groups deliberately occupied churches to gain visibility for their political causes, from spreading word of a workers' strike to demanding the release of certain political prisoners.[2] An occupation meant no masses could be celebrated in the church and people could not stop by to pray, much to Romero's consternation.

Sometimes occupying groups mistreated church property, bringing the archbishop's wrath down on their heads. Romero told the leader of a large grassroots organization:

> Since the Church is the house of God it belongs to everyone, and everyone can use it. But it's not here so that some people, like you, can create chaos and destroy it! You should have seen how you left that church! A bunch of benches broken, graffiti on the walls! You even left one of the saints naked so that someone could wrap himself up with the cloth at night! How can people who call themselves Christians behave like this? You can make denunciations from the church, but you can't show disrespect. I do not accept it, and I'm not going to tolerate it![3]

This leader then cautioned his group prior to another church occupation: "If you damage anything, even so much as one of the damn candles, we're going to penalize you. Monseñor Romero has already scolded us up and down because we've left his churches all filthy and disorderly."[4]

On the other hand, when some parish priests decided to cut off the water supply to force occupying protestors to leave their church, Romero

2. Foreign embassies were frequently occupied by leftist or grassroots organizations for the same reasons, although these occupations also involved the detention of personnel working in the embassies.

3. Monseñor Romero to Odilón Novoa, leader of the February 28 Popular Leagues (LP-28), in López Vigil, *Mosaic*, 250. The LP-28 was linked to the Revolutionary Army of the Poor (ERP), one of the five factions that in 1980 united into the FMLN guerrilla movement.

4. Odilón Novoa to members of LP-28, in ibid.

disapproved. "Think of some other way to do it. It's not right to leave them without water," Romero instructed the priests.[5]

After much consideration, the archbishop expounded on the issue in his homily of September 2, 1979. He had planned to celebrate the highly attended eight o'clock morning mass at El Rosario Church because the Metropolitan Cathedral was occupied. But when a different group occupied El Rosario, he moved the service to the Sacred Heart Basilica.

He opened his message with a query:

"Why are the Cathedral and the El Rosario Church, and the churches in Cojutepeque, Apopa, Suchitoto, and Mejicanos being occupied? Why last night has this list of churches grown to include the churches in Aguilares, San Miguel, and who knows how many more?"

"In a certain sense, we all share the blame," came his unexpected reply to the congregation.

The popular political organizations are blameworthy because they give priority to their own strategies over the peoples' need to worship. "As they occupy our churches, they cry out on behalf of their just demands. . . . I want to remind groups that struggle for just causes that the end does not justify the means." He urged leaders of popular political groups to engage in activities for justice without offending people's religious feelings.

The nation's authorities are also to blame for church occupations, Romero continued. "[People] go before the Legislative Assembly and they are not heard. They go to the different government ministers and they are treated like second class citizens." A pressure cooker without a steam-escape valve will quickly explode, he warned.

The media also share much of the blame, he said. The newspapers and the television and radio stations say nothing of the people's suffering. "Where have we seen published the abuse that our *campesinos* are suffering in Arcatao and Aguilares?" Romero asked. Because the media remains silent, people shout out from within the churches to make abuses known.

"I am not in agreement with this action of occupying the churches," he repeated, "but I try to understand the reasons behind these actions."

"In normal times, no one occupies the churches," he continued. "In normal times when there are normal channels of expression the churches express the religious feeling of the people and nothing else. These are not normal times but rather times of emergency. . . . In times of emergency

5. Francisco Calles, in ibid., 249.

it is not easy to condemn acts which in normal times would definitely be condemned."[6]

Although church occupations would remain a prickly frustration, in this treatment of them Romero did what made him remarkably effective as a bishop: He became flexible as he shed the strict legalism that had guided him as a young priest. He read the gospel from the eyes of the disenfranchised, and he tried to follow Jesus, who had declared that the Sabbath was created for people, not people for the Sabbath.[7]

Father Neto

How closely should priests align themselves with popular organizations? How about with those having armed factions? When did a priest's support for an organization cross the line from the spiritual to the political? This presented an especially thorny issue for Archbishop Romero because many grassroots groups arose from church efforts to help the poor gain dignity and rights.

The question held vital real-world consequences. Too close an affiliation left the church open to accusations of mixing religion and politics. Too loose an affiliation left the groups even more exposed to repression, bereft of whatever limited protection the church could provide. The church would betray grassroots associations if it kept itself safe and out of the fray.

On November 28, 1978, news arrived of the violent death of thirty-year-old Father Rafael Ernesto "Neto" Barrera Motto, a priest who worked closely with laborers and their unions. The government's published report claimed Father Neto was killed with three other members of the Popular Liberation Forces (FPL)—the armed wing of a larger organization[8]—in a five-hour shoot-out with security forces at a house in the capital.

In the mid–twentieth century, a handful of priests in other countries quit the clergy in order to join leftist guerrilla groups like the FPL,[9] but Father Neto's case was not so clear. The priest had not renounced his vows, and the government report aroused suspicion. The account contained at

6. Romero y Galdámez, *Homilies*, September 2, 1979.

7. Mark 2:27.

8. Romero described the Popular Liberation Forces as "considered to be the violent forces of the Popular Revolutionary Bloc" (*Diary*, 104).

9. Erdozaín mentions Camilo Torres (Colombia), Pedro Laín Entralgo (Spain), Gaspar García Laviana (Spanish missionary priest in Nicaragua), "and others" (*Martyr*, 43).

least one blatant lie[10] and the coroner's exam was incomplete,[11] making it difficult for outsiders to piece together exactly what had happened.[12]

Romero sent his "hippie" office assistant, Paco Calles, to the funeral home to take photos of the priest's body. Besides being riddled with bullets, Father Neto's body was covered with burn marks, "like the marks of a cigarettes being extinguished on his body," Paco reported.[13] A forensics doctor confirmed the priest had undergone "atrocious torture."[14]

This evidence of torture led Romero to believe the military had staged the event. As one writer put it, "It would not have been the first time that security forces staged a fake shoot-out and dumped bodies of prisoners killed beforehand."[15]

Soon afterwards, the FPL blanketed the streets with pamphlets carrying its own message: Father Neto was indeed an active member of the FPL, it claimed, in which he was known as "Felipe." He and the other three guerrillas had held off well-armed security forces[16] for five hours while they destroyed printed materials that could have implicated others.[17]

The FPL statement went on: "The heroism with which Father [Neto] Barrera struggled and died as a revolutionary combatant, defending the interests of the working masses with his weapons in his hands, is an

10. The official government report claimed all four men had been killed in the shoot-out. A newspaper photo and TV footage showed one man emerging from the house with his hands in the air. He had been wounded in the throat and could not speak but he answered some reporters' questions in writing. The following day he was dead of a bullet in the head. Brockman writes, "Even though thousands had seen him alive on television, the police declared he had received the mortal head wound in the shoot-out" (*A Life*, 150). Thus, the one person who might have shed light on the event was assassinated by security forces before he was able to do so.

11. "The coroner did not attempt to fix the time of the death of the other men, as he should have done," writes Brockman, ibid.

12. Romero lists many of the official governmental statements that are inconsistent with media reports in his December 3, 1978, homily.

13. Francisco Calles, in López Vigil, *Mosaic*, 261.

14. Romero shared this in his funeral homily for Father Barrera on November 29, 1978.

15. Brockman, *A Life*, 150.

16. The security forces were armed with bazookas, grenades, and machine guns, according to the government report (ibid., 150).

17. As Romero said in his homily of December 3, 1978, citing the investigative reports of his archdiocesan commission on the event: "It seems highly unlikely that four men armed with only two light arms could have confronted for five hours one hundred and fifty members of the Security Forces who were fully armed."

imperishable example for all working people and for all Christians, who now more than ever will understand that there is room in the ranks of the revolution for all those persons who consciously try to struggle against oppression and against class injustice."[18]

Romero did not want to believe this. The statement might have been made by some person or group wanting to embarrass the church by claiming evidence of gun-toting priests. Or, if the FPL had indeed issued it, the group might be using the church's popularity to win support for its own cause.

In any case, the FPL's announcement made Romero's decision about participation in Father Neto's funeral a touchy one. He called together his priests to discuss the matter. Most of them wanted the church to distance itself from Father Neto.

"Don't go. They'll just use it against you," was the majority sentiment.[19] Some said that if he had died as a guerrilla, he was no longer a priest, perhaps not even a Christian.[20]

"When we had all spoken, the bishop surprised us with a question," wrote one priest. "He was pursuing a line of reasoning completely different from ours. 'Don't you think that Neto's mother, without questioning the circumstances, will be next to the body of her son at the funeral? I, as his bishop, must be there also.'"[21]

In the end, Romero could not turn his back on one of his beloved and dedicated priests, to whom he considered himself a father.

In his homily the following Sunday, Romero reported on the funeral, in which sixty priests had presided: "I want to tell you that the celebration of the funeral rites was truly impressive. I believe we heard the voice of the people who love their priests. I was saddened by the inopportune shouts and protests of the Popular Revolutionary Bloc; inside the Church, however, the hymns of the Christian community that prayed and received the message at the time of death were very impressive."[22]

Regarding Father Neto's political associations and activities, he declared, "I can tell you with complete sincerity: I have no personal knowledge

18. As quoted in Brockman, *A Life,* 150–51.

19. Father Astor Ruíz, in López Vigil, *Mosaic*, 262.

20. Francisco Calles, in ibid.

21. Erdozaín, *Martyr*, 45.

22. Romero y Galdámez, *Homilies*, December 3, 1978.

of this matter."[23] He shared the main points of his recent pastoral letter on the topic of the church and popular organizations: namely, that while priests may be drawn to popular organizations, their first concern was to provide guidance in faith and in the justice that faith demands in accordance with Christian principles.[24] And he again condemned guerrilla groups who "preach violence as the only way to achieve justice."[25]

The issue of Father Neto's possible involvement with an armed group did not fade in the media, and Romero addressed it again in his homily the following Sunday: He had no proof the priest was an FPL member. If Father Neto had joined, he had acted without Romero's knowledge as archbishop.[26]

In case the pamphlet was indeed the FPL's, Romero said, "It ought to be very clear that not only is the Archbishop not with the FPL but also the FPL is not with the Archbishop—if they were they would have tried to protect his image and respect his good intention."[27]

In response to that homily, Romero received a six-page letter from FPL leaders. They repeated their claim that Father Neto belonged to the FPL. It lauded his decision. The priest's example, the missive said, should make everyone reflect that being a "loyal member of the church does not argue against the duty to struggle against the tyranny the people suffer from and to achieve the highest acts of heroism in defense of the people's interests . . ."[28]

One journalist described the letter as long-winded and repetitious but intelligent and courteous. "If it was a forgery, it was a clever one."[29]

Romero asked the opinion of a priest familiar with political-military groups, who deemed the letter authentic.

Romero never arrived at a clear conclusion. He remained baffled that FPL leaders accepted the government's account of the implausible shoot-out. He considered that Father Neto may have been an FPL member but not a combatant. Romero did not publish his own diocesan commission's final

23. Ibid.

24. Romero y Galdámez and Arturo Rivera Damas, Third Pastoral Letter.

25. Romero y Galdámez, *Homilies*, December 3, 1978.

26. Ibid., December 10, 1978.

27. Ibid.

28. As quoted in Brockman, *A Life*, 153.

29. Ibid.

report. It had concluded the government faked the confrontation but there were no reasons to doubt Neto was indeed an FPL member.

A month after Father Neto's death, Romero told a group of workers close to the priest: "What the fundamental ideology of this priest was, remains unknown."[30]

Some priests close to Father Neto, however, did know Father Neto had joined the armed FPL. Father Plácido Erdozaín, whom Romero had asked to minister to workers alongside Neto, later said he and other priests encouraged Romero's erroneous interpretation, "because even many of us were not prepared to accept the facts."[31]

That some priests knew Father Neto's "fundamental ideology" squares with the account of another priest. Father Astor Ruíz was one of eight radical priests with whom Romero ate supper the night of Neto's death. Father Ruíz said they "played cat and mouse" with the archbishop, "trying not to reveal too much."[32]

That one of his own priests would opt to join a violent revolutionary group as an armed member—and to do so without consulting him—was clearly beyond the archbishop's comprehension.

The Coup

On October 15, 1979, some young reform-minded military officers, fed up with the armed forces' corruption and extremism, ousted the nation's president in a bloodless coup.[33] Archbishop Romero had expected the coup. In his diary a month earlier, he recorded receiving "three messages from progressive military officers, who are planning—secretly of course—a change of government to a more democratic one. This is very hopeful and I hope that soon El Salvador will breathe better air than the present atmosphere of violence we live in."[34]

30. As quoted in ibid.

31. Erdozaín, *Martyr*, 46.

32. Father Astor Ruíz, in López Vigil, *Mosaic*, 263.

33. The coup ousted General Carlos Humberto Romero, who was not related to Archbishop Romero. General Romero had come to power in 1977 through major election fraud. He had ruled with an iron fist.

34. Romero y Galdámez, *Diary*, 333.

The young officers would replace the president with a junta of both civilian and military members.[35]

After consulting with several priests, Romero decided to issue a statement. Because it was a military coup, the archbishop feared leftist groups would call for a popular uprising. Some had already begun violent responses. Romero also worried that the extreme right, feeling threatened by the coup leaders' promises of economic and social reforms, might respond with heavier repression.

To promote calm, Romero took to the radio early the following morning. To the people, he recognized their suffering and losses of the "last nightmarish years" and encouraged them to "wait and watch before they judge and act."

To the privileged "who have been guilty of so much unrest and violence," he urged them to listen to the voice of justice.

To the popular organizations, he counseled "political maturity and a capacity for dialogue" and to avoid "fanaticisms or idolatry of their own party or organizations."

To the new government, he warned, "This government will deserve the confidence and cooperation of the people only when it demonstrates that the beautiful promises contained in its declaration, issued this morning, are not merely hollow words, but a true hope that will begin a new era in our country."[36]

An ominous wind blew that evening: a priest was taken away among a group of captives to the infamous Treasury Police headquarters.[37] Although security force officials released the priest and apologized to Romero, in his diary the archbishop reported no word on the fate of the others.

35. The five-member junta included Colonels Adolfo Majano and Jaime Abdul Gutiérrez, chosen by the armed forces as their representatives. The civilian members were Román Mayorga, rector of the Central American University; Guillermo Ungo of the Popular Forum (Ungo had run as a Christian Democrat in 1972); and Mario Andino, representing the Chamber of Commerce and Industry.

36. Romero y Galdámez, "Pastoral Statement in Regard to the New Situation in Our Country," in *Diary*, 351–53.

37. Romero y Galdámez, *Diary*, 353. The priest was Father Modesto Villarán, arrested in the Mejicanos municipality of San Salvador Department, in the city of Soyapango. (A month later, in late November 1979, a secret torture cell was located in Treasury Police headquarters; it had been used by the precoup government. Romero spoke of it in one of his homilies.)

Also that evening, Romero met with six seminarians nearing graduation. The students asked Romero in an accusing voice why he had given his blessing to the military:

> "I haven't given my blessing to anyone! Don't manipulate what I've said!!"
>
> "You haven't said that you give your blessing, but you did give a favorable review to the coup, and the government has used your words who knows how many times on the national radio station!! So what are people going to think? They're going to think you're giving your blessing!"
>
> "You guys are seminarians, but you talk as if you were members of the Revolutionary Bloc!"
>
> "And you're the bishop, but you're talking as if you were a participant in the coup!!"[38]

This was a mild opening salvo of the criticism Romero would receive from the left due to his conditional support for the junta. Some Christian base communities believed the archbishop had taken a step backwards in his accompaniment of them.

One day Romero's office assistant went with the archbishop on pastoral visits to three parishes. In each, people grilled the archbishop, arguing with him about his support for the junta. He ended the day frustrated and angry.[39]

The Christian base community of Zacamil parish, close to the capital, protested by ceasing to buy a bulk quantity of the diocesan newspaper *Orientación* to distribute. Members also requested a private meeting with Romero, which he granted. A group of all ages, accompanied by parish priest Father Rogelio Ponseele, a Belgian, sat down with Romero at the cancer hospital where he lived.[40] A young woman who attended later recorded the event:

> We started the meeting and went at it.
>
> "You're putting too much trust in those people!"

38. Exchange as described by Miguel Vázquez, in López Vigil, *Mosaic*, 330–31. Romero also relates the encounter, in milder words, two days after the coup (*Diary*, 355).

39. Francisco Calles, in López Vigil, *Mosaic*, 331–32.

40. Father Rogelio Ponseele accompanied, as an unarmed priest, a guerilla group after war broke out in the 1980s. Father Ponselee can be seen in various YouTube videos, such as at https://www.youtube.com/watch?v=a9rJAURtYLM in which he recalls the massacre of Mozote. María López Vigil wrote an account of Ponseele's life, titled *Muerte y vida en Morazán: Testimonio de un sacerdote* (San Salvador: UCA, 1987).

> "And they're the same old military people as always. Look at all of them in the same position they've always been in. Everyone knows the crimes they've committed! They talked about purging people from the military, but who have they purged? No one!"
>
> "You're going to see how the military people are controlling the civilian friends of yours in the government. You'll see, Monseñor . . ."
>
> "You can't let yourself be deceived, Monseñor, and you can't go on deceiving the people!"
>
> He listened to us patiently for a while, but then he got angry . . . : "You are all so radical. You're extremist about everything! But you can't build anything with radicalism! Give just a little benefit of the doubt to people who don't think like you do. I'm calling you to moderation . . ."
>
> "And we're calling *you* to listen to those who don't think like *you* do!"
>
> He kept getting angrier.
>
> "You don't understand the need to give things a little time . . . And you're not willing to respect authorities unless they take the exact same position that you do!"[41]

The tension lowered when a nun entered to serve coffee. The community members told Romero about a catechist, Osmín, recently disappeared.[42] They told him of the killings of two girls in their early teens. One of the girls had emotionally and spiritually moved Romero when she tendered tortillas and coffee as part of the offering in an earlier mass he had attended in Zacamil, a testament to how people were relating to Jesus's actions in their own lives and time.

Opposition to Romero's conditional support for the junta extended to some of his clergy. Although a majority of the archdiocesan priests approved of their bishop's stance, a group of them, along with some nuns and a few laypersons, wrote a document condemning it. They accused the archbishop of having betrayed the popular organizations.[43]

Romero and his priests devoted several of their senate meetings to the topic. It slowly came to light that a handful of priests felt more committed to the popular organizations than to either the church or the archbishop.

41. Carmen Elena Hernández, in López Vigil, *Mosaic*, 334–35.

42. Romero asked about the disappeared catechist in several of his homilies after this meeting.

43. Delgado, *Biografía*, 147–48.

Romero asked them to seriously consider leaving the priesthood, if such was their conviction.[44]

On January 4, 1980, Romero met with these priests. That night he reported, "I spent this morning in a meeting with five priests from the archdiocese with whom there are some difficulties in our close relations because of the political aspects of their ministry. But in talking in depth and looking sincerely for the solution to these problems and mistrust, I encountered great human, Christian, and priestly merit which we will continue to encourage in further meetings."[45]

Thus, Romero, angered and hurt by these rebel priests, remained open to dialogue, "knowing very well that the group had not reacted in malice, but rather with a desire of being faithful to the poor," as an archdiocesan priest of the time put it.[46]

Romero's clergy likely did not realize just how conditional his support of the junta was. Romero's diary entries of the period testify to the pressure he brought to bear on junta members for speedy reform.[47] Yet he viewed the junta as the country's final hope for peaceful change as war drums beat on the horizon.

The junta's cause was not helped when security forces killed seventy demonstrators of the LP-28 group on October 29. What's more, even before the junta members were publicly announced, the army named the minister of defense and public security of its choice.[48] Through this colonel, military allies took some key government positions.

Then on December 18, the army went a step further. It restructured its entire high command, placing its own people in charge. The high command began to treat the junta "as its servant . . ."[49]

44. Ibid., 148–49.

45. Romero y Galdámez, *Diary*, 433. The five priests were: Fathers Rogelio Ponseele, Benito Tovar, Trinidad Nieto, Rutilio Sánchez, and Pedro Cortéz.

46. Delgado, *Biografía*, 149.

47. The first junta lasted from October 15, 1979 to January 2, 1980. After civilian members began to resign from the junta in early January, a second junta was formed between the military and members of the Christian Democrat party. Romero did not make any statements of support for the second junta. He perceived a growing "psychosis of violence and war" throughout the country in January 1980.

48. Colonel José Guillermo García

49. Brockman, *A Life*, 215.

"In effect it was a countercoup, and the days of the junta were numbered," said one researcher.[50]

On January 2 and 3, 1980, the civilian members of the junta and in the cabinet and other government posts resigned, all protesting the impossibility of implementing the promised reforms of the October coup. One of them, Salvador Samayoa, who had served as education minister, announced he was going underground to join the FPL, the Popular Liberation Forces.[51]

The en masse resignations of civilians from the governing junta, said one observer who had criticized Romero's support for it, "clearly confirmed Monseñor's interpretation, and contradicted our black-and-white analysis. There *had* been people with good intentions behind that effort, and when they couldn't go on anymore, they had the courage to step down."[52]

Leftists have whitewashed this piece of history since Romero's death, contends at least one observer. Writing in 2012, journalist Roberto Valencia commented about the junta's two-month existence: "There was a time in which many of those who applaud Romero now criticized him harshly. They called him an old bourgeois, accused him of forgetting the people, of changing sides. When one raises this issue today, some prefer to tiptoe around it, perhaps to avoid portraying themselves as what they were: people who for weeks or months believed Romero was a traitor."[53]

Despite this disloyalty, however, Romero continued to preach his prophetic words from the pulpit, calling upon both the right *and* the left to look for creative solutions for peace in El Salvador to avoid the bloodbath that was otherwise surely to come.

50. Ibid., 214.

51. Ibid., 219.

52. Ana Guadalupe Martínez, in López Vigil, *Mosaic*, 355–56. Martínez had sent Romero a copy of her newly released book *Las Cárceles Clandestinas* (Clandestine Prisons), in which she described the torture and treatment she and other "dissidents" received from security forces. During a meeting with the archbishop, Martínez criticized Romero's support of the junta. In this anecdote, Martínez also records Romero's fatherly concern for her: "When it was time to go, he gave me a warm hug. 'Take care of yourself, my child, and don't be seen on the streets. They might capture you again, and now that you've written your book, they won't let you out alive. You can't go through that hell again.'"

53. Valencia, "Rutilio Grande." http://www.elfaro.net/es/201203/noticias/7949/Rutilio-Grande-SJ-12031977.htm.

14. A Time to Walk the Global Stage

(1977–1980)

Romero allowed his beliefs to stretch and his horizons to expand while archbishop. He opened himself to relationships beyond Catholic circles and El Salvador's borders. Ecumenical bonds blossomed. A network of worldwide admirers and supporters formed. Romero's new global renown emboldened him to challenge US foreign policy in his country.

Ecumenical Friendship at Home

During his twenty-five years in San Miguel, Father Romero had plenty to say and publish about Protestants, mostly negative, if not nasty. He spoke of the Protestant "poison" spreading in El Salvador and claimed Protestants were not Christians. (*See* chapter 5.) The feelings were mutual. In the pre-Vatican II era, Salvadoran Protestants could be as virulently anti-Catholic as Catholics were anti-Protestant.

When Romero became archbishop, walls between some of the sparring Christian denominations crumbled. A Salvadoran Baptist of the time recalled:

> From the day of the single Mass on, the economic elite had begun an open war against [Romero]. They took out paid ads criticizing him in the newspapers. They made unfounded accusations. They made fun of him. They made offensive remarks. In the midst of all this, we decided to pay him an official visit.
>
> "And what brings you here?" he said to us in greeting.
>
> He was surprised that Protestants would be coming to see him. Maybe it was the first time. We were a good-sized group—the pastor and all of the deacons and their wives representing our little church, Emmanuel Baptist Church.

> We explained to him how much we admired his work, and we told him that we had some good friends among the Catholic priests. . . .
>
> A few days later, Monseñor Romero mentioned our meeting on the radio, calling us the "separated brothers." That was the usual language of the Catholic Church at the time.
>
> We continued to have more meetings, and once when we went back to visit him, [our pastor] called him on the issue.
>
> "You spoke of us in a way we don't like. We do feel like brothers, but we don't feel separated."
>
> Monseñor was pensive for a few moments.
>
> "Let's make a deal," he proposed. "Don't call me Monseñor anymore. Just call me brother. And I won't call you the 'separated brothers' anymore either."
>
> And from that day on, he called us "the brothers from Emmanuel" and we called him "Brother Romero."[1]

The two denominations also organized church unity weeks, with some shared services. A Catholic laywoman recalled: "Monseñor Romero started holding these meetings frequently, calling them 'ecumenical' [interfaith], a word we weren't acquainted with." Sometimes Romero and a Protestant pastor both preached in a joint worship. "You should have heard how the people applauded for both . . . we could see how similar their messages were,"[2] the woman added.

A week of Prayer for Christian Unity in mid-January 1979 involved Protestant leaders from the United States. Six evening ecumenical services took place, alternating between Protestant and Catholic places of worship.

Ecumenical Support Abroad

After the 1977 murders of Fathers Grande and Navarro, and the arrests, torture, and expulsions of priests, Christians worldwide became aware of

1. Miguel Tomás Castro, in López Vigil, *Mosaic*, 134–35. (Heriberto Pérez was pastor of Emmanuel Baptist Church at the time.)

Erdozaín recalls that in the initial meeting the Baptists related that they had been invited to the presidential house, where they were offered money to help with their "mission." "Government officials told them that money that had been given to Catholics would now be given to them. The Baptists refused this kiss of Judas. They wanted to work with the persecuted Catholic Church in order to be on the side of the poor in El Salvador" (*Martyr*, 39).

2. Ernestina Rivera, in López Vigil, *Mosaic*, 215.

church persecution in El Salvador. Romero's "David and Goliath" story of an individual confronting both his government's and the Vatican's entrenched power won him sympathy and solidarity from Christians and non-Christians around the world. Many lent support, and universities and other organizations bestowed honors on him.

The Geneva-based World Council of Churches and the National Council of Churches of the United States sent two leaders to El Salvador in spring 1977 to express concern about the persecution of the Salvadoran church. These organizations hoped greater visibility in the world's eyes might afford Romero and his colleagues a degree of protection.

Presbyterian layman Dr. Jorge Lara-Braud was one of two envoys sent.[3] Romero's appearance did not jibe with what Lara-Braud expected: "He seemed shy and distracted, even a bit intimidated. Was this little man, dressed as a country priest, the controversial firebrand we had heard so much about?"[4]

Lara-Braud, who became Romero's friend over the next three years, later wrote, "[Romero] was a genuine ecumenist. Few things gave him greater pleasure than to welcome representatives from other Christian churches."[5]

Romero shared some of the theological underpinnings of his new ecumenism in his homily of December 19, 1978. The basis of his thinking resided in the Holy Spirit's mysterious workings: "Christ will also say of this Church: outside the limits of Catholicism perhaps there is more faith, more holiness. So we must not quench the Spirit. The Spirit is not the monopoly of a movement, even of a Christian movement or the hierarchy or the priesthood or some religious congregation."[6]

Worldwide Honors

In February 1978, Georgetown University of Washington, DC, granted Romero an honorary doctorate, despite protests from some of the Vatican curia. Founded and run by Jesuits, whose members faced persecution by

3. The other representative was Dr. Thomas J. Liggett. From Jorge Lara-Braud, foreword to *Martyr*, ix. At that time Lara-Braud served as director of the Council on Theology and Culture of the Presbyterian Church in the United States.

4. Ibid., x.

5. Ibid., ix.

6. Romero y Galdámez, *Homilies*, December 17, 1978.

El Salvador's military, Georgetown University took a special interest in the archdiocese.

El Salvador's poor and humble packed the Metropolitan Cathedral on the Tuesday afternoon of the ceremony. "Few had heard of Georgetown University before or knew what an honorary degree is, but they understood that their archbishop was receiving recognition from afar because he spoke for them," noted a biographer.[7]

Also in 1978 Englishman Julian Filochowski, then education coordinator of a British Catholic NGO,[8] gathered the signatures of 118 members of the British Parliament to nominate Archbishop Romero for the 1979 Nobel Peace Prize. "We understood that whether or not he won, just nominating him was a way of providing some protection for him," Filochowski said.[9]

Filochowski noted that neither the Salvadoran government nor its media reported on the prestigious nomination. Finally *La Prensa Gráfica* published the news in a two-inch article buried in its inner pages. Some people in the archdiocese decided it deserved wider attention.

"[They] enlarged the tiny article and turned it into a poster. 'Monseñor Romero nominated for the Nobel Peace Prize' it said," Filochowski related. "Posters were distributed in all of the parishes, and immediately they went up on the walls and doors of churches and chapels around the country. Everyone ended up hearing about it, and almost everyone was happy."[10]Although Mother Teresa of Calcutta won the prize that year, Filochowski succeeded in spotlighting Romero and his progressive diocese.

The nomination ended up strengthening Romero's fight for awareness of his country's situation in a second, unexpected way. It led to a delegation of three British parliamentarians visiting the country in November 1978. The emissaries met a large range of people, individuals holding positions of power as well as victims of violence. In National Guard headquarters, the deputation found a torture chamber. "After their visit they issued a report

7. Brockman, *A Life*, 106.

8. The Catholic Institute for International Relations (CIIR), in London. Now renamed "Progressio."

9. Julian Filochowski, in López Vigil, *Mosaic*, 233. In 2015, Filochowski chairs the London-based Archbishop Romero Trust, which has translated Romero's homilies and pastoral letters into English: http://www.romerotrust.org.uk.

10. Ibid., 233.

that left no doubt that human rights were grossly violated in El Salvador."[11] Word of Romero's and his colleagues' work ranged yet further.

In January 1980, Romero traveled to Belgium to receive an honorary doctorate from the University of Louvain.

Several weeks later, in early March 1980, the general secretary of Swedish Ecumenical Action visited El Salvador to bestow the organization's peace prize—a kind of alternative Nobel Peace Prize—on Archbishop Romero.[12] The Swedish ambassador to El Salvador also attended the March 9 mass at which the honor was presented.[13]

The mass itself became a tragic emblem of the country's anguish: the bodies of a Salvadoran professor and his Danish wife, both in their twenties, located four days earlier, were also present. Witnesses had seen the Salvadoran National Police abduct the couple on February 29. Despite intervention by the Inter-American Commission on Human Rights, they were not released. Their horribly tortured bodies were found on March 5 in an open grave on a beach.[14]

"Roberto's [the assassinated man's] mother had specifically asked for them to be here at this Mass . . ." Romero said in his diary. "She told me that her son had worked hard to improve the situation of the country and greatly admired the stance of our Church. Also, she felt drawn to this Mass and begged that the final prayers for them before they are taken to the cemetery be said here."[15]

During his homily, Romero said, "I am moved by the coincidence that as our companions from Sweden bring us a Peace Prize, a citizen of a neighboring country [Denmark] is laid out before us as though sorrowfully affirming the need to support the work on behalf of peace."[16]

11. Brockman, *A Life*, 149. Brockman supplied the names of the three parliamentarians: Lord Chitnis, Peter Bottomley, Dennis Canavan.

12. The general secretary of Swedish Ecumenical Action at the time was Reverend Per Arne Aglert.

13. The Swedish ambassador at the time was Henrik Ramel. Also present was Anders Kompass, secretary for Latin America of the Swedish Ecumenical Action.

14. The commission's summary of the investigation is at http://www.cidh.org/annualrep/84.85eng/ElSalvador6095.htm. The Inter-American Commission on Human Rights is a unit of the Organization of American States.

15. Romero y Galdámez, *Diary*, 515. The couple was Roberto Castellanos Braña, a twenty-nine-year-old professor, and his wife, Anette Mathiessen Castellanos, twenty-three.

16. Romero y Galdámez, *Homilies*, March 9, 1980.

As in the case of the parliamentarians' visit, the acclaim that brought Swedes to El Salvador underscored the conditions Romero courageously denounced. The visit served to spread knowledge of his efforts to other parts of the world.

Romero calls for justice from the pulpit. (photo credit, CIRIC)

Romero and President Carter

Romero reluctantly and very cautiously stepped into global politics when he felt obliged on his flock's behalf to challenge none other than the world's mightiest nation. The archbishop's acclaim and global platform gave weight to his words.

After the October 15, 1979, coup ousting the ruling general, the need to form a new government gave the United States an opening to further its agenda in El Salvador. The United States favored a ruling coalition of Christian Democrats and the hardline military officers with whom Washington bureaucrats enjoyed well-established relationships.

As observers put it, "Washington's oft-stated desire was to eliminate the extremes of Salvadorean political life and create a center where none had been allowed to exist for fifty years."[17] Oddly, however, rather than eliminate the extremes, the coalition favored by US officials would buoy the extremist elements of El Salvador's armed forces. Likewise, by excluding grassroots organizations, which represented a diverse 80 percent of the population,[18] Washington's plan could never create a true center.

The US government soon settled on Napoleón Duarte, a Christian Democrat, as its choice of key civilian to govern alongside El Salvador's armed forces, despite overt hostility from the military.[19] Salvadoran officers, however, would put up with Duarte if doing so assured US military aid would continue to flow to them.

The United States pushed for an agrarian reform program, which the Duarte–military junta agreed to. A law professor at the University of Washington in Seattle authored most of it, based on a similar program he had devised for the United States in Vietnam. It combined limited land redistribution with repression in order to undercut support for leftist groups in rural areas.[20]

Archbishop Romero understood that by design the agrarian project intended to isolate, if not destroy, the popular groups. The plan also represented yet one more initiative to be imposed on *campesinos* and *campesinas* by US officials and Salvadoran troops. These realizations alarmed the church leader.

Thus, as planned, El Salvador's military began to divide a few haciendas to give land parcels to rural families while it simultaneously unleashed a campaign of terror to destroy peasant organizations and kill their leaders.[21] A civilian cabinet member of the military–Christian Democrat junta resigned on March 26, 1980, citing the repression and giving an example:

17. Armstrong and Shenk, *Face of Revolution*, 138.

18. According to former US ambassador to El Salvador Murat W. Williams, cited in North, *Bitter Grounds*, 84.

19. Armstrong and Shenk, *Face of Revolution*, 138.

20. The professor was Roy Prosterman, PhD, at the University of Washington in Seattle. North, *Bitter Grounds*, 90.

21. Ibid., 85. The government declared a state of siege on March 5, 1980, when it enacted the agrarian reform. The state of siege effectively put the armed forces in charge

> Recently in one of the large estates taken over by the agrarian reform, uniformed members of the security forces accompanied by a masked person pointed out the directors of the self-management group and then these individuals were shot in front of their co-workers.[22]

On March 16, ten days after the launch of the Basic Law of Agrarian Reform, the human rights organization Amnesty International condemned its implementation, which involved troop deployment and terrorizing people in areas with the strongest popular organizations:

> In Chalantenango, a circle of fire was lit around a village to prevent local people from escaping; troops then entered the village, killing some forty people and abducting many others. . . . Troops operating in open coordination with the paramilitary organization ORDEN have shot or abducted peasants, razed villages and destroyed crops in Suchitoto township and Morazán [province], as well as Cuscatlán and Chalatenango.[23]

"To the Salvadorean army, any peasant was suspect, even children were subversive. By May, the 1980 death toll of noncombatants passed 1,400."[24]

In his diary entry of January 26, 1980, Romero stated: "We talked about the perception of El Salvador in the United States . . . It seems that they were alarmed by my last homily, in which I talked about a popular project[25] and did not support the Christian Democrats as much. Because for the United States, the Christian Democrats are the solution; they have promised to help them. We said that we do not have to please the United States or anyone else, but rather to look for the solution that is best for our country."[26]

---

of the reform's implementation.

22. Jorge Alberto Villacorta, undersecretary of agriculture in the second junta, as shared in Armstrong and Shenk, *Face of Revolution*, 146.

23. Amnesty International Report, as quoted in ibid., 145.

24. Armstrong and Shenk, *Face of Revolution*, 157.

25. By "popular project," Romero refers to initiatives by the popular organizations to coordinate their efforts and to unify the many smaller groups into one or more larger organizations.

26. Romero y Galdámez, *Diary*, 461.

While the Salvadoran state terrorized its citizens on behalf of so-called land reform, Archbishop Romero learned the United States planned to send military aid to El Salvador.[27]

After consulting with advisers and spending time in prayer, Romero decided to write a letter to then President Jimmy Carter. On February 17, 1980, the archbishop read the letter in his homily at the Sacred Heart Basilica, saying he would send it "after you [the people] give me your opinion of it."

> Dear Mr. President:
>
> In the last few days, a bit of news appeared in the national press which has disturbed me very much. According to the story, your government is studying the possibility of supporting the junta of our government with military and economic aid.
>
> Because you are a Christian and because you have demonstrated you want to defend the rights of all humans, I want to explain how I, as pastor, see this news and to give you a concrete recommendation.
>
> The information that the United States government is studying the way in which to build up the armaments of El Salvador greatly disturbs me. Reportedly, you plan to send military equipment and consultants to "train three Salvadoran battalions in logistics, communications and intelligence."[28] If in fact this information is correct, the contribution of your government will do nothing to support greater justice and peace in El Salvador. Without doubt, it will intensify injustice and the repression of the organized people who so many times have fought for their fundamental human rights.
>
> Unfortunately, the junta and, above all, the armed forces and the security corps have not shown their capacity to resolve, through practical and institutional politics, our grave national problems. Generally they have simply turned to repressive violence, producing a number of dead and wounded much greater than those of the previous military regimes whose systematic

27. In 1980, the United States remained firmly mired in the Cold War with the Soviet Union, thus responding to any perceived "communist" threat in the hemisphere. That the Sandinistas in Nicaragua, one of El Salvador's neighbors, had won their revolution in July 1979 strengthened US resolve to support the Salvadoran military in efforts to destroy grassroots organizations at any cost.

28. Here Romero is quoting an article: "Ayuda militar a El Salvador estudia Estados Unidos" [The United States considers military aid to El Salvador], *El Diario de Hoy*, February 15, 1980.

> violation of human rights was denounced by the Interamerican Commission on Human Rights itself. . . .
>
> If it is true that last November "a group of six Americans was in El Salvador distributing $200,000 worth of gas masks and bulletproof vests and giving instructions on the use of these against demonstrators,"[29] you yourself must know that from that moment the security corps, with greater personal protection and efficiency, has repressed the people even more violently by using deadly weapons.
>
> As a Salvadoran and as the archbishop of the Archdiocese of San Salvador, I have the obligation to see to it that faith and justice reign in my country. Therefore, if you truly want to defend human rights, I ask you:
>
> - to prohibit the sending of military aid to the Salvadoran government;
> - to guarantee that your government will not intervene directly or indirectly, with military, economic, diplomatic, or other pressures to try to determine the destiny of the Salvadoran nation.
>
> I hope that your religious feelings and your sensitivity to the defense of human rights will move you to accept my request, thus avoiding more bloodshed in this suffering country.[30]

The people approved the letter with their applause, and Romero sent it.

The letter upset both Vatican and Washington officials. Indeed, Romero soon heard that his homily had "caused a furor in Rome."[31] In his diary Romero speculated that the Jesuit provincial for Central America might need to go to Rome to meet with the Vatican Secretary of State "to explain the situation and show how the words of the homily are appropriate to the difficult situation of El Salvador."[32]

A month later, in his homily of March 16, 1980, Romero shared some key points of the US administration's reply to his letter to President Carter and his own feelings about its content:

29. Romero again quotes the military aid article.

30. Romero y Galdámez, *Homilies*. The excerpt is from Romero's proposed letter to President Carter that Romero read to those attending the mass he celebrated on February 17, 1980. In this same homily, Romero also encouraged the Christian Democrats in the governing junta to resign.

31. Romero y Galdámez, *Diary*, 493.

32. Ibid.

> The President's letter expresses his support for the Junta. He states: "It offers the best perspectives." I would say that this is a political judgment that admits discussion. . . .
>
> And then, regarding military aid: "The United States is not unaware of past unfortunate actions of the military." It is enough that these actions are known and so there should be a real fear in lending unconditional assistance.
>
> He also states in his letter that the United States will not intervene in the internal affairs of El Salvador. As we have always said, we hope that actions will verify the truthfulness of these words.[33]

Despite the pledge to stay out of El Salvador's internal affairs, during his last days of office in early January 1981, President Carter authorized $5 million in military aid and the placement of twenty US military trainers in the country. Romero's pleas may have delayed, but they did not stop, the aid that added fuel to El Salvador's tinderbox.

33. Romero y Galdámez, *Homilies*. The letter Romero quotes was written and signed by US Secretary of State Cyrus Vance, in the name of President Carter.

15. A Time to be Loved

(1977–1980)

THE RURAL MASSES OPENED their hearts to Archbishop Romero. Their history in El Salvador helps explain their attachment to him.

Today's *campesinos* and *campesinas* descend from dark-skinned indigenous women[1] and white Spanish conquistadors who arrived in the area starting in the 1520s. While some indigenous enclaves remained relatively untouched, most of the population eventually came to be mestizo, of mixed blood.

Despite this mixed and overlapping gene pool, El Salvador's wealthy families continued to pride themselves on their "Spanish blood" and light skins. They looked down upon peasant farmers, with contempt for their indigenous roots.[2]

In addition to this racist attitude to *campesinos* and *campesinas*, since the 1880s the wealthy found the rural poor's lifestyle—farming corn and beans for family use—inconvenient to their own plans. The elite desired to use the land to raise export coffee in order to modernize the country's economy.

A century after the coffee venture began, a researcher wrote in 1985: "The peasant continues to be an object of derision, despised and regarded as a backward obstacle to development."[3]

Until Vatican II reforms in the 1960s, a "tripod" command of military, government, and church worked in harmony to control the voiceless, voteless *campesinos*. In the 1970s, Father Rutilio Grande, the Passionist

1. Of the native Lempa, Pipil, and Maya peoples.

2. After 1932, the remnant Indian communities hid their Mayan identities. In that year, the Salvadoran army massacred some thirty thousand mostly indigenous Pipil in the coffee-growing highlands of western El Salvador. Survivors abandoned their native dress and ceased to speak their native Nahuatl in public. They wanted to blend in, to avoid being viewed as Indian (Armstrong and Shenk, *Face of Revolution*, 30).

3. North, *Bitter Grounds*, 27.

priests at the Los Naranjos Center, and other diocesan priests throughout the country surprised the poor when they served rural dwellers in a holistic manner. For the first time ever, these priests asked the *campesinos* and *campesinas* their opinions. One leg of the throne began to wobble as progressive members of the church stood beside the poor rather than continue to uphold the status quo.

A woman of Aguilares recalled her first meeting with Father Grande and his team, when they asked if she would help with an evangelization campaign: "I felt happy, included, and ready to help them. You know, a poor person like me really feels like she's been valued when she's taken into account. Up until that day, I imagined priests to be these distant and divine beings. I didn't even consider myself worthy of speaking with them. But these priests asked me to work right alongside them."[4]

In 1977, a man active in a Christian base community felt bold enough to write newly named Archbishop Oscar Romero to ask, "What is your message, Monseñor? We would like to know if you are going to stand with the rich, or with us, the poor."[5] Even fifteen years earlier, it would have been near impossible to imagine a poor Salvadoran daring to question authority.

After the single archdiocesan mass to demonstrate a church united in outrage over Father Grande's murder, the poor learned where Romero would stand. When from the pulpit he denounced depravations they and family members suffered—killings, torture, disappearances—they offered him unstinted devotion.

Romero had always reached out to his parishioners. In both the San Miguel and Santiago de María dioceses, he visited outlying villages to offer mass, marry couples, and preside over first Communions and other sacraments. He called the faithful to him with a loudspeaker installed on his Jeep.

As archbishop, Romero ditched the loudspeakers and opted for more egalitarian face-to-face conversations. He visited communities, often at their invitation. He didn't go as Official Dispenser of wisdom and sacraments, but rather to interact with, even learn from, villagers and Christian base community members, many of them illiterate. Rather than call people to come to him, Romero opted to go directly to them.

4. Ernestina Rivera, in López Vigil, *Mosaic*, 87–88.

5. Moisés Calles, in ibid., 85.

At age sixty, however, he needed to reacclimate himself, physically and emotionally, to the rigors of these outings. A community member recalled how one of Romero's first visits ended on a sour note:

> It was during the intense heat of that day that Monseñor Romero . . . came to visit eight of the *cantones* [hamlets] of Aguilares. They weren't the kind of roads you could travel by car. To get there you had to walk, and he got really tired out from going here and there all day long. . . . Towards the end of the day, he was irritated and dripping with sweat.
>
> We had prepared a surprise for him so that he would feel some relief. "We fixed you some sweet corn *atol* [a beverage], Monseñor. Would you like a little taste?"
>
> "No, I just want to get out of here!"
>
> And he left. He said he wanted to get back to San Salvador as soon as he could, and he even said it like he was mad. We were left standing with the *atol* and the other things we had fixed for him. My *comadre* [close woman friend] and I were so disappointed that we had tears rolling down our faces.
>
> Later we were told that when he returned to the capital he realized how poorly he'd behaved, and was embarrassed about having turned down what we had offered.
>
> One day he returned to our area. He had thought about his mistake so much that he even asked us for forgiveness.
>
> "Please forgive me. I had never seen such poverty. I just wasn't used to it all."
>
> That day when we offered him a big gourd full of *atol*, he accepted.[6]

Romero incrementally learned from his mistakes to avoid hurting others in similar ways. On a later visit to a different community, the archbishop became exhausted after hiking a half hour or so uphill, as a priest accompanying him reported:

> In the distance we saw the outline of an *amate* tree, a promise of respite. When we arrived at the tree, the coolness of its shade restored Monseñor's ability to speak.
>
> "Why don't we stay and have the Mass here where it's cool?" he said, wiping the sweat from his face. "We can call the people to come here to the shade."

6. Rosa Alonso, in ibid., 127–28.

> "All right!" I said. I started to go ahead to let people know about the change, but I'd only taken a few steps when he called out to me:
>
> "Wait. Don't go."
>
> "No?"
>
> "No. I have to make it up there. The *campesinos* shouldn't have to adjust their plans for me. I should adjust my plans for them."[7]

Romero soon relished his visits to outlying communities. Once word spread, he received invitations from all corners of the diocese. Often children would meet him a distance from the community and accompany him on the last leg of the hike.

On another occasion, the archbishop visited a housing project in which people had built their own homes—530 of them. Romero insisted upon stopping at each one: "What you've built with so much effort deserves to be seen," the archbishop exclaimed.[8] He had learned to go the extra mile for those living on society's margins.

The People's Archbishop

How proposals would affect the poor became the yardstick by which Archbishop Romero evaluated plans, whether suggested by the government, the church hierarchy, or other officials. "We will always measure our actions according to how things are going for the people," he told one US official who harped on Romero to cooperate with the Salvadoran government.[9]

The life of Jesus, who was born into a humble family, molded Romero's theology, outlook, and attitudes. In one homily he told the assembled:

> If Jesus would have accomplished his incarnation today, if today he were a man of thirty years and were here in the Cathedral, we would not be able to distinguish him from anyone else. Jesus, a man of thirty years, a *campesino* from Nazareth, present here in

7. Jon Cortina, in ibid., 153–54. The community was El Jicarón.

8. Antonia Ferrer, in ibid., 275–76. Because the community took part in an organized project, the government targeted it for repression. "They're using this house-building stuff as a front to organize subversive activity," Ferrer said of the army's attitude to the community. She said the army killed their entire community council in a single day—and also killed the leaders elected to replace them.

9. Roberto Cuéllar and José Simán, in ibid., 230. The meeting took place in early 1978 with Terence Todman, newly named US undersecretary of state for inter-American affairs.

> the Cathedral like any other *campesino* from our villages—this was the Son of God who became flesh and we did not know him, a person completely like us."[10]

Such a proclamation represents an empowering message for individuals who have been marginalized and looked down upon from their earliest days.

Romero himself came to see Jesus in each humble, suffering peasant. He intentionally put them ahead of others in his priorities. At his office in the capital, he let officials and people with resources wait while he spoke with poor people who came to see him.

He explained why to one of his secretaries:

> I'm always going to receive any *campesino* who shows up here at any time of day, whether I'm in a meeting or not . . . My fellow bishops all have cars. The parish priests can take buses, and they can afford to wait. But what about the *campesinos*? They come walking for miles, face all kinds of dangers, and sometimes they haven't even eaten . . . The *campesinos* never ask me for anything. They just talk to me about the things going on in their lives, and that alone seems to help them.[11]

In return for his attention and advocacy, they flooded him with love. They showed their love with their repeated applause during his homilies. They displayed it by inviting him to visit their homes and communities. And they demonstrated their affection with gifts from what few belongings they had.

Once, an eighty-year-old woman walked sixty-some miles from the Honduran border to San Salvador to give Romero a gift. Having arrived, however, the plaza outside the cathedral was so crowded she could not make her way to Monseñor. A priest offered to deliver her gifts—two eggs and a rumpled one-colón bill, worth forty cents at the time—to the archbishop. Romero thanked her by name in a later mass, which she likely heard on the radio.[12] Niña Remedios trudged a hundred and twenty miles round trip to present her beloved archbishop with a gift from her meager possessions.

A priest related the following anecdote illustrative of Romero's relationship with *campesinos*:

10. Romero y Galdámez, *Homilies*, December 17, 1978.

11. Coralia Godoy, in López Vigil, *Mosaic*, 149.

12. Antonio Fernández Ibáñez, in ibid., 218–20. The woman, Niña Remedios, hailed from Nuevo Edén de San Juan.

> I had to do something at the archdiocesan office one day, I don't remember what. [Monseñor] was in the middle of meeting with some priests, and some *campesinos* came in, bringing him some chickens as a gift. It made me laugh because Monseñor had them there under the table, and they would cluck and make noise and get away from him, and he'd grab them by their feathers and put them back in the box, and they'd get out again. The whole thing was just hilarious.[13]

Despite his many years living in cities and associating with "cultivated" people, Romero was a country person at heart who felt at home with the rural poor—and their animals and their food, especially the beans on which he had been raised. Romero knew from his own childhood what it meant to live without amenities, to have to walk hours and hours carrying wood or bundles. Now, at the peak of his worldly power, he circled around to embrace his roots.

A nonbeliever, a YSAX radio volunteer, related another story expressing Romero's relationship with the poor and suffering. The young woman desired to see a Christian base community, "not for the "religious aspect, but rather to see how people were organized and how it all worked."

> We went to La Libertad by bus, and people were waiting for us there. It was two more hours on horseback. The riding partner assigned to me was an eight-year-old boy, Emilio—he rode in front and I behind. . . .
>
> When the horse started moving, I started to smell a nauseating odor of something rotting. Where was the stench coming from? I noticed the boy's foot. It was one big open wound full of worms.
>
> "Hey, what happened to you there?"
>
> "I cut myself with a machete."
>
> [They arrived in the community high on rocky slopes suitable only to grow sorghum, where they spent the rest of the day.]
>
> When it was late in the afternoon and we were ready to leave, I spoke with Emilio's mother.
>
> "Let me take him to be treated. If I don't, I'm afraid the boy is going to lose his leg."
>
> She gave me her permission, and I took him to San Salvador with me. Emilio had never been out of his *cantón*. When he first saw the cars he asked, "Are we in San Salvador now?"
>
> "This is it? Do you like it?

13. Carlos Cabarrús, in ibid., 212.

"I would like it more if you would do me a favor, ma'am. There's something I'd really like."

[She speculated he might request a bicycle or a trip to the ocean.]

"What is it? Tell me."

"I want to meet Monseñor Romero."

That was what he wanted most in his eight-year-old life.

He had to be in San Salvador for two months for his leg to heal, and in that time he got to know other things: streets, cars, streetlights, escalators, elevators, stores, amusement parks . . .

"Ma'am, do you remember? You owe me a favor," he would remind me from time to time.

One day in the hospital where the nuns were treating him, I saw Monseñor arrive. Emilio saw him too . . .

"Monseñor," I told him, "I'm here with one of your admirers, and what this little guy wants most in life is to meet you."

"Well, let's go get acquainted . . ."

He put his hand on the boy's head and started to walk with him. . . .

He sat down and put Emilio on his lap.

"Tell me about your *cantón*. I've never been there."

I can't describe the look of joy on the face of that child. He was happier than if Santa Claus had appeared on Christmas Day. They spent a good long while talking with each other.

Afterwards, he didn't even want to take a bath because Monseñor had touched him. And from that day on, his main concern was to not forget anything so that when he got back home, he could tell everybody what the two of them had talked about. . . .[14]

Protective Father

One rural woman remarked, "For us, Monseñor was like a father who was always looking out for us."[15]

Thus, *campesinos* and *campesinas* fled to the archdiocesan offices to escape murder in the hinterlands after the military unleashed a campaign of repression in early 1980. (The offensive accompanied a new agrarian reform law—Romero called it a government formula of "reform with

14. Margarita Herrera, in ibid., 268–70. After a cured Emilio went home to share his stories, he lived only two more years. In March 1980, he was killed with the rest of his family when the National Guard attacked and burned down his entire village.

15. María Otilia Núñez, in ibid., 222.

repression," the purpose of which was to eliminate organized, aware communities and their leaders.)

"They were all coming so that Monseñor Romero would protect them from the National Guard, from the repression. They came with so much trust in him,"[16] said one of three doctors attending the displaced. The physician reported some two thousand peasants had already taken refuge in the patios and gardens of the archdiocesan offices, with hundreds more in other church buildings, and an ongoing daily influx of new arrivals. "The only crime those refugees had committed was to be poor and to be part of an organized group," the doctor said.[17]

Romero engaged the Catholic relief agency Caritas to help put his words into concrete actions. With his authorization, Caritas set up various refugee centers to feed and care for the displaced, the great majority of them women, children and elderly persons.[18] In other words, Archbishop Romero both "talked the talk and walked the walk."

As journalist María López Vigil noted, a basic rule of human behavior states that the more authority an official attains, the more he distances himself from the common people. Romero broke this rule in a grand and mighty way, turning it on its head.[19]

For this, El Salvador's poor and marginalized dearly loved him.

16. Francisco Román, in ibid., 388. Women, children, and elderly persons represented 95 percent of the refugees, Román said.

17. Ibid.

18. In his homily of March 23, 1980, Romero cited a recently released Amnesty International report stating at least thirty-five hundred rural poor persons had fled their homes to the capital to escape persecution in the first weeks of March.

19. Palumbo, "María López Vigil," 8–9.

16. A Time to Die

(October 1979–March 1980)

IN THE HANDFUL OF months between the mid-October 1979 coup by young military officers and the early March 1980 breakdown of the second ruling junta, El Salvador hurtled toward derailment. Armed conflict seemed inevitable.

Monseñor Romero refused to accept war. Between the several daily masses he celebrated, as well as the countless religious festivities and observations he attended in parishes, the archbishop was called from one meeting to another to advise, encourage, and mediate among principal players. He hoped to salvage the peaceful change he envisioned when respected civilians first joined military officers in a governing junta.

Romero took a thrashing from many of his supporters for his stance.[1] Even a few of his own priests believed any accommodation or conversation with military men amounted to selling out their vision of a just society. (*See* chapter 14.)

Romero's last four months of diary entries, December 1979 through March 20, 1980, catalog the incredible array and number of meetings to which he was invited in the elusive search for peace. He met with Salvadoran military officers and government ministers and US government envoys; representatives of international church and human rights associations; leaders of people's organizations, including the armed factions; countless journalists from around the globe; workers occupying factories and factory owners; hostages and family members of kidnapped officials; progressive business leaders; and others.

1. On December 19, 1979, for example, Romero recorded, "I went with a delegation of priests . . . to talk with those [members of the February 28 Popular Leagues] occupying the chancery. . . . We talked at length about different matters; I even heard them express great lack of confidence in the way that the Church has acted, as if it had turned around one hundred and eighty degrees—their phrase, . . . as if we had betrayed the interests of the people, which bothers me a good deal given the sincere way that I always try to defend the interests of our people from the perspective of the gospel" (*Diary*, 418).

On December 28, 1979, he noted his regret at missing several events that day, among them a parish feast day celebration, a seminarians' gathering, and a pastoral meeting. "I could not go because there are so many things pending, since many members of the government and the army are coming to consult me. It is an indication of the Church's prestige, and I try to help in all sincerity without abandoning my pastoral role. Because of the political situation of the country, at this time I must be at my post [in his office] to attend to these consultations."[2]

Enormous Hands

Perhaps more remarkable is that Romero maintained this rigorous schedule in an ever-increasingly tense atmosphere. Almost every day brought a new crisis. Refugees fled rural repression. Security forces attacked demonstrators. Guerrilla factions took foreign ambassadors hostage. Right-wing death squads assassinated prominent persons and bombed key buildings. People's organizations occupied churches. Guerrillas and military forces engaged in face-offs, with explosions heard citywide.

The Jesuit provincial put it well when he said, "During those months [following the coup], Monseñor Romero seemed like a pair of enormous hands trying to hold El Salvador together when it was at the point of breaking into a million pieces."[3] War's possibility tormented Romero, the provincial said, and the anguish drove him.

In January 1980, Romero lamented what he termed "a psychosis in the atmosphere . . . an expectancy almost equal to waiting for a civil war." He added, "But our duty as church is to keep hope alive, to stay above all the false rumors . . ."[4]

Keeping hope alive became increasingly problematic, however. On Tuesday, February 19, 1980, the day after he dispatched his letter to President Carter, an urgent phone call awakened Romero. The voice on the other end informed him a bomb had blown up the YSAX radio transmitter. That night another bomb exploded in the library of the University of Central America, run by Jesuits in San Salvador.[5]

2. Romero y Galdámez, ibid., 426–27. Romero sent other priests to represent him at church events he had to miss.

3. César Jerez, in López Vigil, *Mosaic*, 337.

4. Romero y Galdámez, *Diary*, 453.

5. Several weeks later, on Monday, March 10, Father Ramiro Jiménez found an

"Obviously these are the plots of the extreme right against the voice of the church and against the calls for social justice," the archbishop said.[6] Fortunately no one was hurt or killed in either bombing.

The destruction of YSAX engendered worldwide sympathy and financial support for its rebuilding. The event undoubtedly reminded Romero that powerful people wanted him silenced. A number of the archbishop's actions and remarks in the following weeks showed his awareness of the likelihood of violence personally touching him.

Romero had ignored the many death threats he received since taking office in early 1977. He could not disregard a more credible warning delivered after the radio bombing. In his February 23 diary entry, he noted he had debated whether to attend a young people's invitation in the town of Sonsonate in the Santa Ana diocese that day, saying, "The nuncio (pope's ambassador) in Costa Rica has advised me of the danger of threats against me again, and he has told me I should be careful."[7]

Romero did attend the young people's event and was glad he did: "Their reception was very warm; my absence would have caused great disappointment. I tried to fulfill their expectations, later blessing a first aid clinic that they have built on their own initiative. I believe that, even though it is outside my jurisdiction, it is still Church and provides encouragement for the efforts of all humankind."[8]

The YSAX bombing hardly shut Romero up. In his Sunday homily the following day, February 24, 1980, Romero denounced the act with strong words for the oligarchy:

> This attack is an attempt to silence the prophetic and pastoral voice of the archdiocese simply because it is trying to be the voice of the voiceless. . . . The authors of this attack want to prevent people from knowing the truth. They do not want people to acquire criteria that will enable them to judge what is happening in the

---

attaché case containing seventy-two sticks of dynamite at the basilica. It had been set to detonate, but failed to do so, during the previous afternoon's five o'clock funeral mass Romero said for Dr. Mario Zamora, an assassinated civilian who had participated in the junta. Romero recorded, "The bomb, which had been placed near the altar of St. Martha, was disarmed by police experts, who said it was strong enough to have destroyed the entire basilica and everyone who was there at the time" (Ibid., 518).

6. Ibid., 494.

7. Ibid., 500–501. Romero also worried that attending an event in Bishop Barrera's diocese might aggravate tensions between the two men.

8. Ibid., 501.

country. They do not want people to unite and cry out: *Enough! Put an end to the exploitation and domination of the Salvadoran oligarchy!*[9]

In this homily, Romero also shared some of the many messages he received expressing solidarity, sorrow, and renewed defiance in the wake of the transmitter's destruction. A *Who's Who* of Latin America's progressive Catholic leaders signed a telegram the archbishop read to the congregation.[10]

Later in the sermon, Romero returned to the theme of the elite's stubborn resistance to change with yet tougher, more specific, and damning language:

> The dynamiting of YSAX is only a symbol. It shows that the oligarchy, seeing the danger of losing the complete domination that they have over investment and other agricultural exports, as well as their near-monopoly of land, are defending their selfish interests, not with arguments, not with popular support, but with the only thing they have. They use their money to buy weapons and pay mercenaries who massacre the people and strangle every lawful cry for justice and freedom.[11]

9. Romero y Galdámez, *Homilies,* February 24, 1980. The italics, those of the Archbishop Romero Trust translator, reflect Romero's emphasis when he spoke the words.

10. Ibid.: "It is wonderful to see the many expressions of solidarity that have been expressed in our favor as a result of the attack . . . and at this time I want to express my gratitude to all of you. I never imagined that on this first Sunday of Lent that I would have here in my hands the support of a very well-known group of bishops who sent me the following telegram:
Bishop Romero. With great sorrow we have just read about the criminal destruction of the Archdiocesan radio station. We see this as another sign of the persecution that is directed against you and the priests and women religious and the poor and oppressed people of El Salvador. We express our solidarity with your courageous and prophetic homily of February 17. We are grateful to you and to your Church for having faithfully lived the preferential option for the poor. Your brothers in the Episcopate. Helder Cámara, Archbishop of Recife, Brazil; José María Pires, Archbishop of Soa, Brazil; Samuel Ruiz, Bishop of Chiapas, Mexico; Jesús Calderón, Bishop of Puno, Peru; Pedro Casadáliga, Bishop of San Félix, Brazil; José A. Yaguno, Apostolic Vicar of Tarahumara, Mexico; Jorge Hurton, Bishop in Chile; Tomás Balduino, Bishop of Goyas, Brazil; Marcelo Caballería, Bishop of Guarabira, Brazil; Mauro Morelli, Auxiliary Bishop of São Paulo, Brazil; Alfredo Bowok, Auxiliary Bishop of São Paulo, Brazil." (The bishops were meeting in Brazil when they received the news and dictated the telegram.)

11. Ibid., February 24, 1980.

Then Romero included some sobering personal news. His name had appeared on a credible list of people the oligarchy wanted dead:

> I hope this call of the Church will not further harden the hearts of the oligarchs but will move them to conversion. Let them share what they are and have. Let them not keep on silencing with violence the voice of those of us who offer this invitation. Let them not keep on killing those of us who are trying to achieve a more just sharing of the power and wealth of the country.
>
> I speak in the first person, because this week I received notice that I am on the list of those who are to be eliminated next week. But let it be known that no one can any longer kill the voice of justice.[12]

A biographer remarked, "Unless they were well substantiated, Romero did not take threats seriously, much less bother to mention them in his homilies. That he mentioned this one in so dramatic a fashion showed that he regarded it as indeed serious."[13]

Romero and six other priests[14] had planned to go to Guatemala for an annual spiritual retreat the final week of February. El Salvador's deteriorating political situation and concerns over the archbishop's safety led them to decide instead to remain in country. They met at a Passionist Sisters' retreat house in the hills above the capital.[15]

Other than this change of venue, Romero did nothing to protect himself, although the Salvadoran military extended him security on more than one occasion. On September 7, 1979, a colonel had offered the archbishop a bulletproof car. Romero told him he could not ride in safety while his flock lived with no security, and he asked the official to protect people in zones where military operations created terror.[16]

By the time of the late-February 1980 threat, Romero was routinely taking precautions to avoid other people being killed alongside him. He

12. Ibid.

13. Brockman, *A Life*, 233.

14. The six were priests of the Chalatenango diocese: Fathers Fabián Amaya, Efraín López, Eduardo Alas, Sigfredo Salazar, Héctor Figueroa, Gabriel Rodríguez.

15. In Planes de Renderos.

16. Romero y Galdámez, *Diary*, 322. The officer, Colonel Iraheta, served as assistant secretary of the Ministry of Defense. In his earlier July 22, 1979, homily, Romero had publicly stated, "I want to repeat what I have said before. The shepherd does not want security while they give no security to his flock."

drove his car alone whenever feasible and had as few people as possible accompany him to places where he might be targeted.

In his retreat notes, Romero wrote that he had expressed his fear of death to his confessor, the elderly Father Secundo Azcue:

> It's difficult for me to accept a violent death, which in these circumstances is very possible; . . . Father encouraged me, telling me my attitude should be one of giving over my life to God, however my life may end. God's grace will help me through whatever may come. Jesus Christ stood by the martyrs and, if necessary, I will feel him very close when delivering up my last breath. But more valuable than what happens at the moment of death is surrendering all my life to him, to live for him.[17]

Azcue later compared Romero's anguish to Jesus's distress in the garden of Gethsemene when Jesus knew he'd soon be arrested. "Archbishop Romero foresaw his very probable and imminent death. He felt terror at it as Jesus did in the garden. But he did not leave his post and his duty, ready to drink the chalice that the Father might give him to drink."[18]

Mincing No Words

Despite, or perhaps because of, the seeming nearness of death, Romero's March 1980 homilies rank as his most courageous. They are also the best remembered. The archbishop minced no words. In his homily of Sunday, March 23, 1980, the archbishop raised his voice to call for conversion reminiscent of the prophet Jonah imploring Nineveh's inhabitants to mend their ways.[19]

The rebuilt, or "new YSAX," broadcast the March 23, 1980, service, as did the shortwave radio station in Costa Rica that began transmitting Romero's Sunday masses after the bombing.[20] Following a listing of the week's killings and tortures, an especially long, gruesome inventory, and right before his concluding sentence, Romero made a daring plea:

17. Romero y Galdámez, *Ejercicios espirituales*, 41–51. Delgado also provides the Spanish text of Romero's retreat entries (*Biografia*, 188–91).

18. As quoted by Brockman, *A Life*, 233.

19. Jonah 3. Unlike the Salvadoran military's response to Romero, the inhabitants of Nineveh heeded Jonah and dressed themselves in the sackcloth of repentance.

20. Radionoticias del Continente. Its station in Costa Rica had also been bombed.

> I'd like to make a special appeal to the men of the army, and especially to the rank and file of the National Guard, the Police, and the various barracks. Brothers, each one of you is one of us. We are the same people. The *campesinos* you kill are your own brothers and sisters.
>
> When you hear a man ordering you to kill, remember instead the words of God: Thou shalt not kill! God's law must prevail. No soldier is obliged to obey an order contrary to the law of God. No one has to fulfill an immoral law. It is time that you come to your senses and obey your consciences rather than sinful commands.
>
> The church, defender of the rights of God, the law of God, and the dignity of each human being, cannot remain silent in the face of such abominations. We want the government to take seriously the fact that reforms stained with so much blood are worth nothing.
>
> In the name of God, and in the name of our tormented people who have suffered so much and whose laments cry out to heaven, I beseech you, I beg you, I order you in the name of God: Stop the repression![21]

The congregation broke into applause five times during this appeal for civil disobedience and clapped for a half minute at its end, "the most deafening, longest rounds of applause ever heard" in the basilica, according to the radio crew, who at first mistook the buzzing created by the ovations as radio malfunctions.[22] After the service, Romero stood on the steps of the Sacred Heart Basilica to greet the many individuals thronged to speak with him. He then held a lengthy press conference with foreign journalists, followed by a short private meeting.

A biographer describes Romero's ensuing visit with his friends:

> It was after 1 p.m. when he arrived at the Barrazas' house with [his friend] Salvador. He felt satisfied but tired, and he took off his shoes and put up his feet to watch a puppet show on television with the family. This was his favorite place to relax, especially for Sunday dinner. . . . The children drew near and he played and teased with them, throwing drops of water and a pillow or two. Little Virginia, his godchild, mischievously pulled a gray hair from his head.
>
> At dinner he would usually keep watching the puppets on television, but today he did not want to. He was silent and took off

21. Romero y Galdámez, *Homilies*, February 24, 1980.

22. Jacinto Bustillo and Felipe Pick, in López Vigil, *Mosaic*, 399.

> his glasses, which was unusual. At table he was unusually quiet; he gave Eugenia a silent look as though he wanted to tell her something, and tears came to his eyes. The family wondered what was wrong. Then he began to talk about his best friends, recounting their virtues. He lay down to rest after dinner.[23]

In this and a couple other similar interactions, Romero continued to grieve in his garden of Gethsemene, not because, like Jesus, he felt abandoned, but because he would miss life and his friends.

A Single Shot

The next day, Monday, March 24, Romero was scheduled to offer an anniversary mass for Sara Meardi de Pinto, the mother of a friend and newspaper owner whose print shop had been bombed two weeks earlier.[24] Friends expressed concern that the archbishop's name had been published in newspaper announcements as the priest presiding at the six o'clock evening service. The notices also named the venue: the chapel of the Divine Providence cancer hospital, where he resided. Romero refused requests to allow another priest to say the mass in his place. The small gathering consisted of friends and family of the deceased, and some of the patients, nurses, and nuns who worked or lived at the hospital.

Romero concluded his ten-minute homily, as he often did, with an invitation to those present to participate in the sacrament of Eucharist, or Holy Communion: "So let us join together intimately in faith and hope at this moment of prayer for Dona Sarita and ourselves."[25]

A single loud shot rang out.[26]

23. Brockman, *A Life*, 242.

24. The friend was Jorge Pinto, who ran a weekly newspaper, *El Independiente*.

25. As quoted in Brockman, *A Life*, 244–45. In his note 44 for chapter 10 (274), Brockman explains that Romero's "final words about the eucharist may be the reason for false reports that he was shot during the offertory or while elevating the [Communion] host."

26. According to the UN Truth Commission report, Judge Atilio Ramírez Amaya ordered the Polyclinic Hospital to perform an autopsy: "A small entry wound barely five millimeters in diameter in the right thorax indicated the point of entry of the bullet. It had fragmented without exiting the Archbishop's body, causing fatal internal bleeding. Three fragments of the bullet were extracted for further study. Judge Ramírez Amaya maintained the bullet used must have been a .22 or similar. Going by the weight of the fragments, the National Police confirmed the bullet was a .22 caliber but did not reach any more precise conclusions. Following an attempt to assassinate him at his home on

A biographer describes what ensued:

> Archbishop Romero was standing behind the altar, facing the people. He slumped to the floor behind the altar, at the foot of the large crucifix. The congregants were stunned for a moment; some crouched in the pews. Several nuns and other people ran to him, and turned him onto his back. A photographer present for the mass began to take pictures. Romero was unconscious, gasping, blood pouring from his mouth and nose. The bullet had entered his left breast and lodged in his back. Fragments of the bullet scattered through his chest, causing heavy internal bleeding.
>
> Blood was turning the violet vestment and white alb red as the people carried him from the chapel to a small truck outside. Down the drive, down the street, down the hill it went, five minutes, to the Policlínica hospital. In the emergency room, he lay on a table, still gasping, strangling on his own blood, still unconscious, as the nun on emergency-room duty probed for a vein in his arm to start a transfusion. The veins had collapsed from lack of blood. In a few minutes he stopped gasping and was dead.[27]

"Bishop Oscar Romero had already offered his life and, for that reason, they could not take it away from him," one of the archbishop's priest friends commented. "They could only steal it from his people."[28]

March 27, Judge Ramírez Amaya tendered his resignation and left the country" ("Madness to Hope,"120).

27. Brockman, *A Life*, 244–45. Others, including human rights lawyer Roberto Cuéllar, who saw Romero's body at the chapel, say the archbishop was dead before his body was taken to the hospital. See *Last Journey*, chapter 8.

28. Erdozaín, *Martyr*, 2.

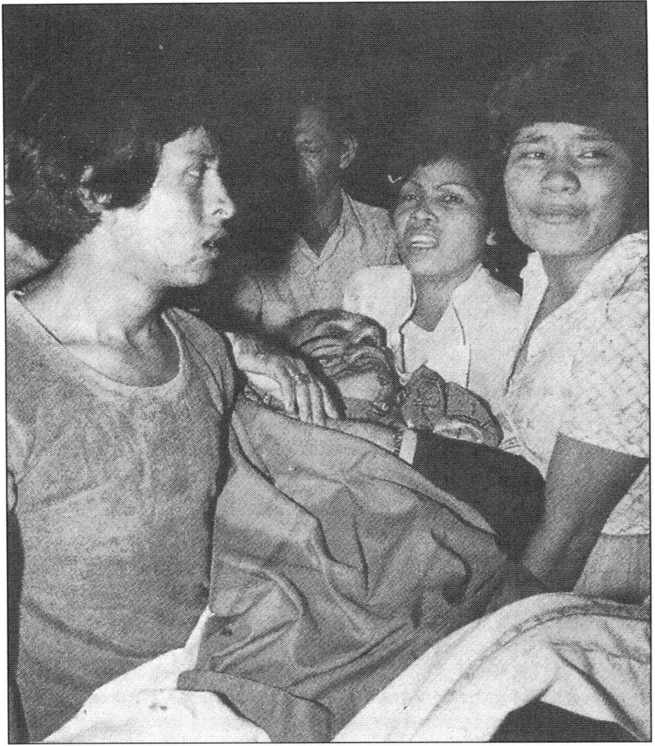

Women carry Monseñor, shot moments earlier, to a vehicle headed to the hospital. (photo credit Eulalio Pérez)

A grand theft it was, and Romero's flock reacted with disbelief and grief. Although all knew of the ongoing threats Romero received, and many heard virulent hate talk about him on TV in the weeks prior to his assassination, the idea that someone would actually murder an archbishop—during a mass, no less—remained inconceivable.

On Tuesday, Romero's embalmed body was taken to the basilica for a mass and viewing.[29] Meanwhile, the organization[30] then occupying the Metropolitan Cathedral cleaned and vacated it so that Romero's wake could

29. Because Romero's heart remained in fairly good shape, after being embalmed it was buried separately at the cancer hospital where he lived. The nuns planted an attractive little grotto next to his house and buried the archbishop's heart below a statue of the Virgin Mary. *See* Valencia, "El corazón."

30. The Bloque Popular Revolucionario, or Popular Revolution Bloc, a coalition of popular organizations.

be held at this larger church, and some priests, nuns, and base community members began a fast in it. Some of them hung a large banner at the cathedral entrance proclaiming that the papal nuncio; bishops Alvarez, Aparicio, Barrera, Revelo, and their secretary Fredy Delgado; members of the ruling junta; and the US ambassador were not welcome inside. Church officials demanded the banner be removed, but the order went unheeded.

On Wednesday, a procession of several thousand accompanied Romero's body as it was moved to the cathedral, where long lines of mourners filed by the coffin from early morning to late at night for the rest of the week. Many left flowers.

One participant recalled, "Arrangements were made for buses, and huge numbers of *campesinos* came to his wake at the Cathedral. Some came on foot. They came from all over the country, from every *cantón*, from every corner. We men cried the same as the women. . . . There were children there, too—little kids who already knew what a great loss it was."[31]

Funeral Mayhem

To accommodate the mourners who jammed the Plaza Libertad for Romero's funeral mass on March 30, Palm Sunday, the organizers turned the cathedral steps into an improvised altar with Romero's coffin present. The nuncio, some thirty bishops, and three hundred priests from El Salvador and around the world concelebrated the mass with Cardinal Ernesto Corripio, of Mexico, sent as the pope's representative. Of the five Salvadoran bishops, only Bishop Rivera y Damas attended.

Corripio was giving the homily when a bomb went off near the National Palace, also located on the plaza. The peaceful ceremony turned into panicked mayhem.[32]

Romero's Protestant friend Jorge Lara-Braud of the US National Council of Churches provided a close-up view of what happened in the cathedral after the explosion:

> The crowd started to run, terrified, away from the Palace. Immediately you could hear the sound of gunfire all around. Thousands of

31. Moisés Calles, in López Vigil, *Mosaic*, 414.

32. Film footage of the funeral, with a voice-over of Romero's March 23, 1980, homily instructing soldiers not to obey orders to kill, can be seen in Carrigan and Weber, *Last Journey*, chapter 9.

> people started running toward us like a massive wave. Behind us, there was only the empty Cathedral. . . .
>
> The San Salvador Cathedral can't adequately hold more than 3,000 people standing up. After half an hour of battle in the plaza, more than twice that many were squeezed inside, and there were still many others outside pushing to get in.
>
> People were standing on all the last available spaces, including the main altar. We couldn't move at all, and soon it got to where we could barely breathe. The building shook with the blasts of bombs, and a terrible echo amplified the noise of the firing guns. All of this was juxtaposed over a background of weeping and prayers rising up from every corner.
>
> I tried to control my panic by looking out for my neighbors, praying with them and trying to keep them calm with comforting words . . .
>
> I was in the second line of people counting from the wall . . . On my left, in the line behind me, a woman was praying to God as she was beginning to die. I could barely turn my head toward her, but that's all I could do. I was a Presbyterian lay person, but I improvised the Catholic last rites. "Your sins are forgiven. Go in God's Peace," I prayed. The woman died but she remained standing. There was no place where she could lay to rest on the floor. In some places, people were able to lift those who'd fainted or died over their heads, but no one knew where to put them. . . .[33]

Most of the up to forty persons who died at the funeral were elderly women trampled or asphyxiated in the "no room to breathe" cathedral.

The cathedral remained packed for two hours while gunfire resounded. Finally, Cardinal Corripio and other bishops and priests were able to get close enough to Romero's coffin—transported fingertip to fingertip over the crowd to where he would be entombed in the cathedral—to continue the funeral service. In the chaos, the Eucharist hosts and wine were lost, as well as prayer books for a responsive reading.

"Then Samuel Ruiz, the bishop of Chiapas [Mexico], took a little book of prayers out of his pocket, and they used that to say a few prayers before burying him. Everything was done in a hurry. The crypt was already open. They put the coffin in quickly. And even more quickly, the masons started to close it over with cement and bricks . . ."[34]

33. Jorge Lara-Braud, in López Vigil, *Mosaic*, 417, 418–19.

34. María Julia Hernández, in ibid., 421.

Later that day, in what one observer termed a "rambling statement,"[35] the government blamed the Coordinating Commission (of the popular organizations) for the bombings and shootings. Twenty-four of the foreign visitors issued a statement contrary to the government's version. Witnesses had seen shooting from the second floor of the National Palace, and many believed the bomb also went off at or near the palace.[36]

Some twenty years later, the United Nations Truth Commission, evidently unable to discern the truth in this case with a high degree of certainty, summarized Romero's funeral violence without naming actors: "A bomb went off outside of the cathedral. The panic-stricken crowd, estimated at fifty thousand people, was machine-gunned, leaving an estimated twenty-seven to forty people dead and more than two hundred wounded."[37]

Others are more precise: "During the funeral, smoke bombs were detonated and snipers fired on mourners from government buildings."[38]

After Romero's Death

Romero's murder and funeral marked the onset of the civil war he had toiled to prevent. Twelve years of hostilities would claim seventy-five thousand lives and destroy much of the country's infrastructure. Two events in particular brought international notice and condemnation: the torture and murder of four US churchwomen on December 2, 1980,[39] and the massacre of six Jesuit priests, their cook, and her teen-age daughter in November 1989.[40]

35. Brockman, *A Life*, 247.

36. Ibid.

37. UN Security Council, "Madness to Hope," 21.

38. Carrigan and Weber. *Last Journey*, chapter 9.

39. "On 2 December 1980, members of the National Guard of El Salvador, on orders from a superior, arrested four churchwomen after they left the international airport. Churchwomen Ita Ford, Maura Clarke, Dorothy Kazel, and Jean Donovan were taken to an isolated spot and subsequently executed by being shot at close range" (UN Security Council, "Madness to Hope," 54).

40. In the early morning of November 16, 1989, under orders from high-level military officers, five soldiers of the Atlacatl Batallion, the US-trained special counterinsurgency unit, entered the Pastoral Center of the José Simeón Cañas Central American University (UCA) in San Salvador. They shot and killed six Jesuit priests: Fathers Ignacio Ellacuría, the university's rector; Ignacio Martín-Baró, vice-rector; Segundo Montes, director of the Human Rights Institute; Amando López and Juan Ramón Moreno, instructors; and Joaquín López y López, founder and director of the Federación Internacional

"The murder of the six Jesuit priests ten years [after Romero's assassination] was the final outburst of the delirium that had infected the armed forces and the innermost recesses of certain government circles," the Truth Commission wrote.[41]

Neither side won a military victory per se. However, the fact that a relatively small number of poorly funded guerrillas took on the full brunt of the Salvadoran military, generously supported by the United States, Israel, Brazil, and a couple of other countries, and brought it to the negotiating table speaks of its effectiveness and persistence. Armed hostilities ended with a UN-brokered peace accord signed January 16, 1992, in Chapultepec, Mexico. The agreement paved the way for a Truth Commission to find and publicize the truth behind the acts of violence committed by both sides during the war.[42]

The Truth Commission verified what most Salvadorans already knew. The "intellectual author" of Romero's assassination was former Army Major Roberto D'Aubuisson, who "gave precise instructions to members of his security service, acting as a 'death squad,' to organize and supervise the assassination."[43]

During a May 7, 1980, raid on a farm in Santa Tecla, a municipality some nine miles from the capital, military officials seized weapons and documents implicating D'Aubuisson in Romero's murder.[44] D'Aubuisson was arrested but released.[45]

Fe y Alegría in El Salvador. The soldiers also killed the center's cook, Julia Elba Ramos, and the cook's fifteen-year-old daughter, Celina Mariceth Ramos. The Atlacatl Batallion was disbanded in December 1992 under the peace accords.

41. UN Security Council, "Madness to Hope," 6.

42. Ibid, 11–13.

43. Ibid., 123.

44. The raid's purpose was to arrest twenty-four current and retired military personnel, among them D'Aubuisson, and civilians formally accused of plotting to overthrow the military–Christian Democrat junta.

45. The UN Security Council stated, "On 7 May 1980, Major Roberto D'Aubuisson was arrested on a farm, along with a group of civilians and soldiers. In the raid, a significant quantity of weapons and documents were found implicating the group in the organization and financing of death squads allegedly involved in Archbishop Romero's murder. The arrests triggered a wave of terrorist threats and institutional pressures which culminated in D'Aubuisson's release. This strengthened the most conservative sector in the Government and was a clear example of the passivity and inertia of the judiciary during this period" ("Madness to Hope," 21).

One of the papers, in D'Aubuisson's handwriting, listed items and personnel needed for "Operation Pineapple," the assassination plot's name: Starlight, 257 Roberts, automatics, grenades, driver, sniper, security. A Starlight is a telescopic sight for the kind of precision rifle, such as a 257 Roberts, needed to accurately shoot from thirty-five meters away, the distance from the street to the altar of the chapel at the Divine Providence Hospital.[46] One member of D'Aubuisson's posse provided the driver and another member, the sniper. The automatics and grenades armed a four-man security detail.

El Salvador's justice system did not investigate Romero's assassination. As the Truth Commission later wrote about the four years between 1980 and 1983, "Civilian and military groups [death squads] engaged in a systematic murder campaign with total impunity, while state institutions turned a blind eye. The murder of Monseñor Romero exemplified the limitless, devastating power of these groups. This period saw the greatest number of deaths and human rights violations."[47]

In that "license to kill" atmosphere, the judge assigned to the case escaped an attempt on his life. One by one, most of the witnesses to and planners of Romero's assassination were eliminated.[48]

Not until November 1987 did Amado Antonio Garay, an ex-soldier and chauffeur, testify about the events of March 24, 1980, bringing details to light. The chauffeur's employer, Captain Alvaro Saravia, recruited by D'Aubuisson to help lead the plot, instructed Garay to drive a red, four-door Volkswagen Passat[49] that evening, first to the Hotel Camino Real parking lot.

Three men, one of them Saravia, followed behind in a white Dodge Lancer. The two vehicles parked in the hotel lot, where a tall, thin bearded man carrying a rifle climbed into the Passat's backseat.

When the Passat arrived at the chapel, the bearded man told Garay to stop in front of it and to bend down and pretend he was fixing something. Garay heard a loud crack and smelled gun powder. He turned to see his passenger holding his rifle pointed at the chapel. The shooter then instructed Garay to remain calm and drive away slowly. Garay dropped off the

46. Dada, "How We Killed." Thirty-five meters represents roughly one-third the length of a football field.

47. UN Security Council, "Madness to Hope," 20.

48. For details, see Dada, "How We Killed."

49. The owner of the Volkswagen dealership, Roberto Mathies Regalado, had donated the car to D'Aubuisson to contribute to the ex-major's anticommunism front (Dada, "How We Killed.").

marksman at a safe house. (The Dodge Lancer had followed the Passat some fifty meters behind, and remained at the chapel until the gunman shot.)

Garay testified that three days later, he drove his boss to see D'Aubuisson and heard Captain Saravia tell the major, "We did what was planned—killed Archbishop Arnulfo Romero."[50]

Garay picked out a 1969 photo with a beard drawn in of Héctor Antonio Regalado as being the closest in description to the gunman.[51] Regalado, a dentist and crack sharpshooter, was D'Aubuisson's right-hand man, serving as chief of the National Assembly's security team when D'Aubuisson headed the assembly. Once again in 1988, the Salvadoran Supreme Court gave excuses for not pursuing judicial prosecution.[52] D'Aubuisson never admitted to his participation. The UN Truth Commission later found insufficient proof that Regalado was the triggerman.

Fearful for their safety, Garay and his wife left El Salvador several months after his 1987 testimony; they entered the US Federal Witness Protection Program.

D'Aubuisson, however, survived and thrived politically. In 1981, he helped found the far-right ARENA[53] party and in 1982 and 1983, he was elected president of the country's Constituent Assembly.[54] ARENA candidate Alfredo Cristiani won the presidency in 1989 and held that position until June 1994. He was succeeded by ARENA member Armando Calderón Sol through June 1999.

When D'Aubuisson died in 1992, age forty-eight, many considered the tongue and throat cancer that took him poetic justice—he had used his mouth to speak vicious lies and hate talk, much of it televised and about Archbishop Romero in the weeks before his murder.

50. Information about the murder and Garay's testimony from Brockman, Dada, and UN Security Council.

51. UN Security Council, "Madness to Hope," 122.

52. Brockman (*A Life*, 253–55) provides a fuller explanation.

53. ARENA stands for "Nationalist Republican Alliance."

54. D'Aubuisson ran for El Salvador's presidency in 1984, losing to Napoleón Duarte. D'Aubuisson did not run for presidency in the next election, in which ARENA's candidate, Alfredo Cristiani, won and assumed the presidency in 1989.

Romero's Memory

Supporters, including many in other countries, have kept Romero's memory alive with posthumous honors and recognition. In July 1998, a statue of Romero was one of ten twentieth-century martyrs unveiled in a row of gothic niches above the grand west entrance to Westminster Abbey.[55] Romero's youngest brother, Gaspar, attended the dedication ceremony in London.

In El Salvador, many colorful murals celebrate Romero's life, and a highway opened in 2012, Central America's first freeway, was named for him.

In early 2014, El Salvador's Comalapa International Airport was rechristened the Monseñor Óscar Arnulfo Romero International Airport. The country's legislature approved the airport name change without the votes of ARENA or the Christian Democratic Party. The airport name-change debate testifies to El Salvador's ongoing political polarization thirty-five years after Romero's murder.

Further evidence of continued divisiveness occurred in late 2014 when San Salvador's ARENA mayor[56] and his city council renamed a main thoroughfare after Roberto D'Aubuisson. The action aroused much controversy.

"To give that person's name to that street or to any other street, avenue, school, public or private place, dead-end alley, passageway, swimming pool, gym, aisle, etc., etc., means declaring oneself against one of the Truth Commission's main recommendations: to honor the memory of those killed or disappeared during the war,"[57] one paper editorialized.

The country's Human Rights Commission agreed. It said the name change violated due process and ran contrary to the 2001 Truth Commission's recommendation that no one identified as responsible for Romero's assassination be honored. Among the first acts of a newly elected city council in May 2015 was to restore the street name to San Antonio Abad.

Street names may be easy to change. A thornier dilemma to overcome consists of El Salvador's economic and political rifts, the entrenched constants throughout the decades.

55. The other nine are: Maximilian Kolbe of Poland, Manche Masemola of South Africa, Janani Luwum of Uganda, Grand Duchess Elizabeth of Russia, Martin Luther King Jr. of the United States, Dietrich Bonhoeffer of Germany, Esther John of Pakistan, Lucian Tapiedi of Papua New Guinea, and Wang Zhiming of China. In July 1998, the Archbishop of Canterbury unveiled the statues in the presence of the Queen of England. (*See* http://www.westminster-abbey.org/our-history/people/maximilian-kolbe.)

56. Mayor Norman Quijano, ARENA party member

57. Alvarenga, "Calle Mártires." http://www.contrapunto.com.sv/opinion/columnistas/calle-martires-de-el-despertar.

Rifts continued in Rome as well. The question of Romero's beatification and sainthood languished for decades in Vatican limbo. Some observers do not blame this on direct opposition by either popes John Paul II or Benedict XVI, but rather to obstructionism on the part of officials, cardinals, and monsignori in various curia, or departments, in Rome.[58]

Others judge Pope John Paul II more harshly, noting that he failed to demand an investigation into Romero's murder. Instead:

> The pope's message [following the assassination] stressed the sacrilege of the killing (Romero was saying mass when he was shot), rather than the martyrdom of the man, and the Vatican denunciation of the crime made no reference to its motives. . . . The first anniversary of his death brought no papal commemoration, and the date passed without mention by the Vatican newspaper *L'Osservatore Romano*.
>
> The pope and his conservative allies have consistently sought to neutralize the meaning of Romero's life.
>
> When the pope paid an "unofficial" visit to Romero's tomb in 1983, he refused to accord him any special distinction . . .[59]

Yet others interpret the pope's spur-of-the-moment 1983 visit differently:

> Although unexpectedly, by completely personal choice, the pope interrupted his planned itinerary and went to the Cathedral of San Salvador. On his knees he prayed at Archbishop Romero's tomb, then praised him as a "zealous shepherd, inspired by the love of God and service to his brethren to offer up his very life, suffering a violent death while celebrating the sacrifice of forgiveness and reconciliation." I have heard that the holy father regards Archbishop Romero as a genuine martyr.[60]

Perhaps, as theologian Sobrino remarked about John Paul II's growth in his understanding of what Romero faced in El Salvador, this pope also grew in his understanding of the significance of Romero's assassination.

58. That neither Pope John Paul II or Pope Benedict opposed Romero's beatification is argued by Julian Filochowski, although he acknowledges the popes' ultimate responsibility for the behavior of the cardinals and monsignori of the Vatican departments to whom the pope delegates authority to act on his behalf. See Julian Filochowski, "Romero: Person and His Charisma with the Pontiffs," in Pelton, *Archbishop Romero and Spiritual Leadership*, 99–110.

59. Huntington, "Between," 40.

60. Sobrino, *Recollections*, 49.

Pope Francis, elected to the papacy in March 2013, opened the road to Romero's beatification on August 18, 2014. He told journalists, "For me Romero is a man of God. There are no doctrinal problems and it is very important that [the beatification] is done quickly."[61]

Francis, an Argentinian and the first Latin American pope,[62] acted swiftly on his assertion and affirmed Romero as a martyr on February 3, 2015. The pronouncement meant Romero could be beatified, or declared holy, without having a miracle attributed to his intercession. Beatification in turn clears the way for eventual canonization as a saint, for which evidence of a miracle is needed.[63]

The beatification took place on May 23, 2015, thirty-five years after the archbishop's assassination. An estimated half million Salvadorans assembled in a plaza in the capital to hear the pope's emissary, Cardinal Angelo Amato, preside at the ceremony.

"Romero, who built peace with the power of love, bore witness to the faith in the extreme by offering his life,"[64] Pope Francis wrote in a letter published the day of the beatification.

Whether or not the Vatican officially names Romero a saint, many Latin Americans already call him "Saint Romero of the Americas."[65] They have not forgotten his sacrificial courage in defending the poor. As Romero paraphrased a gospel verse in his homily moments before he was killed: "One must not love oneself so much as to avoid getting involved in the risks of life that history demands of us. Those who try to fend off the danger will lose their lives, while those who out of love for Christ give themselves to the service of others will live, live like the grain of wheat that . . . allows itself to be sacrificed in the earth and destroyed. Only by giving itself does it produce the harvest."[66]

61. "Pope Lifts."

62. Before becoming pope and taking the name Francis, he was Cardinal Jorge Mario Bergoglio of Argentina.

63. Wooden, "Pope Recognizes."

64. "El Salvador Celebrates."

65. Dom Pedro Casaldáliga, bishop of São Félix, Brazil, first used the term to end a poem he wrote about Archbishop Romero in the week after his murder: "Saint Romero of the Americas, our shepherd and our martyr, no one shall ever silence your last homily." Shared in Sobrino, *Reflections*, 45–46.

66. Romero y Galdámez, *Homilies*, March 24, 1980, at chapel of Divine Providence Hospital. Romero paraphrases John 12:24–25, words Jesus spoke to his disciples before his arrest and death.

Bibliography

Alas, José Inocencio. *Iglesia, Tierra y Lucha Campesina, Suchitoto, El Salvador, 1968–1977*. San Salvador: Asociación de Frailes Franciscanos OFM de Centro América, 2003.

Alvarenga, Luis. "Calle Mártires de El Despertar." *ContraPunto* (November 27, 2014). http://www.contrapunto.com.sv/opinion/columnistas/calle-martires-de-el-despertar.

Armstrong, Robert, and Janet Shenk. *El Salvador, the Face of Revolution*. 2nd ed. Boston: South End, 1982.

Brockman, James R. *Romero: A Life*. Maryknoll, NY: Orbis, 1989.

Carranza, Salvador. *Romero-Rutilio: vidas encontradas*. 1st ed. San Salvador: UCA Editores, 1992.

Cavada, Miguel. *Monseñor Romero: su vida, su testimonio y su palabra*. Illustrated by Oscar Chicas. 4rth ed. San Salvador: Equipo Maíz, 2004.

Clarke, Kevin. *Oscar Romero: Love Must Win Out*. Collegeville, MN: Liturgical, 2014.

Dada, Carlos. "How We Killed Archbishop Romero." Translated by Gretta Siebentritt. *El Faro* (March 25, 2010). http://www.elfaro.net/es/201003/noticias/1416/How-we-killed-Archbishop-Romero.htm.

Delgado, Jesús. *Oscar A. Romero: Biografía*. San Salvador: UCA Editores, 1990.

———. "Romero: un joven aspirante a la santidad." *Orientación* (March 25, 2007) 7–10.

Diez, Zacarías, and Juan Macho. *"En Santiago de María me topé con la miseria": Dos años de la Vida de Mons. Romero: 1975–1976, ¿Años de Cambio?* San José, Costa Rica: 1994. Full text of this book is at: http://servicioskoinonia.org/biblioteca/bibliodatos1.html?gralo1.

"El Salvador Celebrates Beatification of Martyred Archbishop Oscar Romero," *The Guardian* (May 23, 2015). http://www.theguardian.com/world/2015/may/23/el-salvador-celebrates-beatification-martyred-archbishop-oscar-romero.

Equipo Maíz. *Monseñor Romero: El pueblo es mi profeta*. Drawings by Alfredo Burgos and Mario Trejo. San Salvador: Equipo Maíz, 1994.

Erdozaín, Plácido. *Archbishop Romero, Martyr of Salvador*. Translated by John McFadden and Ruth Warner. Maryknoll, NY: Orbis, 1981.

Filochowski, Julian. "Romero: Person and His Charisma with the Pontiffs." In *Archbishop Romero and Spiritual Leadership in the Modern World*, edited by Robert S. Pelton, 99–110. Lanham, MD: Lexington, 2015.

Guest, Iain. *Behind the Disappearances: Argentina's Dirty War Against Human Rights and the United Nations*. Philadelphia: University of Pennsylvania Press, 1990.

Huntington, Deborah. "Between God and Caesar." *NACLA Report on the Americas* (September/October 1985) 37–45.

Jiménez, J., and M. Navarrete. *Monseñor Romero: reseña biográfica*. San Salvador. 1990.

Juliá, Raúl, Richard Jordan, and Ana Alicia. *Romero*. Directed by John Duigan. Los Angeles: Paulist Pictures. 1989. DVD, 105 min. Distributed by Lions Gate.

"La DEA sabía lo que hacía Capister, pero no podía frenar los escuadrones." *Diario1* (October 21, 2013). http://diario1.com/zona-1/2013/10/la-dea-sabia-lo-que-hacia-capister-pero-no-podia-frenar-los-escuadrones.

Lang, Friedl. "Hitler's Visit in 1934 to the Oberammergau Passion Play." *Newsletter of the Association of Contemporary Church Historians* 2, no. 12 (1996) 1–3. http://www.calvin.edu/academic/cas/akz/akz9612.htm.

Lara-Braud, Jorge. Foreword to *Archbishop Romero, Martyr of Salvador,* by Plácido Erdozaín, ix–xxiii. Translated by John McFadden and Ruth Warner. Maryknoll, NY: Orbis, 1981.

Lemus, Efren. "La farsa de la investigación del asesinato de monseñor Romero." *El Faro* (May 23, 2015). http://www.elfaro.net/es/201505/noticias/16994/La-farsa-de-la-investigación-del-asesinato-de-monseñor-Romero.htm.

López Vigil, María. *Oscar Romero: Memories in Mosaic*. Translated by Kathy Ogle. Maryknoll, NY: Orbis, 2013.

———. *Piezas para un retrato*. 1st ed. San Salvador: UCA Editores, 1993. http://www.iglesia.cl/especiales/mons_romero/caminando/Piezas-para-un-retrato.pdf.

Monroy, Daniel Enrique, coordinator. *Cien años de presencia evangélica en El Salvador.* San Salvador: Confraternidad Evangélica Salvadoreña CONESAL, 1996. http://www.prolades.com/historiografia/3-El-Salvador/historia_cien_anos_els.pdf.

North, Liisa. *Bitter Grounds: Roots of Revolt in El Salvador*. 2nd rev. ed. Westport, CT: Lawrence Hill; 1985.

Palumbo, Eugenio. "María López Vigil: Monseñor Romero: la gente le dio fuerza." *Sentir con la Iglesia* (March 15, 1996) 8–9.

"Pope Lifts Beatification Ban on Salvadoran Oscar Romero." BBC news. August 19, 2014. http://www.bbc.com/news/world-latin-america-28845998.

Romero y Galdámez, Oscar Arnulfo. *Archbishop Oscar Romero: A Shepherd's Diary*. Translated by Irene B. Hodgson. Cincinnati: St. Anthony Messenger, 1993. (In Spanish at http://www.romeroes.com/monsenor-romero-su-pensamiento/su-diario.)

———. *Cuadernos de ejercicios espirituales,1966–1980*. Unpublished document. Archives of San Salvador archdiocesan office.

———. *Diario de Oriente*. http://www.romeroes.com/monsenor-romero-su-pensamiento/prensa-escrita/diario-de-oriente.

———. *Homilies*. Translated by Archbishop Romero Trust. London. http://www.romerotrust.org.uk/. Audio versions of many of Romero's homilies are also at http://www.romerotrust.org.uk/ index. php?nuc=homilies. Written transcriptions in both Spanish and English at http://www.romeroes.com/monsenor-romero-su-pensamiento/homilias, the website of the Oficinas de la Causa de Canonización [Offices of the Cause of Canonization] of the San Salvador Archdiocese.

———. *Semanario Chaparrastique*. http://www.romeroes.com/monsenor-romero-su-pensamiento/prensa-escrita/semanario-chaparrastique.

———. *Semanario El Apóstol*. http://www.romeroes.com/monsenor-romero-su-pensamiento/prensa-escrita/semanario-el-apostol.

Romero y Galdámez, Oscar Arnulfo and Arturo Rivera Damas. *Third Pastoral Letter*, "La Iglesia y las organizaciones políticas populares" (The Church and Popular Political

Organizations). August 1978. http://www.romeroes.com/monsenor-romero-su-pensamiento/cartas-pastorales (in Spanish).

Romero y Galdámez, Oscar Arnulfo, Rutilio Grande et al., *Monseñor: The Last Journey of Oscar Romero.* Directed by Ana Carrigan and Juliet Weber. Notre Dame, IN: Kellogg Institute of Notre Dame University. 2011. DVD, 98 min. Distributed by First Run Features .

Sobrino, Jon. *Archbishop Romero: Reflections.* Translated by Robert R. Barr. Maryknoll, NY: Orbis, 1990.

Sullins, D. Paul. *Empty Pews and Empty Altars: A Reconsideration of the Catholic Priest Shortage.* Washington DC: Department of Sociology, Georgetown University. Revised August 2000. http://faculty.cua.edu/sullins/published%20articles/pshort.pdf.

UN Security Council. "From Madness to Hope: the 12-year war in El Salvador: Report of the Commission on the Truth for El Salvador." United States Institute of Peace, January 26, 2001. http://www.usip.org/sites/default/files/file/ElSalvador-Report.pdf.

Valencia, Roberto. "El corazón de Monseñor Romero." *El Mundo* (October 8, 2010). http://www.elmundo.es/america/blogs/cronicascentroamerica/2010/10/08/el-corazon-de-monsenor-romero.html.

———. "Rutilio Grande, S.J. 12.03.1977." *El Faro* (March 12, 2012). http://www.elfaro.net/es/201203/noticias/7949/.

Valencia, Roberto, and Mauro Arias. "Plática con Gaspar Romero, hermano de Monseñor Romero."*El Faro* (August 8, 2011). http://www.elfaro.net/es/201108/el_agora/5019/.

Vatican II. "Constitution on the Sacred Liturgy." December 4, 1963. http://www.vatican.va/archive/hist_councils/ii_vatican_council/documents/vat-ii_const_19631204_sacrosanctum-concilium_en.html.

Wooden, Cindy. "Pope Recognizes Martyrdom of Archbishop Romero." Catholic News Service (February 3, 2015). http://www.catholicnews.com/data/stories/cns/1500492.htm.

Index